Dimensions of Professional Learning

D1741411

Professional Learning
Volume 3

Rationale:

This series purposely sets out to illustrate a range of approaches to Professional Learning and to highlight the importance of teachers and teacher educators taking the lead in reframing and responding to their practice, not just to illuminate the field but to foster genuine educational change.

Audience:

The series will be of interest to teachers, teacher educators and others in fields of professional practice as the context and practice of the pedagogue is the prime focus of such work. Professional Learning is closely aligned to much of the ideas associated with reflective practice, action research, practitioner inquiry and teacher as researcher.

Dimensions of Professional Learning
Professionalism, Practice and Identity

Amanda Berry
Monash University

Allie Clemans
Monash University

Alexander Kostogriz
Monash University

SENSE PUBLISHERS
ROTTERDAM / TAIPEI

A C.I.P. record for this book is available from the Library of Congress.

ISBN 978-90-8790-001-4 (paperback)
ISBN 978-90-8790-002-1 (hardback)
ISBN 978-90-8790-125-7 (ebook)

Published by: Sense Publishers,
P.O. Box 21858, 3001 AW
Rotterdam, The Netherlands
http://www.sensepublishers.com

Printed on acid-free paper

Professional Learning

CONTENTS

LIST OF FIGURES AND TABLES

FIGURES

TABLES

ACKNOWLEDGEMENTS

For the leadership that created opportunities to foster our collaboration and professional learning.

To Brian McKittrick, for his fine and discerning editorial gaze.

To Professor Gaalen Erickson, for his constructive and thoughtful professional advice.

To those who contributed to the writing process, for their co-operative and generous spirit.

SERIES EDITOR'S FOREWORD

This series in Professional Learning has grown out of the recognition of the importance of professional knowledge and its impact on practice. In many ways it illustrates the inherent value in the field of practitioner inquiry and the importance of seeking to better document, articulate and portray the professional knowledge of practice. Professional Learning, as conceptualized and enacted in this series, is concerned with what professionals do and, as a consequence, learn about their own knowledge of practice. As has been noted before, this is in contrast to traditional views of Professional Development because the focus is on that which professionals choose to do to develop and extend their own knowledge in ways that are not always obvious (or expected) in programs and courses designed to deliver information to participants (i.e., in-service training and development). Professional learning is therefore characterised by the role the individual takes in initiating and directing their own growth and development as opposed to being 'trained' to perform particular tasks through 'upskilling' or mandated changes to existing practice to meet imposed policy guidelines.

In order to better understand the nature of professional learning and its impact on professionals, it is clearly important to be able to find new and innovative ways of looking into the knowledge of practice and 'unpacking' it in meaningful ways. In so doing, that which is insightful, challenging, thought provoking and helpful in the development of knowledge for, and of, practice might then be applicable beyond the individual and speak to the broader educational community. In essence, an aspect of professional learning to be encouraged, is that of sharing the wisdom of practice in ways that helps others expand their knowledge of their field beyond that of propositional knowledge and rules alone (although important in their own right). Such knowledge expansion is enmeshed in the subtleties and intricacies of understanding the problematic nature of practice and bringing to the fore the wisdom that underpins actions that may sometimes appear to be habitual or routine as well as those that are innovative and challenging.

There is little doubt that as Fullan (1993; Fullan & Hargreaves, 1991) has noted so well in the past, real educational change requires change in people. Professional learning then offers access to new ways of understanding those changes. By focusing on personal practice, the distinction between the "authority of experience" as opposed to the "authority of position" (Munby & Russell, 1994) becomes an important 'way in' to valuing professional learning and so creates a real agenda for genuine educational change. When professionals explicitly respond to their own needs, concerns and issues there is increased likelihood of change in ways that are not quite so likely when simply responding to the requirements and needs of 'the system'. Such changes are what matter when attempting to document accounts of professional learning. How professional learning might best be portrayed then matters, especially so when the complex world of teaching and learning is the field of study, if the individual learning of the self is to offer similar transformative insights and possibilities for others.

This third book in this series, *Dimensions of professional learning: Professionalism, practice and identity*, purposely sets out to illustrate a range of approaches to, and contexts of professional learning and captures well the need to question the taken for granted and to reframe (Schön, 1983) problems of policy and practice in ways that are responsive to the needs of practitioners. Amanda Berry, Allie Clemans and Alex Kostogriz, in conceptualizing and editing this volume, have created an innovative approach to capturing and documenting professional learning as they have supported and challenged their contributing authors in a push to expand the boundaries of their own learning about practice.

The book is organised in sections, each of which takes up important issues in professional learning. The first section is concerned with the construction of policy and its relationship to professionalism and helps to set an agenda for questioning the taken for granted. It opens with a challenge by Gale and Cross to take critiques of teaching and teacher education seriously and to become actively involved in response. Of course, the very act of so doing, as Kostogriz notes, can be one way of encouraging the development of a standpoint, or of taking a position. Sometimes, to do so is more difficult than anticipated for as Nuttall et al. remind us, language is crucial to developing understanding and therefore vital in the growth of professional knowledge. This point is similarly raised by Gearon and Cross who also introduce the importance of context as a shaping factor for the way in which knowledge might be applied, and helps in transition to the second section of the book.

The second section examines communal sites and the dimensions of professional learning practices and, as Deppeler makes clear, collaborative inquiry offers real opportunities for powerful professional learning outcomes. Tudball adds to these ideas by drawing attention to the value of professional learning communities; offering a further reminder about the roles of context and collaboration. Mitchell further builds on these ideas with a well developed argument about the move from professional talk to teacher research. Mitchell brings a wealth of experience to bear in highlighting the intricacies associated with better understanding practitioner research. Corrigan grasps another vital aspect of the growth in professional learning through a focus on mentoring as she highlights the importance of relationships for the development of shared understandings of practice.

Section three closes the book through the theme of identity, bringing to the surface this issue as a shaping factor in practice and the way in which it is constructed. Williams opens the section with a thoughtful study that builds nicely on the preceding pieces and creates a platform for the chapters that follow. Viete and Peeler challenge singular understandings of identity through their themes of belonging, becoming and being respected which, in many ways, invites new ways of thinking about that which may so easily be taken-for-granted in teacher education. Watt et al. build on the policy implications associated with changing trajectories from teacher education into, and out of, teaching, introduced earlier by Williams. Berry and Scheele further develop the themes of collaboration, professional knowledge of practice and inquiry through a very strong collaborative self-study that illustrates well the rigour necessary to make claims about professional learning and its impact on practice. Clemans explores how issues of context and identity together shape practice in vocational and higher education settings. The section closes by coming full circle as Winter questions what it means to 'keep up' in changing times and to redefine and redevelop as a professional, but she cautions, it is just as crucial to remember that change involves people. As such, interaction is a defining aspect of engagement in professional learning.

In organising the book the way they have, Berry, Clemans and Kostogriz have selected chapters which stand to provide insights into how an individual's professional learning experiences may be applicable and adaptable to other contexts and work roles. Their careful and thoughtful approach to encouraging their authors to work together to critique, question and develop one another's work in order to develop an initial draft of this volume, is itself illustrative of a crucial aspect of professional learning – collaboration – and further highlights the importance of learning with, and through, others that this volume itself encourages.

This series was initiated in response to the growing interest of teachers, teacher educators and others in fields of professional practice that were concerned to develop deeper understandings of the context, identity and practice of pedagogues. Studies in professional learning need to demonstrate a strong commitment to the development of knowledge and ways of constructing and sharing that knowledge with others. Through this book, Berry, Clemans and Kostogriz have, with their team, combined to respond to such needs in a positive and coherent manner.

This book creates multiple entry points to better understanding the complexity of professional learning. It addresses diverse contexts of learning – schools, universities, professional communities, academic and vocational sites. It invites the reader to consider the work of the individual chapter authors, not in isolation, but as a coherent whole. In so doing, the editors hope to encourage readers to reflect on their own practice in light of the studies documented in this text so that their own professional learning might be catalysed and lead to new and meaningful outcomes in terms of both teaching and learning.

REFERENCES

Fullan, M. (1993). *Change forces: Probing the depths of educational reform*. London: Falmer Press.
Fullan, M., & Hargreaves, A. (1991). *What's worth fighting for in your school?* Buckingham, UK: Open University Press.
Munby, H., & Russell, T. (1994). The authority of experience in learning to teach: Messages from a physics method class. *Journal of Teacher Education, 4*(2), 86-95.
Schön, D. A. (1983). *The reflective practitioner: How professionals think in action*. New York: Basic Books.

John Loughran
Faculty of Education
Monash University

PREFACE

Professional learning has long been regarded as a field of inquiry in education and, in this respect, is a place that allows for serious thought about its contours and textures. This book invites re-engagement with educational, social and political realities that shape the local practices of educators and professional communities. To speak about professional learning in local contexts is not merely to speak about its situated nature but also about its broader social situatedness and its individual embodiment. Professional learning as a form of human action, as intellectual and collective practice, is always situated somewhere and related to other historical settings, to its near and distant surroundings. Being inherently situated, it is always contingent upon the variously scaled interconnections, processes and networks that may or may not come into perspective. To capture this multi-scalar nature of professional learning, the book is organized around the following three sections in which multiple dimensions of professional learning are depicted.

Section One, *Political dimensions of teacher professionalism and professional learning*, encompasses the larger scale as it interrogates notions of professionalism and how these come to be constructed and represented by the media, policy makers, politicians and practitioners. Chapters in this section explore the ways that policies and practices mediate the construction of 'a professional' among current and future educators.

Section Two, *Communal sites and dimensions of professional learning practice*, turns to the smaller scale and considers local communal sites. These chapters address important questions about how the practices, designed to advance and develop various professional learning communities, are shaped by virtue of the communal spaces in which they take place.

Section Three, *Dimensions of self, identity and the shaping of practice*, focuses on the nexus of the self and the social as it draws attention to identity formation in professional practice. In these chapters, the authors explore the ways in which professional identity is constructed, sustained and changed, as well as ways in which it is challenged and constrained.

We do not restrict ourselves to the view that these dimensions alone comprise the nature of professional learning. Nor do we consider the dimensions that we have identified as mutually exclusive. On the contrary, these dimensions inescapably connect as issues discussed in the chapters overlap and collide and common themes emerge. For instance, the tensions present in the professional life of educators as they negotiate powerful relations and experience their effects, are felt through political constructions of professionalism, the features of particular learning sites and within the individual her or himself. In fact, it is through the dynamic interrelationship of ideas across dimensions that the nature of professional learning is more fully revealed. Taken as a whole, then, we believe that the chapters provide important insights into the process of 'professional becoming'.

THE WRITING JOURNEY

There are multiple layers of professional learning embedded in this book. It began as a writing project among members of the Professional Learning Research Group in the Faculty of Education, at Monash University. The project was designed to enhance our professional learning as researchers and writers, through a process of collaboration and critique. It took as its reference point the theme which frames the rather disparate interests of researchers who belong to this research grouping. Professional learning is a focus for academics in the Faculty who seek to understand and improve professional education practices and refine our understandings of teaching and learning.

The writing project came at a time in higher education in Australia when there exists a compelling and externally imposed need for research productivity, amidst growing recognition that the isolation of individualised academic work is not the best environment to achieve this. Hence this project was designed to enhance connections among professionals. The project also sought to address the professional learning needs of academics at varying points in their careers – emerging and established researchers – providing possibilities to express our individual and collective scholarly voices to each other and to external communities interested in professional learning.

In a project of this nature, process was everything! Group members were initially invited to construct a brief paper that could form the basis of their contributing chapter for this book. Our brief as a research group was to explore the challenges and dilemmas around professional learning confronting educators in Australia. Meetings and a one-day retreat designed around critical and supportive dialogue were organised to read each other's papers, share ideas, connect and cluster themes and provide constructive critique to each other about content and form. Smaller groupings of papers cohering around distinct dimensions of professional learning soon emerged. Members of sub-groups worked together and were able to offer close, ongoing support to each other as chapters took on their final form.

Each of us, as editors, took responsibility for working with a subgroup to continue to refine ideas and produce final chapters. All participants commented that this experience of collaboration stood out as unique and valuable in a work context that is traditionally individualised and isolated. Little space and few resources are allocated to the development of collective understandings of professional practice, yet few would deny the impact of such opportunities. When they appear, they should be seized!

We see the development of this book, then, as mirroring the development of a professional learning community. In no way is this community homogenous or romantically harmonious. By its nature, it is diverse and difference within it abounds. Individuals carry different disciplinary traditions, values and motivations. We hold varying positions of power within the institution in which we work. It would have been easier to commission 'like minded colleagues' to contribute towards the publication of a book. Yet we found that the value in working with, and through, 'difference' in our professional learning community was profound.

The writing and collaborative process allowed us to make the familiar unfamiliar. By so doing, we came to see afresh our identities as both researchers and educators. We made explicit our values and their shaping of our practices. We honoured our different positions. We articulated our insights into professional learning.

Through the activities of research, writing and sharing our work within our research grouping, we have created a forum for the development of our voice as professional learners, educators and academics. As our voices speak into the public sphere, we invite others to engage with, critique and build on, these ideas.

THE VALUE OF THE BOOK

So why would you read this book? First, it considers the notion of professional learning as associated with professional 'becoming' of those engaged with current or future workplaces. It does not address a particular profession, for example, school teachers, but rather addresses a range of professionals with varying levels of experience – principals, prospective teachers, academics, experienced educators and vocational educators.

Second, it places and addresses professional learning in multiple contexts. It considers 'the professional' and speaks to the nature of professionalism and practices of professional learning that apply as much to schools as they do to other learning settings such as corporate workplaces, universities, vocational colleges and libraries.

Third, this book speaks from the voices of those who are reflective about their own professional learning as they, in turn, reflect on their experiences of leading professional learning programs for others. Most chapters are representative of the writer's professional learning, as individuals responsible for research and teaching associated with the preparation and life long learning of new and experienced educators. The book shares the challenges, tensions and dilemmas faced by professionals as they make sense of their work, identity and practices. It offers ideas for programs and projects designed to enhance professional capacities in a range of learning spaces.

While these chapters begin with local stories, we believe that they make global connections. Policies and practices travel and the themes reflected in what follows are surely felt more globally. Our hope is that these particular dimensions of professional learning offer insights to provoke your own.

The Editors:
Amanda Berry
Allie Clemans
Alex Kostogriz

POLITICAL DIMENSIONS OF TEACHER PROFESSIONALISM AND PROFESSIONAL LEARNING

SECTION INTRODUCTION

Anyone who follows trends in educational policy-making across the globe and in local contexts cannot fail to have noticed a rapid increase of political measures that have worked to redefine teacher professionalism and professional learning. Why is this so? Why is there so much talk about teaching quality, standards and teacher performance? And, how can we explain the rise of governmental interventions in education and teacher professional communities and organisations in times when the state appears to diminish its responsibility for public education? This section of the book endeavours to address some of these political dimensions by focusing on the challenges, contradictions and tensions experienced by teachers and teacher educators in Australia.

Education in Australia, as well as in other so called 'developed' political economies, has undergone profound change over the last two decades. While not desiring to romanticize the past, contributing authors to this section of the book problematise current changes in education to analyse their impact as a result of a broader move to neoconservative political reforms world wide. What has come to be known as 'the neoliberal turn' (Harvey, 2004) represents a shift from Keynesian principles of social democracy and the welfare state to a market-driven model of education where knowledge becomes goods designed for consumption by customers. As such, this model incorporates some major characteristics of hyper-capitalism – with greater emphases on the 'private', the 'individual' and the 'market'. Apple (2006) and Giroux (2003) have asserted that, in these times, government policies have diverted attention away from economics as a source of societal problems and held up social systems such as education as places to find fault. Such an environment has many implications for both the teaching profession and teacher education.

The steady drift towards marketization and deregulation of education since the 1980s has altered the landscape of public education (primary, secondary and tertiary). The gradually diminished social and financial responsibility of the state for education has seen individual schools and universities become responsible for their own performance and economic survival in the marketplace. A new model of governance has emerged. The state has adopted a steering role, managing educational markets and curriculum. This model of governance has often been played out in an environment of 'partnership' where multiple stakeholders are bound together. In reality, however, partnerships are characterised by asymmetrical relations of power among partners whose participation is dependent on the power they hold. Spaces of governance in education then represent arenas of power and conflict in which the neoliberal state continues to play an important role.

How, then, does this political context play out in the lived experiences of prospective and experienced teachers and teacher educators? It is to this context and teachers' and teacher educators' experiences and understandings of professionalism that the chapters in this section speak. They present the challenges experienced by teachers and teacher educators in their current professional practice as they find ways of working with and against the neoliberal turn in education.

Trevor Gale and Russell Cross (Chapter One) reveal the workings of political discourses in delineating teachers and teacher educators as objects onto which social anxieties about traditional values, knowledge and standards can be projected. They focus on the production of effective alliances between neoconservative politicians and the press in establishing the 'context of influence' in education. The authors argue that these voices increasingly dominate the 'contexts of influence' in education policy-making by circumventing the interests of teachers and teacher educators. For these reasons, this chapter deconstructs media discourses that promote a rightward turn in defining ways of being a teacher in Australian schools and, by implication, influence what teachers now need to learn in order to take up their new identities. Their analysis is concerned with naming the messages conveyed around schooling and teacher education and the assumptions that inform them. Gale and Cross conclude that teachers and teacher educators need to learn how to insert themselves and their ideas into the media, given its imperative as a forum for the production of educational policy.

Alex Kostogriz (Chapter Two) shifts the focus from the analysis of neoliberal policy-making to its consequences for teacher education. The argument is made that any discursive-political construction of teacher professionalism also implies the spatial location of learning. By drawing on the works of Henri Lefebvre, Kostogriz explicates the tension between the abstract and differential spaces of professional learning that inform teacher education today. The current emphasis of neoliberal politicians on teaching quality, target-setting and surveillance inevitably reduces the professional learning of pre-service teachers to acquiring technical skills and procedures that appear to be applicable and repeatable across multiple educational settings. This, in turn, presents the location of professional learning in an abstract space that is devoid of social differences and cultural particularities. Instead, this chapter emphasises the value of the multiple and the particular for professional becoming by highlighting, and drawing upon, the everyday experiences of student-teachers in developing their 'practical consciousness' and awareness of what counts as being a teacher in a multicultural society. The differential spaces of professional learning are presented as sites of transformative practice which is responsive to socio-cultural differences and, in this way, represents resistance to the neoconservative restoration of education.

Continuing the topic of contradictions between the universal and the particular in teacher professional learning, Joce Nuttall, Brenton Doecke, Amanda Berry, Bella Illesca and Jane Mitchell (Chapter Three) focus on fieldwork supervision as a site of professional learning for, both, student teachers and those teachers who take on supervisory responsibilities. By drawing on Activity Theory, this chapter examines the professional learning reported by several groups of teachers who met to discuss their experiences of supervising student teachers. It presents fieldwork as a nodal point where the interests of different communities (i.e., activity systems) intersect and where supervising teachers and teacher education students must negotiate the inevitable contradictions. The origin of these contradictions, as the chapter suggests, lies in the unitary representations of learning in schools, centres, and teacher education that are currently circulating as managerialist educational policy. This contributes to a failure of imagination on the part of teacher educators, policy makers and teachers in understanding and reframing fieldwork as a site where all participants can learn from their exchanges with one another. The authors, therefore, lay the groundwork for developing more nuanced programs and practices on the part of teachers and teacher educators when supervising fieldwork.

In the following chapter, Russell Cross and Margaret Gearon also deploy Activity Theory to analyse the construction of professional identity and knowledge of language teachers. This enables them to explicate the formation of professional identity as a process inseparable from teachers' participation in activity and its relation to the wider social, cultural, and historic context from which this activity has emerged. In this regard, Chapter Four focuses on both macro- and micro-processes in understanding teachers' perception of 'good practice'. The authors develop the concept of 'identity-in-activity' that, in their view, captures the contextual particularity of what teachers do in the classroom. Teachers' perception of 'good practice' may differ from its representation in the literature. This has a significant effect on how teachers understand their roles in the classroom. Cross and Gearon, therefore, argue for the importance of producing and disseminating professional knowledge that is more attuned to the workplace contexts within which that knowledge is to be applied. Without doing so, the knowledge base of teachers' professional learning runs the risk of losing its relevance to, and meaning for, teachers.

These chapters call our attention to particular features of, and practices within, education and education policy-making that has been framed by a political context described at the beginning of this introduction. We see the tendency in a neoliberal political environment towards pinpointing the education system as concurrently one of the key sources of, and solutions to, broader social and economic problems. Messages that teachers fail to teach 'traditional values' and that teacher educators fail to 'train' pre-service teachers to transfer the 'correct' knowledge better creates panic. Media constructions of the education system work to permit and justify cuts in social spending to go unchallenged. The work of Stanley Cohen in *Folk Devils and Moral Panics* provides us with a generative sociological analysis to explain the social purpose of panic:

> Societies appear to be subject, every now and then, to periods of moral panics. A condition, episode, person or groups of persons emerges to become defined as a threat to social values and interests; its nature is presented in a stylized and stereotypical fashion by the mass media; the moral barricades are

manned by editors, bishops, politicians and other right-thinking people; socially accredited experts pronounce their diagnosis and solutions; ways of coping are evolved or (more often) resorted to; the condition then disappears, submerges or deteriorates and becomes more visible. (Cohen, 1972, p. 9)

There can be little doubt that such "moral panics" constitute a significant historical moment in the neoliberal politics of education as they simultaneously establish and legitimate a particular set of perspectives on teacher professionalism, professional practice and curriculum.

Overall, the chapters in this section link closely the problems experienced by teachers and teacher educators in their current professional practice within a context of neoliberal reforms in education. The reforms have negatively affected teachers and teacher educators who are often presented as scapegoats for the failure of governments to address educational marginalization and other forms of social injustice. The general mood of civic consent has drawn attention away from social inequalities as matters of socio-economics and promoted, instead, rumblings around teacher professionalism, curriculum and pedagogy. On reading these chapters, one message is clear: alternative and diverse constructions of teacher professionalism do exist in the particularities of practice. Spaces for these need to be made. Critical questions about the agenda need to be continually posed. As the contradictions become more apparent, new possibilities for democratic change emerge.

REFERENCES

Apple, M. (2006). Understanding and interrupting neoliberalism and neoconservatism in education. *Pedagogies: An International Journal, 1*(1), 21-26.

Cohen, S. (1972). *Folk devils and moral panics: The creation of the mods and the rockers.* London: MacGibbon & Kee.

Giroux, H. (2003). Utopian thinking under the sign of neoliberalism: Towards a critical pedagogy of educated hope. *Democracy & Nature, 9*(1), 91-105.

Harvey, D. (2004). *Spaces of neoliberalization: Towards a theory of uneven geographical development.* Stuttgart: Franz Steiner Verlag.

Alex Kostogriz
Faculty of Education
Monash University

TREVOR GALE AND RUSSELL CROSS

1. NEBULOUS GOBBLEDEGOOK

The Politics of Influence on How and What to Teach in Australian Schools[1]

It's not gobbledegook to everyone but it is gobbledegook to the teachers, it's gobbledegook to the students and it's gobbledegook to the parents. These three groups are the only ones that matter. (Greg Williams, co-founder of People Lobbying Against Teaching Outcomes (PLATO); Lewis & Salusinszky, 2006, p. 1).

INTRODUCTION

This chapter provides an analysis of policy and policy making about schooling and teachers' professional learning in Australia. Unlike most policy analyses, it is not focused on a specific policy document – the official "medium for carrying and transmitting a policy message" (Ozga, 2000, p. 33) – but on the "context of influence" (Bowe, Ball & Gold, 1992) that largely produces this message, particularly the "media-tion" (Thomson, 2002) attempted from within the pages of Australia's three major daily newspapers (*The Australian*, *The Age*, and *The Sydney Morning Herald*) during the first decade (1996-2006) of the Howard Federal Government. Approximately 100 newspaper articles were identified and analysed, most appearing in *The Australian* (a neo-liberal/neo-conservative national broadsheet) and dominated by three principal writers: Kevin Donnelly (author of *Why Our Schools are Failing* and former chief of staff for Howard Government minister, Kevin Andrews), Luke Slattery (co-author of *Why Our Universities are Failing*, former education editor of *The Age* and former higher education editor of *The Australian*), and Samantha Maiden (a journalist at *The Australian*).

While many see the media as having a vital role in democracies in reporting on and illuminating the political process, the argument here is that increasingly the media (and particular journalists) are significant players in that process, specifically within contexts of influence that produce education policy and, in this case, in relation to the learning required to know how and what to teach in Australian schools. Fairclough (2003, p. 3) is often cited in similar endeavours for his analysis of the "mediatization" of politics and government, referring to the ways in which the media now affects policy processes and texts, particularly how it has become part of the policy production process in the manufacture of consent;

A. Berry, A. Clemans and A. Kostogriz (Eds.), Dimensions of Professional Learning: Professionalism, Practice and Identity, 5–21.

well illustrated in the activities of the Blair Labour Government in the UK (Fairclough 2000; Franklin 2004). For example, Chistopherson (2002, in Franklin 2004, p. 256) has characterised the Blair Government's communication strategy in terms of three 'Rs'[2]: rhetoric, repetition and rebuttal.

What is intended in this chapter though is more in keeping with Bourdieu's (1998) view that the media has become important in *constructing* policy agendas and is not simply utilised in the service of an existing agenda. Lingard and Rawolle (2004) have theorised the influence of the media on policy production in terms of "cross-field effects", drawing on Bourdieu's notion of field and his text, *On Television and Journalism* (Bourdieu, 1998). In their work, Lingard and Rawolle conceive of a range of cross-field effects: structural, event, systemic, temporal, hierarchical and vertical; categories not intended as entirely discrete or as comprehensive of all effects. In these terms, the hierarchical and vertical effects of the media on education (i.e., the asymmetrical structural links between these fields) provide the chapter's warrant. We share with others the view that the media as a field is increasingly influential or seeking to influence what and how teachers should teach and that this influence warrants analysis as part of the policy making process. This is particularly important given proposed changes to Australian media ownership laws that would see a concentration of such ownership and of its potential influence on policy.

As noted, our analysis differs in that our attention is less focused on the *direct* effects of the media on the production of policy texts (although we are concerned with its potential effects), given that this is yet to be fully realised in relation to policy in this field (although we recognise its effects on the Inquiry into Teacher Education recently conducted by the Australian Federal House of Representatives) and, in particular, such influence is not yet evident in relevant policy texts on teacher professional learning. Rather, we are concerned with analysing the messages *for* policy, as a kind of analysis *of* policy, to rework Gordon, Lewis and Young's (1977) distinction between the two (Gale, 2006a). Alternative views on teaching and teacher education are often evident in commissioned government research providing analysis for policy (e.g., the recent Australian federal government report on *Teaching Reading*; Rowe, 2005), constituting one form of influence on the messages for policy. In this chapter we focus on messages for policy emanating from the media, in particular the print media.

The extent of this influence is necessarily mediated by the particular political and historical context of Australian teacher education. Briefly, formal education (including schooling and higher education) is a residual responsibility of the states retained at the time of Australian federation at the beginning of the twentieth century (in 1901). In the mid 1970s and under agreements reached by the Whitlam Federal Government with the states, financial and administrative (but not legislative) responsibility for universities was transferred to the Commonwealth. Under their respective Acts of State Parliament, universities retained authority to determine their own curricula and award their own degrees. However, the history of teacher education, now located within universities, is somewhat different. In Australia, learning to be a teacher was once done 'on the job' in the context of idiosyncratic master-apprentice relationships and specific employer (usually state department) requirements. As a field – if at that time it could be regarded as having its own distinctive features (Bourdieu, 1993) – teacher education[3] was necessarily and strongly influenced by and located within teaching practice, which itself was informed by broader educational policy. Later, when the initial lessons of learning to be a teacher were removed from the school classroom, through their transfer to state-controlled teachers colleges and colleges of advanced education (creating pre-service education), teacher education was inevitably afforded greater autonomy, albeit still under the authority of government departments of education and, increasingly, in tandem with departmental professional development ('PD' or in-service education) of teachers and sometimes for them (Gale, 2006b).

We could attribute these changes to systemic effects – "broad changes [over time] in the values underpinning social fields" (Lingard & Rawolle, 2004, p. 369) – but this would be to miss more significant structural changes that distinguished teacher (pre- and in-service) education as a field, albeit related and with similar origins. As Australian teacher education developed its own "logic of practice" (Bourdieu, 1990) – more recently reflecting the academic freedoms of the Unified National System (UNS) of Australian universities into which it was incorporated in the late 1980s and early 1990s under the Dawkins reforms – much education policy and practice became far less influential in determining the education that teachers receive in universities, so much so that it is now mundane to note the seemingly endless reviews of teacher education that failed to have impact. For example, Gregor Ramsey noted in the most recent New South Wales government review of teacher education that:

> Unless new approaches are developed in a number of important areas, my belief is that like the twenty previous reviews of teacher education of national significance over the same number of years, little will happen as a result of this Report. (Ramsey, 2000, p. 3)

Despite its apparent ability to ward off outside challenges in the past, the current teacher education settlement is under siege. While others attempt its renegotiation, teacher educators' "strategic orientation toward the game" (Bourdieu & Wacquant, 1992, p. 99) has tended to delay or to stall the renegotiation of interests (Gale, 2003). Ignoring or "standing tough" against "outsiders" as a form of crisis management (Offe, 1984) may have worked up until now but it is a strategy fast outliving its usefulness. In short, crisis management in schooling and in teacher education is in crisis. Those who seek change and who increasingly dominate contexts of influence in education policy making (Bowe, Ball, & Gold, 1992) are out manoeuvring or circumventing (Gale, 2003) the interests of teachers and teacher education, taking their concerns to forums (such as the media) with potential influence in reconfiguring teacher education policy and practice. For these reasons, this chapter takes seriously (without being convinced by) recent media reports that champion new ways of being a teacher in Australian schools and, by implication, what teachers now need to learn in order to take up their new identities. The analysis is concerned with naming the messages for schooling and

7

teacher education and the assumptions that inform them.

The chapter is organised into two main sections. The first reports on the apparent "crisis" in school curriculum, assessment and pedagogy, as identified within our collection of newspaper articles. Bernstein (1971) refers to these domains as three message systems of education, with pedagogy centrally located in a complex three-way relationship (Lingard et al., 2001). Lingard (2006) suggests that "historically, educational policy has had more to say to and about curriculum and assessment than to pedagogies" (p. 3), although inevitably policy of this kind still speaks to pedagogy given its intimate connections with the other two. For example, Lingard (2006) points to the production of "defensive pedagogies" developed in response to standardised testing policy in US schools (McNeil, 2000). Ball (2006), drawing on Lyotard's (1984) notion of performativity, has also argued that pedagogy is increasingly the explicit interest of education policy. In our analysis of the context of influence producing school policy, we note in the data a strong focus on curriculum and assessment (and their implications for pedagogy) whereas discussions of pedagogy tend to dissolve into attacks on teacher educators rather than consider how teachers teach. Each of these message systems is addressed in turn.

The chapter's second and shorter section distils the assumptions and implications embedded in the data about teachers, teaching and teacher education. In Lingard and Rawolle's (2004) terms, we see structural effects between schooling and teacher education, specifically the effects of schooling and its logic of practice on teacher education, as this is imagined by the media reports under examination. The assumptions and implications are primarily about where the problems with schooling lie, what teaching should entail and what these say about the nature of education. Our intention is to raise these issues to the surface rather than to engage with them at great length, given our primary interest in their politics.

We conclude with a brief discussion which argues that rather than an evidence-based engagement with the problems of schooling and therefore with teacher education, the 'problems' raised in the Australian media over the last decade have tended to have more to do with politics than with education. However, we caution teachers and teacher educators against dismissing these accounts out of hand. Influence in policy making is not confined to substantive evidence and rational argument. Instead, teachers and teacher educators are encouraged to take the debates seriously and learn how to engage effectively with these in media forums.

MEDIA MESSAGES FOR SCHOOLING AND TEACHER EDUCATION

Claus Offe (1984) has noted that the way in which crisis is named by opponents of current political, economic and social arrangements generally indicates its potential resolution. In similar fashion, media reports of crises in education rarely stop at reporting the 'facts'. This is evident in the analysis below of articles in Australian newspapers over the last decade, which provide a coherent, consistent, and sustained 'attack' on teaching and teacher education as well as 'messages' about how things should be. We have organised these messages into three categories – curriculum, assessment and pedagogy (Bernstein, 1971) – as a way of analysing the claims that are being made in relation to teaching, teachers and their education. It is important to note that these claims are often made without evidence, the use of research is selective, and claims in one article often counter claims made in another (sometimes by the same author), although through our analysis we have aimed where possible to bring coherence to such accounts. Indicative of the imagined sense of crisis, emotive language abounds and often substitutes for the lack of evidence and reasoned argument.

This framing and naming of values – not simply what is legitimated by research and practice – is what constitutes policy making in contexts of influence (Gale, 2006a). Couldry (2000) has written similarly about the media's production of legitimate and naturalised accounts:

> He suggests that media power is exercised through processes of *framing*, *ordering* in terms of hierarchical implications of framing; *naming* in the sense of the media as the principal authority as the principal source of 'facts'; *spacing*, in the sense that media is distanced from most people's lives; and *imagining*, in terms of the "imaginative and emotional investments in the symbolic hierarchy of the media frame" and how it taps into our sense of identity. (Blackmore & Thomson, 2004, pp. 313-314, emphasis original)

Each of these strategies – framing, ordering, naming, spacing and imagining – are evident in the attempted influence on teaching in Australia through the newspaper extracts examined below.

Curriculum: Back to Basics

The principal criticism in the media levelled against the current school curriculum is that it is crowded with 'non-essentials' and ideologically loaded material. Donnelly, for example, describes it as "broad" and "nebulous" with the goal of indoctrinating young, impressionable students into a questionable "left-wing" world-view fed by "wacky" and "new-age" values (2005d, p. 14; 2005f, p. 8). The solution, in his view, lies with a return to "the basics" (p. 14), especially the ability to read and write. Debates over the status accorded to literacy in the curriculum appear to be something of a perennial issue for Australian education, with one of the earliest in our survey of newspaper articles on teaching and teacher education inciting a "war" on the "serious literacy problem in Australia" (Moore, 1997, p. 13):

> Can our children read or not? Worrying illiteracy levels have governments, educationalists and parents up in arms. Here, experts argue it is time to deploy resources and funding in a more strategic plan of attack, and that parents are the front-line troops.

Debates around the nature of this 'literacy crisis' suggest that the issue is less to do with a 'lack' of literacy skills being taught in schools and more with defining what exactly we mean when we speak of 'being literate'. And the recent attack on English curricular from several Australian states implies that the main point of contention lies with the *critical literacy* movement. Denigrated as a "virus" (Norrie, 2005, p. 10), critical approaches to literacy and its postmodern proponents have been slated for "'mumbo jumbo' teaching" and the spread of "cryptic jargon", "outdated literary theories", and "cappuccino courses" (Norrie, 2005; Slattery, 2005a, 2005b). McIlroy's (2005) disquiet with English as it is currently taught in schools is that it has been corrupted by "the ideology of the Left, represented by social-critical literacy, feminist and gender theory, and deconstruction[ism]" (p. 11). The former Federal Minister for Education, Brendan Nelson, has similarly described the "infiltration" (Slattery, 2005b, p. 5) of critical approaches in education as an ideological menace. As it has been reported elsewhere in the national press:

> The promulgation of a bastardised version of postmodern literary theory in schools – just when its fashion is on the wane in universities – is one more example of the insidious politicisation of our educational institutions by the cultural Left … Before students embark on any kind of interpretation, deconstructive or otherwise, they need the basic tools of comprehension and written expression. Thanks to the dumbed-down curricula in our schools, they are missing out on these skills. More disturbing, however, is the way the 'critical literacy' establishment inculcates the view that the values embedded in Western literature, from the children's classics up, necessarily exist to justify unequal power relationships based on gender, class and race. (Schools Should Foster the Love of Reading, 2005, p. 6)

In reaction to the critical literacy "establishment", Donnelly (2005a, 2005b, 2005e, 2005g, 2005h) and others have called for literacy to be stripped of its post-modern "mumbo jumbo" and for schools to "go back to basics" (Milburn, 2004, p. 6). Portraying critical literacy's position as one in which "reading is subjective [and] there can be as many interpretations of a text as there are readers" (McIlroy, 2005, p. 11), opponents claim that critical approaches deny students the basics since it "[ignores] the reality that there is a right and a wrong way to teach children how to read and … no amount of edu-babble can disguise the fact that reading is highly unnatural and totally unlike learning how to speak" (Donnelly, 2005e, p. 26).

Instead, those who oppose critical approaches to literacy argue for a phonics based approach that they claim as being "the most scientific way" (Maiden, 2005d, p. 4) to teach reading and writing. Taking her lead from US initiatives that only fund literacy programs that have been "scientifically proven", Buckingham (2004) contends that:

> … researchers and educators want to see research-based methods adopted in teaching … Teaching has been described as an art and a science. Yet some believe there is too much art and not enough science, especially in reading instruction. (p. 14)

Similarly, Macquarie University Professor Max Coltheart dismisses a recent critique of the phonics approach by children's author Mem Fox on grounds that she "doesn't know anything about reading at all", because "she's not a scientist" (Maiden, 2005d, p. 4).

These 'right/wrong', 'research based' and 'scientific' discourses surrounding the literacy debate have had a flow-on effect to related arguments on the need for "detailed, concise and unambiguous" (Donnelly, 2005d, p. 14) *syllabi* in schools. In contrast to "wacky" *curricular* frameworks that have been criticised for being "broad and nebulous", "designed to inculcate new-age values" and "politically correct" (ibid, p. 14), a traditional syllabus would leave teachers "in no doubt as to what to teach". In their ideal world:

> There is a syllabus for each year level; teachers are expected to teach, not facilitate; there is regular testing to monitor standards; and the focus is on essential learning ... There is an expectation that students master essential knowledge, understanding and skills at each year level. (Donnelly, 2005d, p. 14)

Donnelly's call for a 'teacher friendly' syllabus looks more like 'teacher proofing' schooling, particularly from a federal perspective. Brendan Nelson, for example, when responsible for the federal education portfolio, was vocal in the national press on the need for "state and territory education ministers to get a tighter grip of the school curriculum" (Slattery, 2005b, p. 5) and the importance of exercising "centralised power over curriculum" (Maiden, 2005a, p. 17). Similarly, the current Federal Minister for Education, Julie Bishop, wants "to take school curriculum out of the hands of the ideologues in the state and territory education bureaucracies and give it to a national board of studies" (Topsfield & Rood, 2006, p. 1). She claims there is a need for a common "commonsense curriculum with agreed cores subjects such as Australian history and a renewed focus on literacy and numeracy" (Topsfield & Rood, 2006, p. 1).

Advocated here are tighter controls by government over school curricula, under the cloak of "giv[ing] parents 'greater confidence' in what is being taught in schools" (Topsfield & Rood, 2006, p. 1). The claim is that this requires a curriculum framework that does away with the cultural relativity of post-modern critical theory where notions of 'right' and 'wrong' are not as clear, objective or definitive, and replacing these with the "scientifically credible" and "research-based method" offered by phonics with its much narrower "direct", "explicit" and "systematic" (Devine, 2006, p. 11) focus on "code-breaking skills" (Maiden, 2005g, p. 3).

Assessment: Centralised Checks-and-Balances

Many of the themes that underpin current debates concerning curriculum also come through in arguments about assessment. For example, "left-wing views of education" are ridiculed as "the politically correct approach" in which "it is wrong to make students learn correct answers" (Donnelly, 2004), questions are "dumbed down", and exams are made "so user-friendly anyone can succeed" (Donnelly,

2005b, p. 14). Like curriculum, assessment is portrayed as "nebulous" (2005d, p. 14), "subjective" (McIlroy, 2005, p. 11) and littered with "cryptic jargon" (Norrie, 2005, p. 10). Donnelly (2004), for example, argues that "what passes as student assessment is often so vague and nebulous that parents, and students, are unable to get a clear and succinct statement of what has, or has not, been achieved". Quoting the Commonwealth report on *Reporting on School and Student Achievement*, Donnelly concurs that "parents consider there is a tendency ... to avoid facing or telling hard truths ... There is a lack of objective standards that parents can use to determine their children's attainment and rate of progress".

Likewise, opponents of the current approach to criterion-based assessment in schools – or "non-competitive" or "non-graded" assessment, as it is more commonly referred to in the popular press (e.g., Donnelly, 2005f, p. 8) – have similarly faulted the model for lacking any "scientific credibility" (Milburn, 2004, p. 6). As Moore's (1997) disparaging portrayal of criterion-based assessment reads:

> The case put by this lobby [who control teaching] in Australia is easily summarised. Norm-referenced tests cause children undue stress and are, in any case, unhelpful. Overseas research studies have limited relevance to us and, unfortunately, research undertaken on local school premises interferes with academic freedom and spontaneity. Educators who want hard evidence of student achievement are thinly disguised reactionaries. Political leaders care only about costcutting – hence whatever they say about failures in school programs should be dismissed without a second thought. (p. 13)

If we follow the argument of Donnelly and others, the solution to present inadequacies with assessment is "graded" measures of attainment. In other words, shifting from the current criterion-based model in which "grades give way to vague and generalised descriptive comments such as 'attained', 'shows evidence', or 'not always achieved'" (Donnelly, 2004), to a competitive approach which instead provides an "objective" or, as Donnelly puts it, "fair and honest" measure of success based on how students "rank" in relation to each other. Here, the relationship between assessment and curriculum becomes especially clear, since a 'competitive' and 'objective' model of assessment leaves no room for 'relative' or 'subjective' curriculum content. From this perspective, the basis for the determination of 'right' and 'wrong' begins with a curriculum framework that is clear, simple, and unambiguous, not vague, broad or nebulous; in short, a return to "an emphasis on teaching and assessing correct grammar, punctuation and spelling" (Donnelly, 2005b, p. 14).

Here are the spurious foundations for a 'teacher friendly' (cf. 'teacher proof') framework for schooling referred to earlier in relation to curriculum. Not only will such changes make it possible to get a "tighter grip" (Slattery, 2005b, p. 5) over the nature of the content taught in classrooms, but competitive norm-referenced testing of that content – regardless of state, local, or individual peculiarities – will allow for a national framework of standardized or 'benchmark' examinations that can be administered, it is claimed, to all students equitably and without bias. As Donnelly (2004) maintains in response to "left-wing teachers [who] argue that [competitive assessment] is socially unjust":

> Forgotten is that one of the benefits of a competitive, academic curriculum, when it is allowed to operate, is that it provides a social ladder by which those who are less fortunate can achieve a higher standard of living and a fruitful career. (¶2)

Much of this discourse on competitive assessment focuses on the advantages it has to offer, to parents in particular, in terms of "transparency" and its capacity to reveal the "true level" (Shanahan, 2006, p. 8) of standards in schools. It is a "quest for national uniformity" (Shanahan, 2003, p. 1) in the shape of a national framework of checks-and-balances to redress decades of claimed damage caused by "powerful ideologues [who] have disguised the effects of one of the most appalling con jobs in the history of education ... when hundreds of ordinary children do not know how to write all the letters of the alphabet" (Moore, 1997, p. 13).

Pedagogy: Practical Strategies for the Classroom

While responsibility for perceived problems with school assessment and curricula (described above) are primarily attributed in the data to teachers, problems with teachers' pedagogy tend to be attributed to the poor standard of their education. In fact, very little direct comment is made about pedagogy itself, with discussions quickly moving on to the inability and/or inattentiveness of universities to provide meaningful instruction about instruction. Hence, teaching styles that were once the staple of popular imageries of schooling – memorisation, rote learning, and testing – are lamented in public debates on the state of pedagogy in schools as having now become "[things] of the past" (Donnelly, 2005f, p. 8). As with the demise of "right or wrong answers" (ibid, p. 8), similarly "ignored is the reality that there is a right and a wrong way to teach" (Donnelly, 2005e, p. 26). Milburn (2004), for example, points out that many graduate teachers report having "no practical strategies to use in the classroom" (p. 6), although her understanding of "practical strategies" is clearly linked with her vision of curriculum, and of literacy in particular:

> I've had young teachers say they've never heard of phonemic awareness," says Dr Kerry Hempenstall, senior lecturer in psychology at RMIT University, who runs in-service workshops for about 500 primary and secondary teachers each year. "I have a great respect for teachers; it's the quality of their training that's the problem. When they're told what the scientific research says, they're often upset that they've not heard about it before." (p. 6)

Buckingham similarly lays the blame squarely with those responsible for teacher education. In one recent article, which suggests that not much has changed since a former Victorian Minister for Education, Phil Gude, was quoted as saying almost a decade ago that the problem with education is that "we do not train [teachers] properly" (*The Age*, July 22, 1997), Buckingham (2005a) accuses universities of being "negligent", and asserts that "perhaps the reason teachers claim they had no literacy training is because the training they received was unrecognisable as such, or it was not useful" (p. 18).

In short, the principal criticism lies in the purported "'mismatch or disjunction' between universities and classrooms" (Rood, 2005b, p. 3). With the transformation of education faculties into "quasi-sociology departments" (Guerrera, 2005, p. 3; Norrie, 2005, p. 10; Rood, 2005b, p. 3) steeped in "half-baked social theory" (Learning What the Teachers are Taught, 2005, p. 14), the purported problem with teacher preparation is that "teacher training is no longer simply learning how to teach" (Donnelly, 2005h, p. 18). As Donnelly (2005e) argues elsewhere, the educational research upon which teacher education is based is "far removed from the reality of the classroom and the needs of hard-pressed teachers" (p. 26), a critique echoed in Buckingham's (2004) claims that:

> A lot of what goes on in the classroom still lacks a solid empirical-research base. But this may be due to the quality and usefulness of educational research rather than neglect ... Education research has tended to be small case studies, funded as one-off initiatives and not part of a larger research agenda. (p. 14)

Lane (2005) sums up the basic critique made against educational research that underpins teacher education when he writes, "education academics turn out research that bears little relation to classroom reality" (p. 37), citing one example of a teacher who had taken a unit on racism then, when confronted with racism in her classroom, said later: "None of that sociology at university was of any use to me".

With graduate teachers therefore open to the accusation of being "not ready for reality" (Buckingham, 2005b, p. 7), the solution proposed is a shift from an academic model of teacher "education" to a practice orientated mode of teacher "training". As Victor Perton, the Victorian Opposition spokesman for Education, argues: "teacher training is exactly that, teacher training, and universities have turned it into a completely academic study" (Rood, 2005a, p. 5). Consequently, calls to increase the number of hours teacher trainees spend in schools saturate the press (Buckingham, 2005b; Jones, 2001; McGilvray, 1999; Rood, 2005a, 2005c), with Jacobsen (1998) noting as much as a decade ago that schools and principals "have been arguing for years that universities really aren't doing their job, because they had to finish it off for them" (p. 14).

In short, the problem with the state of teaching in schools is portrayed as resting with those responsible for teaching the teachers: "Second-rate sociologists who'd drop dead with fright if parachuted into a Year 9 classroom" (Taylor, 2005, p. 28).

ASSUMPTIONS ABOUT AND IMPLICATIONS FOR TEACHERS, TEACHING AND TEACHER EDUCATION

These calls for reforms to establish *practice* at the "heart" of teacher education (Buckingham, 2005b, p. 7) highlight a number of assumptions about and implications for how we understand teaching as a profession and, just as importantly, the role of teachers and education in society. Our reading of these assumptions and implications canvasses who is to blame for our current problems, what knowledge and skills are seen to be required to be a teacher, and the nature of education this implies for students and their teachers. Our intention is to uncover the politics that informs the concerns about schooling raised in the media; to highlight these as political matters first and foremost, not just matters of educational debate. In particular, the argument is made that this re-imag(in)ing of teachers (already in progress) is in danger of reducing or narrowing what it means to be a professional teacher, not simply by diffusing the governance of schooling by inserting new voices (of authority) into the mix, but because it renders teachers' accumulation and generation of knowledge redundant or irrelevant.

Finding Fault

What is not as clearly articulated in the data we canvass above is the shift in responsibility for education away from government to 'someone else', although this is certainly implied through the absence of references to government responsibility. As a way of locating the problem, teachers are a logical choice although pragmatically they present as a problem that is difficult to do much about. In part this is because teaching is one of the largest occupations in the nation[4]; the sheer number of teachers mean that any attack on them cannot be sustained long-term: they are well unionised, are in regular contact with and many are well respected by the public, and they would be hard to replace en mass.

In such circumstances, it is far easier and more palatable to blame the education that teachers receive (as illustrated above); hence prescribing the solution to retrain teachers and provide pre-service teachers with a different curriculum. Note, for example, that Julie Bishop's attack on current school curricula (discussed above) is framed as "directed not at teachers but education bureaucrats" (Topsfield & Rood, 2006, p. 1). If the above accounts are to be believed, teacher trainers are the root of all problems in teaching and the education system as a whole. By taking a position that at least appears sympathetic to teachers, protagonists have been able to argue that the solution for resolving 'the problem with teachers' lies with 'fixing the problem with teacher trainers'.

It is not surprising, then, to find that those responsible for 'teaching the teachers' have been maligned throughout these public discourses as 'second rate' academics who engage in pointless educational research that apparently lacks 'scientific credibility'. Indeed, educational research is denigrated as being little more than esoteric fodder which sustains the egos of academics, rather than being concerned with what is best, necessary, or of most use for teachers: a thorough understanding of the content they teach and a set of practical classroom skills. Likewise, teacher trainers are characterised as 'edu-crats' whose reality is far removed from that of real classroom concerns, espousing out-dated, irrelevant, and pointless research that lacks any relevance for practice. Teacher trainers – and it is interesting to note that they are almost never referred to as teacher 'educators' within any of these

15

commentaries – are therefore discredited 'ideologues' pushing their own political interests: a 'left-wing' socialist agenda and subversive political orientations to text and literature in the guise of what they call 'teacher education' for the sake of their own conceited status within the academe instead of what 'really matters' for teachers in the realities of day-to-day classroom life.

What's Worth Knowing?

What knowledge really matters is a consistent theme in the data. The act of teaching (and therefore teacher development) is portrayed as reducible to the delivery of content knowledge and skills: primarily and narrowly, 'the basics' of reading, writing, and numeracy. The underlying assumption is that teaching is the sum of its parts (and no more). Hence, a theory or knowledge of teaching or education more broadly – whether it take the form of 'half-baked social theory', 'quasi-sociology', 'mumbo-jumbo', or 'edu-babble' – is seen as unnecessary in teacher preparation and in ongoing professional development.

Iyengar (1991, p. 3) refers to this as the "framing effect" of the media, which (often simplistically) presents problems in ways that "profoundly influence decision outcomes" – in this case, that contemporary education theory is an unnecessary and even unhelpful aspect of teachers' professional learning – through "subtle alterations in statements" or the "presentation of judgement" in the absence of evidence or even reasoned argument. In our data, journalists often employed dichotomies ("scientific/non-scientific", "evidenced based/non-evidenced based") that seemed designed to generate a perception within the public that teaching and teachers' professional knowledge are somehow 'soft', lacking in rigor and credibility.

A further message produced within these discourses is that teachers themselves lack any ability to 'be professionals'. Repeatedly, they are characterised within these debates – whether implicitly or explicitly – as illiterate, unskilled and incompetent, with a low aptitude for academic excellence as well as an inability to work autonomously unless guided by clear direction from higher authorities. (See Leigh and Ryan (2006) and also endnote (5) below.) This is clearly evident, for example, in calls for curricular reforms by Donnelly and others that take the form of rigidly prescribed "road maps" to ensure teachers have fail-safe directions for classroom instruction. Hence, it is frequently advocated that the responsibility for assessment be shifted to centralised authorities as a check-and-balance measure to hold teachers accountable (especially to parents) for instances of "gross incompetence". As Lingard (2006, p. 3) notes in relation to England and which also appears evident in the discourses in the Australian press:

> Ranson (2003) has shown how a regime of professional accountability has been replaced by a regime of neo-liberal accountability, which has witnessed an increasing specification of curricula and classroom practices, which has reached into the pedagogic core of teachers' work, as well as ensuring the secret garden of the curriculum is secret no more.

What is 'Education'?

Evident too in these commentaries are messages about the nature of education itself, since this is, essentially, at the heart of teachers' professional work. As Lingard (2006) argues, "it is through pedagogies that education gets done" (p. 3). On the one hand, the argument is presented that teaching is little more than the black-and-white transfer of skills and traditional discipline, knowledge, and ways of thinking (neo-conservativism) while, on the other, we see calls for a platform of individual competition that would have us believe all things are equal and, hence, naturally 'just' (in a neo-liberal sense). Lost in these accounts is any suggestion that education should be emancipatory in its nature, or concerned with social justice, transformation, and redressing social inadequacies.

In taking this position, it has been necessary to reduce the act of teaching to something that appears, at least, to be apolitical. That is, rather than challenging the status quo with critical or transformative orientations as the basis for teacher preparation (i.e., the teaching of critical literacy or pedagogical practices that are conscious of social inequalities and the need for social justice), teaching and teachers' professional knowledge are characterised as purely instrumental in nature: a set of basic skills and the subject knowledge that is necessary to certify graduates of teacher education programs as being 'classroom ready'.

CONCLUSION

One conclusion we can reach from reading these media texts is that there is a problem with the teaching in our schools: (i) with *what* is taught (which is heavily influenced by teachers), (ii) *how* it is taught (the defining characteristic of teaching) and (iii) *how* (in what manner and with what result) students' abilities are assessed (the proxy for measuring teacher and school effectiveness). Problems with the latter are often used to demonstrate the inadequacies of the former two (curriculum and pedagogy). At the very least, recognising this (as a) problem requires a belief in a direct and linear relationship between teaching and learning and that all learning is derived from teaching in the context of schooling. It also requires a belief in decontextualised curriculum, assessment and pedagogy so that when students are assessed for one thing when something else has been taught, their 'failings' are attributed to inadequate pedagogies rather than an acknowledgement of legitimate differences across time and space in what is taught and how.

Of course, there are several problems with these conceptions of the problem. One is that what and how teachers teach do not account for all differences in students' academic achievements. Even the teacher effectiveness literature, which tends to focus narrowly on metrics to make determinations about teaching and learning relationships, reports that "switching from a teacher at the 10th percentile [of teacher quality distribution] to a teacher at the 90th percentile would raise a student from the median [point of student achievement; i.e. the 50th percentile] to the 60th percentile" (Leigh & Ryan, 2006, p. 2).[5] If teaching is *the* difference and the only variable in student achievement then one could reasonably expect a

17

greater improvement in their achievement than this.[6] Certainly, the quality of teaching makes *a* significant difference but it is not *the* difference (Gale, 2006b; Hayes, Mills, Christie, & Lingard, 2005) between poor and outstanding student achievement that is often claimed.[7] A second problem with the 'teacher problem' is that Australian students have a history of very high academic achievement in literacy and numeracy compared with students in other OECD countries. For example, in the most recent Programme for International Student Assessment (PISA) tests (OECD 2004), Australian students ranked second on literacy and fifth on numeracy among all OECD nations. In such circumstances, claims that all is not well with what is being taught in Australian schools, the performance of its students, the quality of their teachers and, by implication, the quality of teachers' learning, seems more like media hype. Lynne Kosky, the Victorian Minister for Education, expressed this well in responding to her federal counterpart's recent call (see above) to centralise the formation of Australian school curricula: "Victoria has record average low class sizes, we have completion rates that are the best of any Australian state, literacy and numeracy rates at or above benchmarks – why should Victorian parents trust Canberra [the city that is home to the nation's parliament]?" (Topsfield & Rood, 2006, p. 1).

Given the inadequacies of teaching in Australia that are persistently bemoaned in the press, a second and alternative conclusion is that teachers and, particularly, teacher educators can no longer afford to ignore calls in the media for change. This is not simply about ceding to neo-conservative requests; it is more about engaging in debates in the media and developing understandings about how education policy is now formulated and the arenas in which this occurs. In our view, this is the learning that teachers and teacher educators now need. Of course, this is not to discount the critique (some of it valid) offered regarding teaching and teacher education. We cannot continue to stall on addressing problems within Australian teacher education (Mitchell, Murray & Nuttall, 2006). And there is work to do on the teaching front as well. However, addressing these matters in themselves will not guarantee well-informed teaching and teacher education policy and practice. We also need to engage with contexts of influence in the production of messages for policy, as cognitive activists. Elsewhere Gale (2006a) has argued that cognitive policy activists are:

> ... in the business of taking their laboratories to the farm, as Bruno Latour (1983) would say. This requires translating the central concepts of a critical education science into terms used by the dominant, so that working on their terms is also working on the field. The place to begin is not with *their* framing but with one's own and then to reconceive of the relative importance of these terms in keeping with one's own frame. Having made the translation, the task becomes one of naming what the field lacks and then to become the source of its resolution. (p. 10)

The "new basics" conceived by Allan Luke as Deputy Director of Education Queensland in the wake of and building on the Queensland School Reform Longitudinal Study (Lingard et al., 2001) is a good example of this cognitive policy activism at work. Utilising neo-conservative terms, the "new basics" agenda attempted to reconfigure traditional notions of school curricula to address a globalised world and new knowledge forms seen to be important for students' futures. It was successful in a way that many other curriculum reforms have not been and within a broader neo-conservative climate. Further and perhaps one reason for its success is that teachers in the state were encouraged to contribute to its conceptualisation and implementation in schools. In contexts of influence, then, "framing is more about constructing the right place to be in, rather than waiting for some serendipitous moment that thrusts us into the spot light for all the right reasons" (Gale, 2006a, p. 9). This is the kind of engagement with education commentary in the media now required of teachers and teacher educators.

NOTES

[1]   We wish to acknowledge Scott Bulfin's contributions to an early conversation conceptualising aspects of this chapter.

[2]   This is a telling echo of the three 'Rs' of a traditional education (reading, 'riting and 'rithmetic).

[3]   A related yet nevertheless distinct field from education, as Ladwig (1994) has argued in relation to the US context.

[4]   In 2004, 2.7 percent of the Australian workforce or 264,919 (233,065 equivalent full-time) people were teachers (Australian Bureau of Statistics, *Schools, Australia 2004. Cat. No. 4221.0* Table 64.)

[5]   We quote this DEST commissioned report with some trepidation. It laments the decline in teachers' "academic aptitude" (a proxy it uses for teacher quality) over the last twenty years, measured (narrowly) as "the literacy and numeracy performance of teachers in standardized tests while they were themselves at school" (Leigh & Ryan, 2006, pp. 5-6) and "assumes that the [academic] aptitude of an individual teacher does not change over time" (p. 6). It then speculates that teachers' aptitude could be increased (despite the assumption that this remained constant in the populations studied) by the introduction of merit or performance pay, even though this has not proven to be successful in the US.

[6]   One Australian independent school recently found itself on the receiving end of a lawsuit instigated by a parent of one of its students, because the school had claimed it could teach children to read but the child in question remained largely illiterate. The matter was resolved out of court.

[7]   The Australian Department of Education, Science and Technology (DEST) website quotes teacher effectiveness research suggesting that up to 70% of the variation in students' academic achievement can be attributed to teacher practices.

REFERENCES

Ball, S. (2006). The necessity and violence of theory, *Discourse, 27*(1), 3-10.
Bourdieu, P. (1990). *Logic of practice*. Stanford, CA: Stanford University Press.
Bourdieu, P. (1993). *Sociology in question*. London: Sage.
Bourdieu, P. (1998). *On television and journalism*. London: Pluto Press.
Bourdieu, P., & Wacquant, L. (1992). *An invitation to reflexive sociology*. Cambridge: Polity Press.
Bowe, R., Ball, S., & Gold, A. (1992). *Reforming education and changing schools: Case studies in policy sociology*. London: Routledge.
Buckingham, J. (2004, May 24). Putting science into art of teaching. *The Australian*, p. 14.
Buckingham, J. (2005a, February 28). The problem with educational research. *The Australian*, p. 18.
Buckingham, J. (2005b, March 1). Trainee teachers "not ready for reality". *The Australian*, p. 7.
Buckingham, J. (2005c, February 18). We're still in the dark, so bring on the spotlight. *The Australian*, p. 5.

Department of Education, Training, & Youth Affairs (DETYA). (2000). *The impact of educational research*. Canberra, ACT: Author.

Devine, M. (2006, March 16). Phonics – Sounds like a great idea. *The Sydney Morning Herald*, p. 11.

Doherty, L. (2005a, August 10). Enter the super teacher, fit for schools and unis. *The Sydney Morning Herald*, p. 1.

Doherty, L. (2005b, August 16). A teacher problem that's multiplying. *The Sydney Morning Herald*, p. 9.

Donnelly, K. (2004, August 12). *Our education system is lacking competitive assessment* (Previously published in the *Weekend Australian Financial Review*, June 26, 2004). Retrieved June 5, 2006, from www.onlineopinion.com.au/view.asp?article=2440

Donnelly, K. (2005a, November 25). The literacy and numeracy crisis in our classrooms. *The Australian*, p. 14.

Donnelly, K. (2005b, October 21). Literacy lagging behind. *The Australian*, p. 14.

Donnelly, K. (2005c, December 19). Perils of multicultural education. *The Australian*, p. 8.

Donnelly, K. (2005d, September 28). Top marks to syllabus road maps. *The Australian*, p. 14.

Donnelly, K. (2005e, November 19). Unsound approach won't take us far. *The Australian*, p. 26.

Donnelly, K. (2005f, March 7). The wacky curriculum. *The Age*, p. 8.

Donnelly, K. (2005g, November 10). Whole language diehards need the facts in words of one syllable. *The Sydney Morning Herald*, p. 13.

Donnelly, K. (2005h, March 8). Why correct is so wrong. *The Herald-Sun*, p. 18.

Fairclough, N. (2000). *New Labour, new language*. London: Routledge.

Franklin, B. (2004). Education, education and indoctrination! Packaging politics and the three 'Rs'. *Journal of Education Policy, 19*(3), 255-270.

Gale, T. (2003) Realizing policy: The *who* and *how* of policy production. *Discourse: Studies in the Cultural Politics of Education, 24*(1), pp. 51-66.

Gale, T. (2006a) Towards a theory and practice of policy engagement: Higher education research policy in the making. *Australian Educational Researcher, 33*(2).

Gale, T. (2006b). How did we ever arrive at the conclusion that teachers are the problem? A critical reading in the discourses of Australian schooling. In B. Doecke, M. Howie & W. Sawyer (Eds.), *Only connect ...: English teaching, schooling and community* (pp. 99-119). Kent Town, SA: Wakefield Press.

Gordon, I., Lewis, J., & Young, K. (1977). Perspectives on policy analysis. *Public Administration Bulletin 25*, 26-35.

Guerrera, O. (2005, February 18). Nelson orders review of teacher training. *The Age*, p. 3.

Hayes, D., Mills, M., Christie, P., & Lingard, B. (2006). *Schools and teachers making a difference? Productive pedagogies and assessment*. Sydney: Allen and Unwin.

Inyengar, S. (1991). *Is anyone responsible? How television frames political issues*. Chicago, IL: University of Chicago Press.

Jacobsen, G. (1998, October 26). Program aims to prepare teachers for the reality. *The Sydney Morning Herald*, p. 14.

Jones, P. (2001, May 9). Educators face generation lag. *The Australian*, p. 7.

Ladwig, J. (1994). For whom this reform? Outlining educational policy as a social field. *Journal of Sociology of Education, 15*(3), 341-363.

Lane, B. (2005, November 16). No reality on classrooms. *The Australian*, p. 37.

Learning what the teachers are taught. (2005, 16 February). *The Australian*, p. 14.

Leigh, A., & Ryan, C. (2006). *How and why has teacher quality changed in Australia?* Retrieved September 20, 2006, from econrsss.anu.edu.au/~aleigh/pdf/TrendsTeacherQuality.pdf

Lewis, S., & Salusinszky, I. (2006, April 21). PM canes 'rubbish' teaching. *The Australian*, p. 1.

Lingard, B. (2006). *Pedagogies of indifference: Research, policy and practice*. Keynote Address, BERA Conference, University of Warwick, UK.

Lingard, B., Ladwig, J., Mills, M., Bahr, M., Chant, D., Warry, M., Ailwood, J., Capeness, R., Christie, P., Gore, J., Hayes, D., & Luke, A. (2001). *The Queensland School Reform Longitudinal Study* (Vols. 1 & 2). Brisbane: Education Queensland.

Lingard, B., & Rawolle, S. (2004). Mediatizing educational policy: The journalistic field, science policy, and cross-field effects. *Journal of Education Policy, 19*(3), 361-380.

Lyotard, J. (1984). *The postmodern condition: A report on knowledge*. Manchester: Manchester University Press.

Maiden, S. (2005a, November 26). In a class of his own. *The Australian*, p. 17.

Maiden, S. (2005b, February 18). Inquiry puts teachers to the test. *The Australian*, p. 5.

Maiden, S. (2005c, December 8). Literacy war back to basics. *The Australian*, p. 1.

Maiden, S. (2005d, December 9). Nelson concedes phonics alone won't lift standards. *The Australian*, p. 4.

Maiden, S. (2005e, February 18). Nelson puts focus on teacher respect. *The Australian*, p. 4.

Maiden, S. (2005f, September 16). Nelson warns of teaching shakeup. *The Australian*, p. 5.

Maiden, S. (2005g, November 11). Testing blitz in reading reforms. *The Australian*, p. 3.

McGilvray, A. (1999, June 30). Better training for teachers. *The Australian*, p. 40.

McIlroy, A. (2005, February 10). Who's for Shakespeare? *The Australian*, p. 11.

McNeil, L. (2000). *Contradictions of school reform: Educational costs of standardized testing*, New York: Routledge.

Messina, A. (1997, July 22). Deans hit back at minister's attack. *The Age*, p. 3.

Milburn, C. (2004, November 8). Reading between the lines. *The Age*, p. 6.

Mitchell, J., Murray, S., & Nuttall, J. (2006). Teacher education: What are its prospects? . In B. Doecke, M. Howie & W. Sawyer (Eds.), *Only connect ...: English teaching, schooling and community* (pp. 321-334). Kent Town, SA: Wakefield Press.

Moore, S. (1997, September 19). Why teacher training fails the test. *The Australian*, p. 13.

Norrie, J. (2005, August 6). Deconstructing Buffy leaves Nelson clueless. *The Sydney Morning Herald*, p. 10.

OECD. (2004). *Learning for tomorrow's world: First results from PISA 2003*. Paris: OECD Programme for International Student Assessment (PISA).

Offe, C. (1984). *Contradictions of the welfare state*. Cambridge: MIT Press.

Ozga, J. (2000). *Policy research in educational settings: Contested terrain*. Buckingham: Open University Press.

Perry, L. (2005, February 14). Nelson flags teacher training inquiry. *The Australian*, p. 5.

Ramsey, G. (2000). *Quality matters. Revitalising teaching: Critical times, critical choices*. Sydney, NSW: Department of Education and Training.

Rood, D. (2005a, September 6). Experts to step to head of the class state recruitment drive for teachers. *The Age*, p. 5.

Rood, D. (2005b, December 3). Teacher training out of touch, Kosky warns. *The Age*, p. 3.

Rood, D. (2005c, March 1). Unis attacked over teacher training. *The Age*, p. 9.

Schools should foster the love of reading. (2005, July 25). *The Australian*, p. 6.

Shanahan D. (2003, June 23). Nelson plan to reform schools. *The Australian*, p. 1.

Shanahan D. (2006, February 8). New bid to lift basic skills of all students. *The Australian*, p. 8.

Slattery, L. (2005a, August 4). 'Mumbo jumbo' teaching to end. *The Australian*, p. 1.

Slattery, L. (2005b, August 6). Nelson joins battle for plain language. *The Australian*, p. 5.

Slattery, L. (2005c, August 18). Theory of teaching faces test of reality. *The Australian*, p. 7.

Taylor, T. (2005, December 14). Why school's out at uni. *The Australian*, p. 28.

Thomson, P. (2002). *Schooling the rustbelt kids: Making the difference in changing times*. Sydney: Allen & Unwin.

Topsfield, J., & Rood, D. (2006, October 6) Lib calls for national curriculum. *The Age*, p. 1.

Trevor Gale
Russell Cross

Faculty of Education
Monash University

ALEX KOSTOGRIZ

2. SPACES OF PROFESSIONAL LEARNING

Remapping Teacher Professionalism

[T]he present epoch will perhaps be above all the epoch of space. We are in
the epoch of simultaneity: we are in the epoch of juxtaposition, the epoch of
the near and far, of the side-by-side, of the dispersed. (Foucault, 1986, p. 22)

INTRODUCTION

In recent years, an increasing number of teacher educators and educational
researchers have been concerned with fundamental changes in the politics of
teacher professionalism and professional learning (Ball, 2001; Sachs, 2001). Since
the release of *A Nation at Risk* in the USA in the early 80s, teacher professionalism
has been debated in the Western world, and the rhetoric of declining standards over
the last two decades has been instrumental in reshaping the governance of
education (Furlong, 2005; Gewirtz & Ball, 2000). To understand the current
changes and their implications for teaching profession and teacher education, as
many educational researchers argue, the new politics of teacher professionalism
needs to be placed in a broader context, notably in the context of neo-liberal and
neo-conservative economic and political reforms (Gewirtz, 2002; Phillips &
Furlong, 2001; Tomlinson, 2001). Central to these reforms is a historical shift from
the Keynesian welfare state to the model of social governance that is based on the
principles of market economy. Neo-liberal policies have been justified by the
corporate need to maximize profits through the privatization of the public service
provision, and education is seen now in many countries as a 'choice' market where
'better providers' compete for more capable students, leaving less capable or
disadvantaged ones for less favoured educational institutions. Not only do socially,
economically and racially uneven educational markets contribute further to
'undemocratic' schooling, they also shift responsibility for educational
marginalization on teachers, teacher educators and disenfranchised communities
(Apple, 2004; Teese & Polesel, 2003). Teachers and teacher educators are made
accountable for an alleged decline in education standards, traditional values and
literacy.

In the circumstances of diminishing state responsibility, market mechanisms are
seen both as a means of improving schooling and as a model of governing teacher
preparation. As the public-service ethos in education gives way to the customer-

*A. Berry, A. Clemans and A. Kostogriz (Eds.), Dimensions of Professional Learning: Professionalism,
Practice and Identity, 23–36. © 2007 Sense Publishers. All rights reserved.*

oriented one, the concept of a professional becomes radically reshaped, too, reflecting the values of global market economy. Talking about the affects of global capitalism, Guattarri (2000, p. 33) argues that in current conditions people are "crushed by the dominant economic relations" and are "mentally manipulated through the production of a collective, mass-media subjectivity." In this regard, as rigid accountability mechanisms in education have emerged from the dominant economic relations of consumerism and privatization, the production of teachers' professional identity becomes increasingly mediated by the discourses of a market-regulated professional community that seeks to ensure improved performance and normative practices for its members. A key to this process is the idea of a 'new professional' – the one who is sensitive to the demands of the market and is motivated to produce quality and accept accountability. However, the paradox of market-driven discourses in education is that, in putting emphasis on self-regulation and personal accountability, they in fact erase the professional singularity of teachers and inscribe instead their identity (or rather pseudo-identity) as a 'managed' professional.

In the managerial construction of professionalism, it is not expected that new professionals question the aims and means of producing uneven educational markets (e.g., see Gale & Cross, this volume). Market economy is interested more in people who have technical rationality and are instrumental in raising performance and standards set by bureaucrats. Even though educational authorities may recognize that professional standards should be owned and developed by teachers and can initiate wide-scale consultations with other stake-holders, the relations of power in this process cannot be wished away. There can be little doubt that discourses of 'new professionalism' are inextricably linked to the new forms of governance in which state bureaucracy plays a strong coordinating role in relation to strategic educational projects. Educational markets necessitate, therefore, significant intervention into the professional lives of teachers and teacher educators by the state in defining what and how to teach to meet the demands of a stake-holding community, particularly those 'clients' who are prepared to pay for better quality services. This new form of meta-governance blurs the boundary between the economic-political and the educational spheres and produces a new workplace and teaching culture that is driven predominantly by externally conceived standards and measures of performativity (Ball, 2001). It is for this reason that the production of professional knowledge and curriculum is no longer the 'turf' of professional communities detached, as it were, from public accountability. And it is for this reason that teachers and teacher educators have attracted the anxious gaze of neo-liberal governments in order to impose regimes of scrutiny and regulation in the face of public concern and 'lost trust' (Frowe, 2005).

This chapter, therefore, examines an alternative vision of professionalism drawing on the spatial analysis of learning as situated within the networks of social relations and practices. It looks at the ways in which the spatial dynamics of student-teachers come to re-write their professional identities as split, plural and conflicting selves, as they seek to come to terms with a political impetus of neo-liberal outcomes ideology. The beginning teacher is thus seen to be located in a complicated nexus between policy, ideology and practice. Epistemologically, the chapter offers a deconstruction of spaces of professionalism and criticizes the reductive typologies in the production of what counts as learning. Politically, it reaches towards a more nuanced account of professional identities, stressing the local, situated and dynamic nature of professional learning, and the inescapable dimensions of diversity in becoming a teacher. The chapter emphasises the importance of student-teachers' distancing themselves from the normalizing and abstract notion of collective professional identity through singularization. This, arguably, has major implications for re-modeling teacher professionalism in terms of vectors of professional becoming that are related to the existential spaces of learning.

THE SPATIAL PRODUCTION OF TEACHER PROFESSIONALISM

If we agree that the notion of teacher professionalism is not pre-given but socially produced, then we can also say that this process occurs in a social space. The history of this space, of its production, is not to be confused with a chain of historical events. Many would be tempted to understand teacher professionalism through an evolutionary representation of its history. But then we inevitably run into a number of problems; one of them is what events, memories, experiences and political circumstances should be included in, and what should be excluded from, this representation. To minimize this problem time should be connected with space. That is to say, the production of professional space should be tied to the social forms of teachers' work, to the forms of its organization, control and measurement of its effectiveness and, of course, to the ideology of what counts as professionalism and what comes to be valued as professional knowledge. Without these foci it would be difficult to reveal the contradictions of professional space and to imagine other possibilities in learning and teacher education.

We should begin the exploration of professional space with the study of "natural rhythms, and of the modification of those rhythms and their inscription in space by means of human actions, especially work-related actions" (Lefebvre, 1991, p. 85). Every rhythm of pedagogical practice implies the relation of time to space, the localized time-space that mobelizes and maintains specific social relations, particularly relations of knowledge and power in teachers' workplaces. And as we look at the history of mass schooling, the production of professional space has been characterized by certain continuities and disruptions in the rhythmic organization of teachers' work. It is not a ground-breaking assertion, therefore, that the rhythms of educational practices reproduce and validate the basic organizational patterns of the larger social system of production. As Britzman (2000, p. 200) rightly points out, "the old question of what schooling is for becomes utterly entangled with what it means to think about school and teacher education as part and parcel of the world." In a similar vein, Vygotsky (1997, p. 55) argues that:

We only have to glance over the various educational systems in their historical development in order to discover that the goals of education have, in fact, always been entirely specific and fundamental, and have always corresponded to the ideals of the epoch and of those particular economic and social structures of society that define the whole history of the epoch.

Hence, education is an inherently spatial phenomenon that is historically related to different social formations, most notably to the production of its spatial scale by nation-states.

As Anderson (1991) reminds us, a nation-state is the 'imagined community' that is tied together by the print-based media. This allows people who never know most of their fellow community members to imagine a horizontal communion. Needless to say that education, particularly language and literacy education, plays a crucial role in the reproduction of a nation-state – its cultural, social and linguistic politics. Complicating the spatial nature of education is the production of other scales of education such as, for example, the global scale of educational policy-making that is transnational in its nature and the local scale of pedagogical practice that reflects the particularity of teachers' work in urban, ethnic, rural and other communal places. The work of educators is always situated, therefore, within the politics of multiple scales that has to do with the construction of educational *teloi* for people within certain territorial boundaries. Any territorial unit, be it a nation-state or a local community, would also inscribe identities to those whose social role is to make sure that these teloi are realized.

Since the 19th century, when schooling in most Western countries became state-sponsored and policy-regulated, teacher identity has been congealed as fixed, if not natural, within a bounded space of the nation-state. It should be clear, however, that this construction of identity has been contested on other spatial scales (e.g. local) due to its abstractly conceived representation that manifests fixity out of the multiplicity. Other reasons for contestation have been contradictions between the global and the local as well as between the old and new conditions of teachers' work. In this regard, one can approach shifting understandings of teacher professionalism historically, from the point of view of time, as a resolution of these contradictions if one conceives of the national scale of education as a closed system. Alternatively, one can draw on the spatial analysis of professionalism to examine productive uncertainties and unresolved tensions commensurate with a politics of both space and identity. Hence, it is important to raise some ontological issues in thinking about the uncertain or contradictory production of professional space.

Talking about the production of social space, Lefebvre (1991, p. 73) argues, that "space is not a thing among other things, nor a product among other products: rather it subsumes things produced, and encompasses their interrelationships in their coexistence and simultaneity – their (relative) order and/or (relative) disorder." Importantly, he sees any social space as a projection of social relationships that become inscribed in the process of producing that space itself. It is both a field of action and the basis of action (Lefebvre, 1991). Thus, when we recognize that the space of teacher professionalism encompasses the contradictory and uncertain nature of its production, we can see how the forces of unification or ordering and fragmentation or dis-ordering operate today in restructuring our understanding of what counts as professional practice and knowledge. The current re-construction of teacher professionalism reveals a spatial tension between representations that are over-inscribed – the dominant codes of professional practice – and those that are deliberately concealed, negated or marginalized. The resulting spatial texture of professional space today is characterised by the tension between the abstract codes and differential codes of professional practice; the former is attempting to homogenize teacher education and practice though the standards that fail to adequately reflect the everyday life of teachers, while the latter fragments the production of abstract space and resists homogenization by emphasizing local specificities and differences.

The contradiction between the abstract and differential codes of professional practice figures prominently in the literature on teacher professional practice as researchers try to understand, and respond to, the current neo-liberal politics in education (Sachs, 2003). Central to the critical work in education is the idea of changing social relationships between elements that constitute professional space as an abstract code of practice. The teacher, the classroom or other context, the content and the view of learning are all codified so that teacher professionalism appears as a technical concept that reflects the values of an 'audit society' (Power, 1999). As a result, we are witnessing the rise of a neo-liberal culture of performativity that puts emphasis on the 'how to' rather than on the critical 'why' in teachers' work. It is for this reason that the production of abstract professional space is inseparable from "the language of technocratic rationality" that validates a singular form of professional knowledge and practice as universal (Mansfield, 2005, p. 214). This is contested, however, in the everyday life of teachers and teacher educators for, as Sachs (2001, p. 150) contends, "there [can be] no singular version of what constitutes professionalism or teaching as a profession" that is shared by professionals in the diverse contexts of education (Sachs, 2001, p. 150). It would seem therefore vital to engage in a mode of education that is responsive to the differential spaces of professionalism. This can be instrumental in unravelling the production of abstract space – i.e., the politics of universal professional knowledge and standards and the essentials of teacher education such as a pre-packaged set of basics skills – by emphasising the heterogeneous vectors of learning and becoming. And if educational bureaucrats try to submerge these subtleties of teacher professionalism within instrumentally rational managerialist discourses, the question becomes: where else, if not through teacher education, do we address the effects of managerialism on professional learning?

THE DIFFERENTIAL SPACES OF PROFESSIONAL LEARNING

One starting point for developing a spatial conception of professional learning is to analyse the tension between the abstract and the differential space of teacher professionalism. In so doing, I refer to a research project in which my colleagues and I explored the challenges of implementing critical writing pedagogy in conditions of increasing cultural and textual uniformity of literacy education in the post 9/11 world. Counter to the current conservative backlash in this area of professional learning, we emphasized through this project the need for a pedagogy that takes into account the heteroglossic nature of writing space and its relation to the multiple textual and cultural practices of student-teachers (Doecke & Kostogriz, 2005; Doecke, Kostogriz & Charles, 2004). Our previous publications have examined the impact produced by abstractly defined professional standards for the graduates of Education Faculties on teacher education. These standards arguably construct their identities as professionals who deliver education, trivialising the professional learning of pre-service teachers as a matter of acquiring the 'basic knowledge' needed for such a service delivery (see Doecke & Kostogriz (2005) for a critique of the Victorian Institute of Teaching (VIT) guidelines). Furthermore, this understanding of professionalism does not leave sufficient room for preparing future teachers for work in multicultural and multilingual classrooms. In this way, our research project was a response to a managerial approach, most notably to its narrow view of literacy as developing basic skills in English and a professional culture of universalistic standards in 'delivering' literacy skills. Through our research project we endeavoured to capture the contradictions and complexities of our work as teacher educators as we sought to make 'critical movements' across the spatial-discursive sites that our students occupy and encouraged them to become reflexive about their own values and beliefs. This chapter draws on the data gathered in this project to consider the spatial nature of professional learning.

Student-teachers in our project were enrolled in 'Language and Literacy in Secondary School', a subject in which they engage with socio-cultural perspectives on language and literacy learning. One of the central goals of this subject is to sensitize student-teachers to the increasingly diverse range of textual practices in which people engage in a postmodern world and, in turn, to build their critical awareness of socio-cultural differences in meaning-making in contemporary schools. After reading and discussing some texts of the key thinkers in the New Literacy Studies (e.g., Gee, Heath, Street, Luke), student-teachers were invited to write narrative accounts of their early literacy experiences and to share these with other students. We, therefore, expected them to develop a broader understanding of literacy as social practice and to transcend traditional psychological notions of learning how to read and write. But, most importantly, we wanted them to consider the way literacy practices – including their own – are situated in specific socio-cultural domains; spaces that legitimize particular 'ways with words' and modes of meaning-making. The outcome of this exercise was to reflect on whether or not their literacy experiences prepared them for schooling and encouraged them to think about relationships between literacy events in other social settings and classroom literacy practices. To illustrate this, I draw from our more extensive analysis of students' narratives (Doecke, Kostogriz & Charles, 2004).

Students' narratives in our study usually involved vivid evocations of places from their past that contrasted with their present circumstances. These spatial perspectives on literacy practices included stories of physical movement through time and space, diverse accounts of boundaries between family practices and schooled practices, and metaphorical and literal references to journeys, pathways and trajectories. Writing such narratives for students became more than reconstructing moments from the past, but, as Deleuze and Guattari (1988) put it, it resembled a process of 'surveying' and 'mapping' in which students conceptualized literacy learning spaces by choosing certain spatial domains to tell stories about their early literacy experiences. Even though the majority of our student-teachers were from middle-class, Anglo-Saxon families, quite a few represented other social and cultural backgrounds. This diversity ensured that representations of literacy domains could be traced across a number of spaces and, consequently, across multiple uses of literacy.

Many student-teachers' narratives describe their early literacy experiences as situated in the textual practices of middle-class families. Typical to this literacy domain are the textual practices of the nuclear family in which both parents play significant roles in developing 'ways with words'. Middle-class parents usually provide a variety of social and cultural resources that are conceived to be important for becoming a member of a 'literate society'. One participant describes her literacy experiences in an interview, arguing that what she learnt depended on the occupation and social status of her parents. In particular, she reflects on the role of her father who is a journalist:

My dad, he always encouraged us to write. So he'd sit down at the typewriter and we'd talk, like before I could read, before I could write. And he would just type as we spoke. And then he would sort of print it off on a page and he'd put a spare page between and we could draw pictures, so we were creating books from the age of 3-4. And so we've got these stories that my sister and I wrote. And so not only was reading encouraged right from an early age but writing was. And so there's sort of a sense of just playing around and being really proud and producing something. And so like we were taught very young to be proud of what we wrote. (Flo)

Important for this literacy domain is the dialogical interaction between school and home literacy practices. As many participants argue this is particularly visible in their socialisation to the culture of bed-time stories. They identify story-reading as a major literacy event that is central to their preparation for the kinds of learning and displays of knowledge expected in school. Furthermore, many parents from middle-class families are aware of school requirements and their understanding of literacy development underpins how they engage in activities with children at home. Jane describes the involvement of her mother as follows:

Mum always encouraged us to read and more so than write, but writing was important later on. We used to have our own sort of dictionary with words we didn't know and mum would write down words that we didn't know and we'd learn ... It was a model based on reading, I think. Just my mum was a primary teacher and she just made us read a lot more so than write.

By way of contrast to scenes that feature bed-time stories and home settings, some students narrate about other places, such as annual family road trips to the beach:

> Every Christmas holidays our family would cram into our tiny white 1978 Toyota Corolla and head for the beach. With our suitcases, towels, swimmers, sand buckets, shovels, cricket sets, beach bags and assorted belated Christmas gifts all packed in, we were left with very little breathing space, let alone seating space...After eventually getting on the road mum would reveal the novel and try to excite us with the blurb. (John)

We can see how bits of literacy can be found in different spaces. In John's case, literacy is present amidst a pile of sand buckets and other objects and is formed by his relationships with his siblings. In this way, most narratives described and reflected upon literacy events that presented home or other places as the sites of literacy learning. A spatial take on literacy learning enabled student teachers to differentiate the ways of conceiving and practising literacy in and outside of schools and recognize the value of differential spaces of learning.

Even though early literacy experiences of our student-teachers were affected by schooled literacy, homes provided semiotically richer and socio-culturally diverse spaces for learning. These included literacy mediated by languages other than English and by children's popular culture (e.g., games and TV shows). Parents, grandparents, older siblings and neighbours brought their own stories to the worlds of our participants, influencing their text-making experiences. Student-teachers from working class families emphasised the wealth of other funds of knowledge that their parents brought to them. These included work and sport related activities and resources that were described as different from the 'mainstream' ways of literacy learning. As Sophie reflects:

> My pre-school learning involved and was centred on the traditions, skills and capacities that my parents knew and were able to offer, i.e., talking, listening, showing and doing... My memories are of my mother teaching me how to create things through sewing, watching and helping my father tend to his vegie patch out in the backyard, of listening to the chitchat and discussions between my parents and their Italian friends, telling stories of the good old days ... This is my experience of 'literacy'. One that is quite different to many children of my age from other social and cultural backgrounds.

Sophie delves into family history in her narrative, as a way of making sense of her childhood literacy experiences. Her account offers an insightful glimpse of the socially situated nature of literacy practices that may not be necessarily print-based and, hence, conceived as unofficial and even hidden. Sophie situates these practices outside what she considers 'the norm'. In a reflection following her narrative, she explains: '[M]y early childhood learning was not the norm and so as a consequence my transition to school was not quite so progressive.' She views this disjuncture in a positive light, and observes:

> Literacy is much more than being able to read and write at a specific level judged or dictated by a mainstream educational system... Literacy is about who we are as individuals and how we explore our worlds in terms of our

interactions with different people, places, books, things, traditions, values, beliefs, norms, languages – our whole environment.

Sophie provides a definition that ties literacy learning to identity – i.e., when she considers literacy she also considers identity. Both literacy learning and identity are situated in social and cultural spaces of meaning-making and, because these spaces are multiple and differential, both identity and literacy are multiple and differential as well. What this illustrates is that in the contemporary world of great semiotic and socio-cultural complexity the lived experiences of literacy can not be represented by the one-dimensional and homogenizing frameworks of education. The narratives of our student-teachers not only demonstrate the limits of such frameworks for professional learning but also present an alternative understanding of their professional becoming that entails never-ending movement across and between multiple spaces of literacy, across different communication networks and related to these semiotic codes and social languages. This means that teachers today should know and be able to draw upon different spaces of literacy. To do this they should develop a particular kind of awareness – a knowledge of the everyday plane of literacy events where different socio-cultural spaces and identities collide.

TRANSFORMING THE ABSTRACT SPACE OF PROFESSIONAL LEARNING THROUGH THE EVERYDAY

In the process of writing their narratives and discussing these in the classroom many student-teachers in our subject have developed a particular kind of critical awareness, something that Williams (1977, p. 130) defined as "practical consciousness." This type of consciousness becomes fundamental for professional learning as it arises from the multiple identities and experiences of student-teachers in making sense of the social uses of literacy. The practical consciousness of pre-service teachers has originated from the differential spaces of literacy practices and everyday experiences of making flexible transitions across literacy spaces that they highlighted in classroom discussions. As such, it appears to be different from "official consciousness" (Williams, 1977) that underlies the idea of managed teacher professionalism and that arises from the abstract space of thinking about teacher professional attributes. In fact, the relations between the practical consciousness of our students and the official consciousness articulated in the discourses of quality teacher education become exceptionally complex. Here we can see a clash between the two models of professional learning – the everyday and the abstract.

Practical consciousness emerges from lived experiences, where ideas about multiple social and cultural spaces of literacy learning described in our student-teachers' narratives appear to be new for them and cannot be reduced to the official and often rational-psychologistic views of teacher professional knowledge about literacy. Practical consciousness in professional learning includes elements of their own social and cultural experiences of literacy that may lie beyond teacher attributes articulated by educational authorities. These aspects of everyday literacy events, which can be described as more informal or unofficial textual practices,

31

arguably inform students' professional learning through writing narratives in a very different way to the more official and traditional forms of professional learning such as, for example, through writing academic essays. Narratives enable students to talk about literacy events that are diverse, socially situated and dispersed across time and space. Because of this, student-teachers' awareness of differences and diversity in literacy learning does not rely entirely on the institutional context of professional learning, but materializes through their writing about informal spaces of the home, the church, the street, playgrounds, ethnic schools, sporting grounds, shopping malls and other such spaces of text-mediated practices. In this way, our student-teachers became aware that school is just one place where literacy learning occurs and recognized that forms of literacy could be different. This made them also aware of interrelationships between their participation in multiple literacy practices, the construction of their multiple identities and their professional practice. They infused their narratives with multiple senses of belonging to a particular social class, cultural or religious group or youth culture and, through this, embedded parts of themselves in their understanding of teaching. Equally, in the concluding sections of their narratives, many pre-service teachers emphasised how learning is always and everywhere filtered through identities and everything students bring to the classroom.

At the same time, when we analyzed students' final essays in this subject, particularly written pieces where they articulated their vision of managing socio-cultural differences in the classroom, many of them reversed from the practical to the official consciousness of normalizing differences through teaching 'decontextualized' literacy (Street, 1993). This is not to say that we, as teacher educators, failed to re-inscribe the abstract space of professional learning through the differential spaces of literacy learning. Rather, the discourse of managerial professionalism has shaped the overall teaching culture and students' learning experiences to such an extent that it was difficult to break the mould of decontextualized literacy and learning in this subject alone. One reason for this is that the project of neo-liberal professionalisation dismisses the plural and endorses unification in the 'production' of qualified graduates. Knowledge and skills of student-teachers are therefore typified, staged and judged in the process of their training so that they can be seen as moving progressively towards an imagined construct of 'the professional'; one who can demonstrate specialized knowledge and skills in making her own judgments and acting with responsibility to ensure certain outcomes (Pels, 2000; Shore & Wright, 2000). With regard to literacy, for example, this means that graduates are expected to deal with literacy problems in the classroom in such a way that standardized criteria set for students' performance are met, contributing to the school's formal accountability processes. In such a context of teacher education, a decontextualized model of literacy becomes appealing as it claims to provide a relatively straightforward framework for the solution of literacy problems, such as developing decoding skills rather than learning how to deconstruct the dominant codes of meaning production. The production of official consciousness in teacher education becomes, therefore, inseparable from the current emphasis on the psychologistic model of literacy learning in schools and from the 'outcomes' culture in teacher education that promotes reproduction of official views as evidence of teachers' professional readiness to work in conditions of managed professionalism.

In such a context of tensions between official and everyday consciousnesses in professional learning some questions remain: Is it possible to transform the production of professional space in teacher education so that social diversity, multiliteracies and multicultures of students are officially recognized? Is it possible to imagine professional learning in terms of the co-presence of different socio-cultural spaces? And, can this be a vehicle for implementing critical pedagogy in teacher education? I would argue that the answer is yes to all, if we draw more extensively on a socio-cultural approach to professional learning. From our analysis of students' narratives and essays, the possibility of transcending the managerial and abstract construction of professional learning outcomes hinges not only on the critical awareness of how the spatiality of professionalism is played out in a dialectical tension between the material-symbolic configuration of teacher education by bureaucracy and the multiplex spatiality of students' social and textual experiences. This requires a re-mediation of student-teacher learning by providing new textual resources and concepts about learning that would enable transformative practice to occur. Lefebvre (1991), for example, is optimistic about the transformation of an abstract space. The possibility of transformative action lies, in his view, in the possibilities of differential spaces to generate new social relations, where we recognize differences and oppose the homogenization of abstract space.

This is essentially about changing power-knowledge relations in the spaces of professional learning. Power relations in these spaces always intervene so that some resources are more readily available for mediating learning than others. Spatial units such as classroom communities or professional communities are not harmonious constructions. By providing certain resources and knowledge for learning they produce differential privileges for some while marginalising others. This is, for example, the case when asymmetrical relations between official and unofficial knowledge as well as between abstract and everyday concepts in professional learning become the domain of disciplinary power employed in teacher education (cf. Foucault, 1977). Student-teachers learn in a specific socio-cultural context, and their contextual meaning-making – the ways they use knowledge – is nested within the space produced by the dominant ideology of professionalism. The local production of spatiality in teacher education cannot avoid using building materials from policy documents and broader managerial discourses that are produced by power apparatuses seeking to provide a particular vision of teaching and learning. As Edwards and Usher (2000, p. 4) point out, this vision is often constructed and cast in economic terms, with educational institutions being required to work in "more commercial and market-like ways." This means a more direct control over curriculum content and performance measures, normative allocation of resources, emphasis on standards, increasing tuition fees and reducing education costs.

Therefore, recognising this debilitating politics of professionalism, the challenge is to re-mediate teacher education so that it is geared toward exploring other ways of professional becoming; those that are informed by differential spaces of meaning-making and everyday experiences. This is necessary for expanding the possibilities of professional learning outward (e.g. by focusing on textual practices of home, school and community and how these sit in relations of power). This kind of re-mediation requires a recognition of the professional learning in teacher education as multiple and relational. It does not occur exclusively in an isolated and bounded space of classrooms, lecture halls or even school practicum; it rather is a site of relations to other spaces. The material-semiotic configuration of learning acquires meaning only when this involves meaningful connections to other socio-cultural spaces.

A spatial perspective on professional learning acquires then a particular significance for it encourages teacher educators to think more carefully and critically about both the situated nature of learning and its relationship to other domains, emphasizing the role of multiple mediating resources in making sense of what counts as a professional otherwise than represented by the abstract space of teacher professionalism. This is not to argue that abstract concepts are not important; these are necessary constituents of any knowledge. The value of the Lefebrian perspective on spatial transformation lies precisely in his instance on the dialectics of the abstract and the everyday. The focus on the interplay between official and unofficial knowledge in learning uncovers teachers' professional becoming as multidimensional and related to their daily lives. Just as the institutional spaces of learning are currently made more open to interventions and official codification by neo-liberal governments, so too these spaces can be counterbalanced by the differential spaces of everyday life. Expanding the scope of professional learning by critically rebalancing bifurcations between the abstract and the everyday through an emphasis on differential spaces of pedagogical practices and ways of knowing – these are the challenges that constitute an important agenda for teacher educators today. The transformation of the official through the unofficial and the everyday can be seen in all aspects of teachers' everyday life in schools and should be also reflected in the discursive and spatial mapping of professional learning in teacher education.

CONCLUDING REMARKS

Few would deny that our understanding of professional learning and teacher professionalism occurs in some context. The concept of space, as I have tried to argue in this chapter, enables us to take into account not only the contextual situationality of professional learning but also its dynamics based around the ontology of relations between, and movement across, multiple spatial domains. In encouraging teacher educators and others to think spatially about learning, I am not suggesting that old and familiar ways of thinking and doing should be discarded, but rather this is an invitation to question them in new ways. Examining how the space of professional learning is produced, what knowledge is legitimized and for what purposes, looking at the spatial contradictions and political tensions – all this can open up and expand the scope and critical sensibility of already established perspectives on student-teacher learning. For pre-service teachers, whose learning (and learning about learning) has been re-mediated by critical texts or other resources, professional knowledge is about developing a standpoint or taking a position. In current conditions of neo-liberal managerialism many of them realize that their position is necessarily embedded in the politics of professionalism. As one of the students in our study (Doecke, Kostogriz & Charles, 2004) argues:

> I will be working within a system that expects a certain standard and measurement of competence. So the questions I ask myself are, to what degree will I impose the dominant mainstream view of competence? Will I be able to detach myself from my expectation, and consider diverse students and what they bring to the classroom? Will I look outside the 'square'? ... I suppose being conscious and aware of these issues puts me one step closer to the type of teacher I hope to be. (Sophie)

In this passage there is a glimpse of hope situated, as it should be, in the perception of lived professional space. The student-teacher makes a strategic choice that is aimed at constituting resistance to the dominant neo-liberal conception of teacher professionalism, which in itself can be empowering and potentially emancipatory. Talking about this kind of resistance, Soja (1996) emphasizes the radical role of marginality in building a shared spatial consciousness and a collective determination to take greater control over the production of our lived spaces. Today, when neo-conservative and neo-liberal approaches to teacher professionalism have significantly disempowered both teachers and teacher educators, the lived space of pedagogical practice can mediate our resistance. It can do so for one simple reason – it can never be contained within the spatial politics of performativity; it acquires its meaning only as fully lived and, hence, it will continue to mobilize critical imagination and the re-visioning of a new and different understanding of professionalism. This might be the most powerful source of opposition to the 'right turn' in teacher education today.

REFERENCES

Anderson, B. (1991). *Imagined communities*. London: Verso.

Apple, M. (2004). *Ideology and curriculum* (3rd ed.). New York: Routledge.

Ball, S. (2001). Performativities and fabrications in the education economy: Towards the performative society. In D. Gleeson & C. Husbands (Eds.), *The performing school: Managing, teaching and learning in a performing culture* (pp. 210-226). London: Routledge.

Britzman, D. (2000). Teacher education in the confusion of our times. *Journal of Teacher Education, 51*(3), 200-205.

Deleuze, G., & Guattari, F. (1987). *A thousand plateaus*. B. Massumi (Trans.). Minneapolis: University of Minnesota Press.

Doecke, B., & Kostogriz, A. (2005). Teacher education and critical inquiry: The use of activity theory in exploring alternative understandings of language and literacy. *The Australian Journal of Teacher Education, 30*(1), 15-26.

Doecke, B., Kostogriz, A., & Charles, C. (2004). Heteroglossia: A space for developing critical language awareness? *English Teaching: Practice and Critique, 3*(3), 29-42.

Edwards, R., & Usher, R. (2000). *Globalisation and pedagogy: Space, place and identity*. London:

Routledge.

Foucault, M. (1977). *Discipline and punish: The birth of the prison*. A. Sheridan (Trans.). Harmondsworth, UK: Penguin.

Foucault, M. (1986). Of other spaces. *Diacritics, 16*(1), 22-27.

Frowe, I. (2005). Professional trust. *British Journal of Education Studies, 53*(1), 34-53.

Furlong, J. (2005). New Labour and teacher education: The end of an era. *Oxford Review of Education, 31*(1), 119-134.

Gewirtz, S. (2002). *The managerial school*. London: Routledge.

Gewirtz, S., & Ball, S. J. (2000). From 'welfarism' to 'new managerialism.' *Discourse, 21*(3), 253-268.

Guattari, F. (2000). *The three ecologies*. London: The Athlone Press.

Lefebvre, H. (1991). *The production of space*. Oxford: Blackwell.

Mansfield, J. (2005). Certainties and censure: Teacher education in a changing terrain. *Policy Futures in Education, 3*(2), 212-222.

Pels, P. (2000). The trickster's dilemma: Ethics and the technology of the anthropological self. In M. Strathern (Ed.), *Audit cultures in accountability, ethics and academy* (pp. 135-172). London: Routledge.

Phillips, R. & Furlong, J. (Eds.). (2001). *Education, reform and the state*. London: Routledge.

Power, M. (1999). *The audit society*, (2nd ed.). Oxford, UK: Oxford University Press.

Sachs, J. (2001). Teacher professional identity: Competing discourses, competing outcomes. *Journal of Educational Policy, 16*(2), 149-161.

Sachs, J. (2003). Teacher professional standards: Controlling or developing teaching? *Teachers and Teaching, 9*(2), 175-186.

Shore, C., & Wright, S. (2000). Coercive accountability: The rise of audit culture in higher education. In M. Strathern (Ed.), *Audit cultures in accountability, ethics and academy* (pp. 54-89). London: Routledge.

Soja, E. (1996). *Thirdspace: Journeys to Los Angeles and other real-and-imagined places*. Cambridge, MA: Blackwell.

Street, B. (1993). Introduction: The New Literacy Studies. In B. Street (Ed.), *Cross-cultural approaches to literacy* (pp. 1-21). Cambridge, UK: Cambridge University Press.

Teese, R. & Polesel, J. (2003). *Undemocratic schooling*. Melbourne, Australia: Melbourne University Press.

Tomlinson, S. (2001). *Education in a post-welfare society*. Buckingham: Open University Press.

Vygotsky, L. (1997). *Educational psychology*. R. Silverman. (Trans.). Boca Raton, FL: St. Lucie Press.

Williams, R. (1977). *Marxism and literature*. Oxford, UK: Oxford University Press.

Alex Kostogriz
Faculty of Education
Monash University

JOCE NUTTALL, BRENTON DOECKE,
AMANDA BERRY, BELLA ILLESCA AND JANE MITCHELL

3. FIELDWORK SUPERVISION

A Space for Professional Learning

INTRODUCTION

Supervision of fieldwork in teacher education programs provides a site for professional learning not only for student teachers but also teachers who take on supervisory responsibilities. Yet accounts of the learning of teachers who supervise fieldwork pre-service teachers are largely absent from the research literature on teacher education. This chapter analyses the professional learning reported by several groups of teachers who met to discuss their experiences of supervising student teachers, and seeks to better understand the conditions and nature of that professional learning within the current Australian policy context. Our aim is to reach a more refined understanding of professional learning within a theoretical framework deriving from cultural-historical activity theory (Engeström, 1987, 1994). By reconceptualising the fieldwork experiences of supervising teachers within this framework we resist falling back upon accepted understandings of professional learning that continue to frame both teachers' supervisory practices and our own as teacher educators and attempt to conceptualise fieldwork differently. We thereby lay the groundwork for developing more nuanced programs and practices on the part of teachers and teacher educators when supervising fieldwork.

Classroom teachers who work with beginning teachers in fieldwork settings play a critical role in pre-service teacher education (Haigh & Ward, 2004; Hastings & Squires, 2002; Glickman & Bey, 1990; Sanders, Dowson, & Sinclair, 2005). Yet, as Wideen, Mayer-Smith and Moon (1998) observe, "supervising teachers are frequently missing in the research" on teacher education, and it is timely to focus on how such players "affect the landscape and process of learning to teach" (p. 169). Moreover, the professional learning that comes from being a supervisor, and the formal and informal ways that this learning might be recognised and given currency, have not been considered in any detailed way, either in the research literature on professional learning or in practice.

During 2005, we conducted a large-scale survey and then a series of group interviews that focused on teachers' preparation for the role of supervising teacher, the learning they experience through this role, and the incentives and recognition associated with being a supervising teacher. We begin this chapter by returning to

A. Berry, A. Clemans and A. Kostogriz (Eds.), Dimensions of Professional Learning: Professionalism, Practice and Identity, 37–52. © 2007 Sense Publishers. All rights reserved.

the design phase of the initial survey, when we, as practising teacher educators, attempted to crystallise our views on the variables we felt were important in the professional learning of supervising teachers, in order to develop the survey instrument we administered.

Analysis of the resulting survey data, as well as critical reflection on the survey instrument itself, provided us with both a stepping-off point and a set of challenges for the conduct of a series of focus group conversations with supervising teachers drawn from early childhood, primary, and secondary school settings. The bulk of this chapter will analyse what the teachers who participated in these focus group discussions said about their experiences of supervision, paying particular attention to the tensions and complexities that are bound up with their work as supervisors. We argue that these partly derive from the managerial discourses that are so much a feature of contemporary educational settings in Australia and elsewhere, although we also identify dimensions of professional learning that point beyond our current policy setting. We conclude the chapter by raising questions about the potential for developing alternative relationships and conversations, between campus-based and in-school teacher educators, in order to redefine our respective professional roles.

Our data analysis is located within a theoretical framework deriving from cultural-historical activity theory (Engeström, 1987). Such an analysis allows us to identify and make sense of the contrasts between teacher education as enacted within universities, and teacher education as it is understood and experienced within schools and early childhood settings. Supervising teachers, almost as much as teacher education students, must negotiate the inevitable contrasts and contradictions that occur when these complex activity systems meet during fieldwork. Vygotsky's original articulation of Soviet activity theory (1978) has been reframed by subsequent theorists and is now in its 'third generation' (Engeström, 1987, 1994). In activity theory, the aims (or *object*) of an individual or social group (the *subject*) are explained in terms of the cultural practices in which they engage and the *community* in which they are embedded. These explanations attend to the *rules* that guide the group's shared activity, the *division of labour* the group employs to achieve the activity, and the *tools* (both artefacts and ideas) used to implement the activity. This understanding of the socially mediated character of all human activity enables us to develop a better understanding of the complexities of the working relationships between campus-based and in-school teacher educators, as well as the possibilities for changing existing arrangements.

In the case of schools and early childhood centres, *tools* include statements of philosophy, school charters, curriculum and program plans, government policies, formats for reporting to parents, theories of learning and development, and methods of observing how children or adolescents learn and grow (e.g. the learning continua that have recently been developed by governments at both a federal and state level in Australia). These, in turn, support and are sustained by particular rules and divisions of labour within these educational settings. Within teacher education institutions, by contrast, important tools include methods of assessing and reporting pre-service teacher learning (both within course work and during fieldwork), manuals advising supervising teachers about aspects of fieldwork supervision, and modes of maintaining contact with supervising teachers during fieldwork blocks. Teacher education faculties are also increasingly subjected to managerial tools imposed by (and on) the university sector, including graduate outcomes statements and other types of accountability, such as professional standards for entry to the profession which have recently been developed by state authorities around Australia (see, for example, those specified by the Victorian Institute of Teaching, www.vit.vic.edu.au). Through systematic identification of these aspects of cultural practice, research within an activity theoretical framework aims to both explore and explain the possibility of transforming the way that groups operate within institutional settings and wider community networks.

The challenge is one of understanding the interrelationships between the two distinct activity systems that constitute teacher education. Although early childhood settings, schools, and universities might be said to share a common goal with respect to fieldwork, namely to educate a new generation of teachers, they achieve this common goal in different ways. Indeed, the goal is 'common' only at the most general level of renewing the teaching profession. Teachers and teacher educators do not necessarily understand this goal in the same way, because their professional knowledge and practice are each the product of distinct activity systems, including rules, tools, and divisions of labour that are not necessarily transparent to each other.

Indeed, it could be argued that the policy agendas driving schools and universities have diverged in significant ways over the last two decades in response to neo-liberal managerial imperatives. As Smith (2000) notes, University agendas are increasingly dominated by commercialisation, research and resource cut-backs; and the school sector is increasingly sceptical of the relevance of research and theories embedded within the content of teacher education programs. The supervisory practices that are part of fieldwork components of teacher education programs represent one clear site in which such diverging agendas have become manifest. Supervision of fieldwork represents a significant cost for faculties of education. As part of industrial awards created in the 1980s teachers in Australia are paid for their role as supervisors of pre-service teachers. While the payment for individual teachers is relatively small, the overall costs to faculties can be large and over the years, and in line with concerns for cost-efficiency, many faculties have reduced the amount of supervision provided by university staff and devolved more responsibility for supervision to teachers in schools. Thus, using the concepts derived from activity theory, the rules and division of labour in relation to supervision have changed. Yet how those rule changes have been communicated and understood by those within and across the school and university sectors remains open for question.

Much is at stake in any attempt to reconceptualise the relationship between educational settings (such as early childhood centres and schools) and teacher education faculties within such a theoretical framework, including the way universities have traditionally been positioned as the sites of knowledge and research. For all the work that has been done under the banners of 'reflective practice' and 'action research' (Schön, 1983), teacher education is still fractured by a binary between 'theory' (as the province of the university and specifically teacher education faculties) and 'practice'. We shall see how this binary continues to frame the views and practices of the supervising teachers who participated in this study. We shall also acknowledge the ways in which this binary continues to frame the work of teacher educators. Activity theory provides a basis on which to rethink the nature of professional knowledge and practice, including the complex mix of teachers' values, beliefs and life experiences (Connelly & Clandinin, 1988), formal theories they have acquired during teacher training (Edwards, 2003), the micro-politics of their workplaces (Kelchtermans, 2004), government policy imperatives, and reflection on experience (Korthagen, 2003). It also provides a framework for teacher educators to reflexively consider their role in relation to fieldwork.

MAPPING TEACHER EDUCATORS' ASSUMPTIONS
ABOUT THE PROFESSIONAL LEARNING OF SUPERVISION TEACHERS

In mid-2005, 1,192 supervising teachers on Monash University's data base of supervising schools and early childhood centres responded to a survey asking them about their experiences as supervisors. Analysis of the survey results have been reported elsewhere (Clarke, Mitchell & Nuttall, 2006). In this chapter we focus on the way our assumptions as teacher educators shaped this survey, and what these assumptions reveal about how we are ourselves located within the activity system of university-based teacher education. The tertiary world that we occupy contrasts with the professional contexts of teachers as they subsequently described them to us in follow-up group discussions, when they evoked the complex (and often contradictory) activity systems they must negotiate in their day-to-day practice.

The survey began with a series of demographic questions: respondent age (the largest single group were aged 50-54 years); gender (70% of respondents were female); school or centre location (65% worked in suburban Melbourne); the age group of the children taught (just over 700 respondents worked with 12 to 18-year-olds); years of teaching (fairly evenly spread from less than five years to more than 25 years); their date of graduation (over one-third graduated from their teacher education program in the 1970s); where they graduated from (82% studied in Melbourne and only 4% graduated overseas); how long they had been supervising student teachers (one-third had done so for less than five years and only 60 had done so for more than 25 years); the number of students they had supervised (the single largest category had supervised five or fewer students); and whether they would be supervising a student this year (only 16% were a definite 'No').

As with all survey designs, these questions reflected preconceptions held by the research team regarding the likely nature of survey respondents and, in particular, important demographic variables with respect to supervising teachers as a group. These included the assumption that supervising teachers would reflect the aging cohort of Australian teachers generally (true) and would be mainly female (also true). Some of our assumptions were, however, clearly inaccurate, at least in the case of these respondents. We assumed, for example, that there would be a positive correlation between length of service and commitment to student supervision.

Instead, respondents were most likely to have been teaching for between six and ten years, supervising students for less than five years, and to have supported less than five students.

A further series of questions explored the supervising teachers' motivations for taking on student supervision and the sources of their understandings about the role of student supervision:

No. of teachers

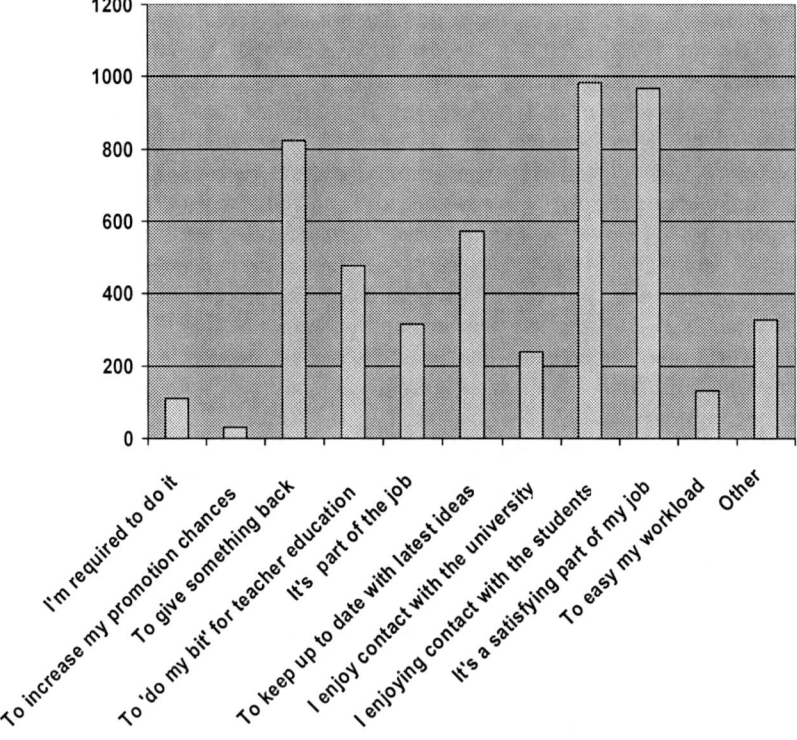

Figure 3.1. Reasons why teachers took on the supervisory role

Whilst some respondents selected more than one category, the four most likely responses were: 'I want to give something back to the profession', 'I want to keep up with the latest ideas', 'I enjoy the contact with students', and 'The satisfaction of seeing student teachers develop'. Teachers were least likely to identify 'For promotion purposes', 'Easing my classroom workload', or 'I'm required to supervise students'. These responses, and qualitative responses to questions that invited survey respondents to expand on their selected motivating factors, signalled to the research team that many supervising teachers subscribe to a professional

41

ethic that involves responsibility for inducting new members into their professional community. This contrasted with the prominence that we had given to other factors the research team had discussed at length when preparing the survey. In hindsight, the selection of variables for the survey is also remarkably silent with respect to the potential for professional learning for the teachers, which was, after all, the focus of the study. Why did we not include response options such as 'I learn more about my own thinking and practices' or 'I value learning from students and university colleagues'?

The obvious answer to this is that the survey reflects teacher educators' assumptions about the rules, tools, and divisions of labour that frame the practicum from *our* perspective. This is unremarkable given the absence of literature on the perspectives of supervising teachers, but it does seem to be an interesting oversight. Because of this absence of an empirical base, we largely relied on anecdotal evidence from our own experience, the reported experiences of students, and our regular contact with supervising teachers. One finding that highlighted the gap in the survey design between anecdote and actual practices in schools was the response to the survey question: 'How often do you meet with student teachers during fieldwork blocks?' Anecdotal evidence from students suggested that meetings are often infrequent; by contrast, 91% of respondent to this question answered 'Daily'. Although both perceptions might in fact be false, this response suggested that supervising teachers had their own views about desirable supervisory practice that were not necessarily congruent with our sense of the way they perceived their role.

One of the most important questions in the survey (from our perspective) asked the supervising teachers where they got information and advice about the role. Just over one-third relied on the fieldwork handbooks supplied by the various universities whose students they supervised; five percent of respondents reported they had had no advice or information at all; and only three percent had attended some type of in-service course related to the role. Rather than seeking information about supervising students from these sources, almost twenty percent of respondents indicated that they actively sought advice and feedback from colleagues in the school, usually more experienced supervisors and sometimes senior staff. The professional learning implications of this response struck us immediately. Our survey had presupposed that supervising teachers were dependent on the university when it came to understanding their role – a traditional model of professional development that is open to critique (as something that is 'delivered' to teachers by outsiders who are supposedly more knowledgeable). By contrast, the supervising teachers implicitly affirmed the value of professional learning that was situated within their workplaces, involving relationships with other colleagues (i.e. a model of professional knowledge that is constructed in schools).

LISTENING TO SUPERVISING TEACHERS TALK ABOUT FIELDWORK

Both the volume and nature of the survey responses made us more self conscious when planning the follow-up focus group discussions. We were, after all, taken aback by the supervising teachers' preparedness to respond to the survey (we had anticipated a much smaller number of respondents). This, combined with the actual survey results, suggested that teachers were taking their roles as supervisors far more seriously and reflectively than we had imagined. They were raising questions about their roles, and – as the focus group discussions revealed – they clearly valued the opportunity to get together to share their experiences and construct professional knowledge about supervision (cf. Mercer, 1996; Clarke, 2001). The focus group discussions gave us the opportunity to go to the heart of issues of professional learning within fieldwork supervision, as they were understood by groups of teachers who self-selected to speak with us in these forums. Over four hundred returned an additional survey response, in envelopes provided exclusively for this purpose, indicating their willingness to participate, even though we initially required only 24 teachers to take part.

We decided to engage the teachers in conversations that both coalesced around the following questions and offered opportunities for supervising teachers to identify important factors we might not have considered:

– How do you establish and maintain a working relationship with student teachers?
– What range of practices do you use in working with student teachers?
– Why do you do what you do?
– How did you learn to do this?
– Does a good teacher also make a good supervisor?
– What sort of preparation have you had for your role as supervisor?
– Tell us about what you have learnt about your teaching as a result of supervising student teachers.
– Why is that important to your professional learning as a teacher?
– How is the role of supervisor recognised in your school/more broadly amongst profession?

MAPPING THE ACTIVITY SYSTEMS OF SUPERVISING TEACHERS

The following analysis of the focus groups concentrates on three tensions within their professional practice with implications for the supervision of student teachers, as described to us by supervising teachers who contributed to these discussions. These tensions are symptomatic of the way teachers simultaneously engage with the managerialist discourses of contemporary educational policy and the highly situated nature of their experiences as members of particular school communities. From an activity-theoretical point of view, these teachers are grappling with a fundamental contradiction within the broad activity system of contemporary educational provision: the local and particular needs of learners (children, families, student teachers, professional colleagues) versus the unitary representations of learning in schools, centres, and teacher education that are currently circulating as educational policy. We explore these tensions through three sets of questions that have been prompted by an analysis of the focus group conversations. These questions relate to the *communities of interest* served by teacher education, the *rules* that guide knowledge production in fieldwork settings, and the *division of labour* in conceptualising alternative models of fieldwork supervision.

1. What *communities of interest* does teacher education serve? More specifically, how do we simultaneously prepare student teachers to operate within a local policy environment whilst also equipping them to take their place in a globalised teacher workforce?

Tensions with respect to the communities that teacher education serves emerged in the focus group discussions when the primary school teachers invoked the Victorian Early Years program. This system-wide initiative that the Victorian government maintains is grounded in quality research. Although this claim has been challenged by a number of researchers and classroom teachers (Davidson & Perkins, 2000), the teachers involved in the discussions repeated it several times. For them, the apparent lack of knowledge about Early Years shown by pre-service teachers was a sign of the distance between their university studies and the professional demands they face in schools:

> I ask [students on fieldwork] about the Early Years Program, third and fourth year students … [but] … no, it's not being taught in universities. And I get frustrated because I feel that this is an important component of a teaching classroom, you know, practice. And our students, our graduates … are coming to us and they know very little about something that is really the substance of our classroom teaching at this particular time, even in the junior schools. And I think it's really important they get that instruction in university and come out with it and feel that – oh yes, I know what she's talking about … [Teacher A, Primary focus group #2].

This teacher is positioning policy-makers alongside teachers as key players in the education community. By implication, teacher educators are outside this community, something that was made explicit when another primary school teacher shared this anecdote:

> I had a student that told me – because I actually said the same thing, 'Do you know about Early Years? – and this particular student said that they went to a lecturer here at Monash and said, 'Why aren't you teaching us about Early Years?' and his response was, 'It'll be out in a couple of years, I don't need to'. So it's supposed to be latest practice but the lecturers don't appear to be up with what the latest practice is [Teacher B, Primary focus group #2].

Subsequent comments introduced another layer of complexity into the discussion of Early Years and other government initiatives:

> I was told that they weren't implementing it because it was an Australia-wide teaching practice [that] you learn at university and Early Years is Victorian. So they haven't implemented it because teachers, once they're trained, should

be able to teach anywhere in Australia and the Early Years is specific to Victoria [Teacher C, Primary focus group #2].

Potentially, teacher education serves communities at local, national and international levels. So the alleged lecturer's comment related by one of the teachers (that teacher education should enable pre-service teachers to do more than implement Early Years) should not be read simply as a refusal to engage with policy issues at a local level. There is a much higher proportion of international students in faculties of education than when these teachers completed their initial teacher education. Increasing mobility amongst young professionals generally since the 1970s also means that many young teachers spend the early years of their careers off-shore. Teacher preparation must respond both to these demographic pressures, with their inherent pedagogical implications, as well as to the local conditions that frame the majority of fieldwork settings. This means that teacher education faculties need to work alongside schools and supervising teachers in order to understand the internationalisation of teacher education (including the best ways to work with international students in fieldwork settings), and how issues of internationalisation and globalisation can be addressed within local settings.

Yet these supervising teachers' frustration about the lack of knowledge shown by pre-service teachers with respect to Early Years also reflects a situation where teacher educators are arguably failing to grasp the pressures that teachers have been under to implement such policies. Whether the university lecturer's reportedly cynical view of the likely life-span of Early Years makes this lecturer out-of-date, as claimed, or highly up-to-date, the comment exposes a significant disjunction between the professional world of teachers and that of university lecturers. The research underpinning Early Years is largely vindicated by the fact that it has been translated into a system-wide policy initiative, even though the knowledge claims made by the research have never been subjected to rigorous scrutiny or scholarly debate. However, the government's claim that Early Years is research-based was repeated several times by these teachers in the course of their discussions. What should we make of this?

To simply dismiss Early Years, as some of our university colleagues are reported to have done, is to turn a blind eye to developments in recent years which have produced a changing relationship between research, policy, and professional practice of the very kind that we have been discussing. Wave after wave of top-down reforms have resulted in a radical restructuring of teaching and learning in schools and other educational settings. There is evidence that, while teachers continue to believe in the value of practitioner research and the situated nature of their professional knowledge (as we shall see in the next section), they are increasingly obliged to meet the demands for accountability embedded in such reforms (Early Years, for example, is linked to improved performance on standardised literacy tests). They are increasingly obliged to accept 'knowledge' that is arriving from elsewhere, via the conduit of policy reform (cf. Connelly & Clandinin, 1995).

With respect to the question of internationalisation or globalisation, this produces a tangle of conflicting perceptions and practices, both on the part of

45

supervising teachers and teacher educators. On the one hand, Early Years might indeed be judged to be a parochial matter in the face of the changing demographic of student teachers and their increasing mobility. On the other hand, as a significant example of managerial control and accountability, Early Years is hardly parochial at all, but takes its place alongside similar forms of managerialism that are currently being implemented by neo-liberal governments across the globe (cf. Mahony & Hextall, 2000). Teachers themselves are the focus of such reforms, and those reforms cannot simply be dismissed because they fail to meet what teacher educators deem to be rigorous research standards. Teachers are obliged to operate within an increasingly complex policy environment, and teacher educators should be trying to understand that environment better, tracing the network of relationships that constitute this activity system, and the forms of subjectivity that such an environment produces.

2. What are the *rules* that frame knowledge production within teacher education? Can such (largely generic) knowledge about teaching and learning productively engage with the knowledge and practice of teachers within their local settings? What is the status of locally-generated professional knowledge in relation to the policies and programs that constitute teacher education?

The teachers' descriptions of the specific demands posed by their workplace conditions revealed a further, related tension with respect to their role as supervising teachers. For these teachers, their concrete, everyday experiences in their educational setting were a key source of professional insight, influencing the way they think about the supervision of students:

Teacher A: [Pre-service students] need to also have exposure to different types of schools. They come to our school and they've been in similar schools and they think teaching's easy.

Teacher B: Where are you?

Teacher A: [Names a primary school in a wealthy bay-side suburb of Melbourne].

Teacher B: Teacher heaven.

Teacher A: It is; it's teacher heaven. But it's not …

Teacher B: I mean, when we all came out we did the [names two schools in low socio-economic status areas of Melbourne] and all of those, which was fantastic as a young teacher but it [the school in the wealthy area] is lovely-land.

Teacher A: Yeah.

Teacher B: And it's not real because they need to have a contrast…not only in grade levels, but, you know, this is what happens in other schools too.

Like, do the nice schools, because they have issues too, they have lots of issues [Primary focus group #2].

These teachers have experienced the contrasts between schools located in different socio-economic communities, and they know that each type of setting offers significantly different opportunities for professional learning for pre-service teachers, not to mention teachers who are at other stages of their careers. In their conversations, they repeatedly affirmed the situated nature of any professional learning, and the fact that 'knowledge' constructed in one location cannot automatically be transferred to another setting. This perspective contrasts with their insistence on the value of a system-wide reform like Early Years, providing a small window on the types of contradictions and complexities that these teachers must negotiate in the course of their professional lives. Yet there is no doubt that the professional knowledge of these teachers, as it is represented through key artefacts, rules, and practices in specific educational settings, provides a rich resource for pre-service teachers, if it can be made explicit to them in ways that have meaning for them.

The supervising teachers described the ways in which they attempted to make these local complexities explicit to students, outlining how they established their relationship with a student new to the school or early childhood centre:

Initially … you know, where's the toilet, where's the coffee, where do you put your bag, that sort of thing. We'll clarify their hours, what I expect from them in their dress, what they need to bring like lunches and sunhats, that sort of basic stuff. Any paperwork I need to sign to get it started, I'll get that all organised. A bit of a run through of what's happening in the room at the moment, what activities we're doing, what theme we might be working on, any [particular] children that might be coming in the door today … [Teacher A, Early childhood focus group].

Although this teacher describes these practices as 'basic stuff,' she is clearly articulating to the student the rules, tools, and divisions of labour that frame professional practice in her preschool. The factors which she mentions cannot be treated simply as elements of the context in which she is operating, as though her professional practice can somehow be conceptualised apart from the social relationships and physical spaces in which it occurs. Her day-to-day professional practice should, rather, be understood as a function of these relationships and conditions, an action that forms an integral part of the activity of early childhood education as it is enacted within this setting (cf. Leont'ev, quoted in Engestrom, 1999/2003, p.4).

Many of the teachers in the focus groups also indicated how they attempted to find out about the student teachers' lives, including their education and work experiences, thus avoiding treating them as blank slates (an important professional maxim, whether you are working with children, adolescents or adults):

I usually find out something about the students, what they're doing, what course they're doing, whether they've come straight from school, or whether they've worked first. You know, try to get to know them a bit personally … Usually there's five staff within our centre and usually we would make sure that the first lunchtime we would sort of all sit down and have a chat, a really casual sort of thing [Teacher B, Early childhood focus group].

Supervising teachers from large school settings described going to considerable lengths to position student teachers as professional colleagues and as members of an extended professional community:

I'll take them down the street for a coffee and tell them [that] probably the next day they're going to be interviewed by me in front of house. So, over that coffee, I'll get some kind of picture of them and then say, 'Well, I'll start by asking you, and then I'll ask you', just do a Tom and Jerry act … So they get to know me a little better. And they quite enjoy telling [the children] where they've been, what they've done … this in front of maybe a hundred kids, some of whom are going to see them in the classroom [Teacher A, Secondary focus group].

[In] the staffroom we're very mindful of making sure that they're welcomed formally. And beforehand, at a staff meeting, everyone knows who's coming into the school and who is having that student … So we make sure that all of us, if we've got something that we do in a particular theme or policies, we make sure that we give them everything from every area that we can to fully arm them … [Teacher A, Primary focus group #1].

For the supervising teachers, this initial emphasis on introducing students to the school or centre is clearly more than a polite formality, but a vital element in establishing a context for a generative professional dialogue with student teachers. The web of organizational practices, the physical spaces of buildings, the social relationships that constitute any institutional setting – all these dimensions frame the highly localised and situated nature of professional learning as pre-service teachers and their supervising teachers experience it. First and foremost in the minds of these supervising teachers is the need for pre-service teachers to establish good relationships with the children or students in their care, implying a larger vision of schooling than a managerialist focus on measurable outcomes.

This recognition of the situated nature of professional knowledge and practice exposes a fundamental contradiction between the activity systems of schools and the assumptions about professional learning reflected in many teacher education settings. We need only think of the way that teacher education students are usually assessed individually, particularly in fieldwork settings, to be confronted by a common practice within teacher education that flies in the face of the situated nature of professional learning, which these teachers were jointly articulating (and enacting) in the course of their conversations. Although increasing attention is being given to the socially distributed nature of professional learning within the research literature (Russell, 2002/2004), we continue to be mindful of a set of practices within teacher education that reduces learning to teach to an aspect of individual growth, somehow situated in the mind of the student. Indeed, the much celebrated 'reflective practitioner' (Schön, 1983) has arguably come to convey such a model of professional learning, at the expense of acknowledging the socially situated nature of any learning – this is despite the value of Schön's original attempt to formulate an epistemology of practice that might do justice to the complexities of learning within professional settings (cf. Kemmis, 2005).

The perspectives of supervising teachers show such an individualistic model to be false, particularly during fieldwork. Respondents to the survey overwhelmingly prioritised 'establishing relationships with children', 'classroom management', and 'personal organisation' as skills and abilities for student teachers to develop during fieldwork. Supervising teachers who participated in the focus groups emphasised personal dispositions, including a capacity for reflection, curiosity, enthusiasm, risk-taking, and even 'madness' in students who strive to generate a truly dynamic and engaging classroom situation. In speaking of these dispositions, which acknowledge the sophisticated knowledge, skills, and attitudes necessary to 'read' classroom settings, as well as an ability to handle the social relationships of any educational setting, these teachers repudiate the notion that classrooms are constituted by children who present with relatively stable and measurable variables or outcomes. Instead, they reveal the way in which the development of student teachers is a fundamentally intersubjective, and therefore risky, undertaking and that each student teacher has a personal stake in participating in the pre-existing community of the classroom.

3. How might we better conceptualise the *division of (intellectual) labour* during fieldwork? How can we move beyond the novice/expert model that underpins most teacher education policies and programs? Can fieldwork provide a space for the co-construction of knowledge and collaboration between supervising teachers, pre-service teachers, and teacher educators?

The teachers who participated in the focus group conversations consistently positioned themselves as co-constructing knowledge with student teachers, rather than treating those student teachers as novices who were being 'trained'. Supervising teachers saw themselves as not only supporting students, but learning through their exchanges with them:

> I enjoy taking [student] teachers because I feel that it does help my teaching a bit and I think it's important to get younger teachers in and let them have a meaningful contribution to what we're doing as well ... [Secondary teacher A, Teleconference focus group].

Some participants acknowledged that students made a direct contribution of new theories and practical suggestions:

> I really enjoy the input that they bring into the classroom. And they challenge me because it makes me look at my teaching practice too [Primary teacher A, Teleconference focus group].

For others, the benefits were more to do with not becoming stale:

[W]hen you've been teaching a long time … you just go into remote control and often once you're on your set topic or your theme or whatever, it really makes you think … And because you're modelling for the time when they're observing you, you have to really think about, okay, am I doing all the things I really should be doing and I often even think that I expect the student teacher to do [Secondary teacher B, Teleconference focus group].

One supervising teacher even related the experience of speaking with a student teacher about the dubious value of prepared worksheets for children, only to look down into her own hands at the worksheets she had just photocopied for her class. Her sense of irony in relating this anecdote showed how experienced teachers reflexively monitor their practices as they negotiate classroom situations from day to day.

Comments such as these prompted the research team to ask whether our own teacher education program actively supported such co-constructive partnerships or remained locked into a model which positioned student teachers as novices – a paradoxical conclusion, given the way the rhetoric of reflective practice typically challenges any hierarchical relationship between professional knowledge and academic knowledge, affirming the way both experienced and inexperienced teachers learn by reflecting on their professional practice.

This paradox leads us to consider again the division of intellectual labour and professional practice that actually frames fieldwork settings. What is the nature of the knowledge of classroom teachers? How might this knowledge be successfully appropriated by pre-service teachers? How might university-based teacher educators draw on this knowledge during interactions around fieldwork? How might classroom teachers draw more effectively on the knowledge that teacher educators bring to the fieldwork situation? How might the various participants in these overlapping activity systems expand the object of their work in order to redefine knowledge about teaching, and about learning to teach? These questions are not new. They have been asked many times (they are arguably at the heart of Schön's original investigation into the nature of professional knowledge and inquiry). Our research, however, suggests that we are presently experiencing a failure of imagination on the part of all the key players in teacher education (teacher educators, policy-makers, and teachers) in understanding and reframing fieldwork as a site where all participants can learn from their exchanges with one another.

CONCLUSION

The use of fieldwork as a pedagogical strategy, designed to support the learning of pre-service teachers, has traditionally assumed that supervising teachers and teacher educators share a common object, at least where the practicum is concerned. Our exploration of supervising teachers' perspectives on fieldwork suggests that this assumption of a common object is highly unstable, or at least more complex than first thought. This is due not only to the contradictions inherent *within* schools, early childhood centres, and teacher education settings as distinct activity systems, but the contradictions that are emerging *between* these systems. Each sector has been subjected to a series of reforms that have radically recast the way teachers and teacher educators respectively engage in and understand their work.

Paradoxically, although these reforms might loosely be grouped together as examples of managerialism, they have not produced a greater understanding across the sectors of teacher education, schools, and early childhood settings as participants in each sector have grappled with the language of performance appraisal and other forms of accountability. To the contrary, each sector seems to be finding it increasingly difficult to appreciate the pressures that the other is experiencing; the example of the way teachers and teacher educators view the Early Years initiative in Victoria shows the kind of breakdown in communication that can occur. A further paradox is that current policy discourses increasingly construct teaching and learning in abstract, generic terms, without any acknowledgement of the situationally specific nature of these activities as they are enacted in diverse settings. Such managerial discourses mediate the professional practices of both teachers and teacher educators in powerful ways, preventing either sector from satisfactorily grappling with the deeply contextualised nature of professional learning and jointly developing a knowledge that might do justice to the complex ways in which professional learning is bound up with professional practice. Cultural-historical activity theory provides not only a means of identifying the contradictions within and between the sectors. It also offers a way of seeing those sectors differently.

Our study has brought home to us that neither the rhetoric of teacher educators nor that of teachers captures the complexity of the professional practices in which we are presently engaged. Teachers and teacher educators alike need to develop a new language that enables us to grapple with the present and future complexities posed by the concrete situations in which we are working. Together, we need to develop a better understanding of the socially mediated nature of learning, and to resist the way managerial ideology and processes position people as abstract individuals and treat the social and historical conditions in which they work as being of no real consequence when it comes to engaging in productive forms of pedagogy.

REFERENCES

Clandinin, J. D., & Connelly, M. F. (1995). *Teachers' professional knowledge landscapes.* New York: Teachers College Press.

Clarke, A., Mitchell, J., & Nuttall, J. (2006). *Pedagogy and the practicum: A comparative analysis of the profile and perspectives of Canadian and Australian cooperating teachers.* Paper presented at the Annual Meeting of the American Educational Research Association, San Francisco, California.

Clark, C. M. (2001). *Talking shop: Authentic conversation and teacher learning.* New York: Teachers College Press.

Connelly, F. J., & Clandindin, D. J. (1988). *Teachers as curriculum planners: Narratives of experience.* New York: Teachers College Press.

Edwards, S. (2003). *"The curriculum is ... " Early childhood educators' conceptions of curriculum and developmentally appropriate practice. A comparative case study across two Victorian early childhood educational settings.* Unpublished PhD thesis, Monash University, Melbourne, Australia.

Engeström, Y. (1987). *Learning by expanding: An activity-theoretical approach to developmental research.* Helsinki, Finland: Orienta-Konsultit.

Engeström, Y. (1994). Teachers as collaborative thinkers: Activity-theoretical study of an innovative teacher team. In G. Handal & S. Vaage (Eds.), *Teachers minds and actions: Research on teachers' thinking and practice.* London: Falmer Press.

Engeström, Y., Miettinen, R., & Punamäki, R. (Eds). (1999/2003). *Perspectives on activity theory.* Cambridge, UK: Cambridge University Press.

Glickman, G., & Bey, T. (1990). Supervision. In R. Houston (Ed.), *Handbook of research on teacher education.* New York: Macmillan.

Haigh, M., & Ward, G. (2004). Problematising practicum relationships: Questioning the 'taken for granted'. *Australian Journal of Education, 48*(2), 134-148.

Hastings, W., & Squires, D. (2002). Restructuring and reculturing: Practicum supervision as professional development for teachers. *Asia-Pacific Journal of Teacher Education, 30*(1), 79-91.

Kelchtermans, G. (2004). *Valuing vicissitude and vulnerability: Tracking the micropolitical learning of new teachers.* Paper presented at the Annual Meeting of the American Educational Research Association, San Diego, California.

Kemmis, S. (2005). Knowing practice: Searching for saliences. *Pedagogy, Culture and Society, 13*(3), 391-426.

Korthagen, F. A. J. (2003). *Practice, theory and person in life-long professional learning.* Paper presented at the Biennial Meeting of the International Study Association for Teachers and Teaching, Leiden, The Netherlands.

Mahony, P., & Hextall, I. (2000). *Reconstructing teaching: Standards, performance and accountability,* London: RoutledgeFalmer.

Mercer, N. (1996). *The guided construction of knowledge.* Adelaide, South Australia: Multilingual Matters.

Perkins R., & Davidson, J. (2000). What do we value ... Where do we stand? Special Joint Issue *English in Australia,* 129-130 and *Literacy Learning: The Middle Years, 9*(1), 17-23.

Russell, D. R. (2004). Looking beyond the interface: Activity theory and distributed learning. In. H. Daniels & A. Edwards (Eds.), *The RoutledgeFalmer Reader in Psychology of Education.* London: RoutledgeFalmer.

Sanders, M., Dowson, M., & Sinclair, C. (2005). What do associate teachers do anyway? A comparison of theoretical conceptualizations in the literature and observed practice in the field. *Teachers College Record, 107*(4), 706-738.

Schön, D. A. (1983). *The reflective practitioner: How professionals think in action.* New York: Basic Books.

Smith, R. (2000). The future of teacher education: Principles and practices. *Asia-Pacific Journal of Teacher Education, 28*(1), 7-22.

Vygotsky, L. S. (1978). *Mind in society: The development of higher psychological processes.* Cambridge, MA: Harvard University Press.

Wideen, M., Mayer-Smith, J., & Moon, B. (1998). A critical analysis of the research on learning to teach: Making a case for an ecological perspective on inquiry. *Review of Educational Research, 68*(2), 130-178.

Joce Nuttall
Brenton Doecke
Amanda Berry
Bella Illesca
Jane Mitchell

Faculty of Education
Monash University

RUSSELL CROSS AND MARGARET GEARON

4. THE CONFLUENCE OF
DOING, THINKING, AND KNOWING

Classroom Practice as the Crucible of Foreign Language Teacher Identity

IDENTITY AND FOREIGN LANGUAGE TEACHER EDUCATION RESEARCH

While identity has been a topic of interest within the field of general teacher education for quite some time, second language acquisition research – the knowledge base upon which foreign language teacher education relies – has historically confined studies of identity to language learners and learning (see, for example, Norton & Toohey, 2002; Ricento, 2005), rather than to studies of language teachers or teaching. Indeed, as Vélez-Rendón (2002) concludes in her recent critique of foreign language teacher education research, there is still much we do not know of language teachers and their work: "what they do, how they think, what they know, and how they learn" (citing Freeman & Richards, 1996, p. 465). Varghese, Morgan, Johnston and Johnson (2005) have similarly identified the topic of language teacher identity to be "an emerging subject of interest" (p. 21) within the broader field of second language education, and conclude that future research in this area will ultimately depend upon studies that take into account conceptions of language teacher identity as both 'identity-in-practice' and 'identity-in-discourse':

> In 'identity-in-practice,' teacher agency is seen as action-oriented and focusing on concrete practices and tasks in relation to a group and mentor(s). In 'identity-in-discourse,' agency is discursively constituted, mainly through language … there needs to be a recognition that in language teacher education we must incorporate simultaneously a focus on shared practices in communities as well as individual "meta-awareness" (Ramanathan, 2002). (Varghese et al., 2005, p. 39)

While we concur with Varghese and her colleagues' fundamental premise that research on language teacher identity requires both an understanding of identity as concrete, action-orientated practice, as well as how that practice has been discursively constituted by the community within which it occurs, our point of departure in this chapter lies in their suggestion that these two lines of inquiry might somehow be understood as independent or separable. Instead, drawing on Vygotsky's thesis of human development which has as its core the dialectic between (practical) activity and the broader social, cultural-historic (discursive)

A. Berry, A. Clemans and A. Kostogriz (Eds.), Dimensions of Professional Learning: Professionalism, Practice and Identity, 53–67. © 2007 Sense Publishers. All rights reserved.

context from which that activity emerges, we propose an alternate frame of reference for understanding language teacher identity which captures both conceptions – practice and discourse – as inseparable domains of development within a notion of 'identity-in-activity'[1].

IDENTITY-IN-ACTIVITY

Sociocultural theory is concerned with the social formation of the mind. In sum, the idea that (cognitive) mental development is not purely the product of biological maturity, but is dependent upon ongoing interaction with the (social) world around us (Vygotsky, 1978, 1987). For Vygotsky, humans do not act directly upon their world but, through the use of mediatory tools and other cultural artefacts, they interact with the world around them to regulate their environment through activity.

While Vygotsky never explicitly dealt with the concept of identity himself (Varfolomeeva & Gearon, 2006), we would agree with Penuel and Wertsch's (1995) assertion that sociocultural theory nevertheless provides a useful basis for researching and understanding identity. By this, we understand identity to be a fluid and ongoing developmental process that involves the formation of one's (individual) 'self' in relation to a broader set of social practices and shared cultural experiences. As Roth (2004) puts it, "identity is something that is continuously made and remade in [mediated] activity; it is a being in continuous becoming" (p. 8). Our orientation to identity therefore reflects an understanding of identity that occupies much of the literature on social and cultural theory; that is, identity as a culturally constructed sense of one's self (Butler, 1990; Buzzelli & Johnston, 2002; Hall, 1996; Norton, 2000) in relation to a situated context of shared social, political, and historical practices (Gee, 1996; Lave & Wegner, 1991). Hall's (1996) conception of identity, for example, is consistent with that offered by Roth in his assertion that identity is concerned with "questions of using resources of history, language and culture in the process of becoming rather than being ... what we might become" (p. 4). Similarly, as Penuel and Wertsch (1995) argue from a Vygotskian perspective:

> Identity formation must be viewed as shaped by and shaping forms of action, involving a complex interplay amongst cultural tools employed in the action, the sociocultural and institutional context of the action, and the purposes embedded in the action. Taking human action as the focus of the analysis, we are able to provide a more coherent account of identity, not as a static, inflexible structure of the self, but as a dynamic dimension or moment in action, that may in fundamental ways change from activity to activity, depending on the way, in each activity, the purpose, form, cultural tools, and contexts are coordinated. (p. 84)

Hence the idea of activity – the process of 'becoming', and not simply 'being' – is pivotal in how we might approach an understanding of identity from the perspective of Vygotskian sociocultural theory.

Mediated Activity: A Unit of Analysis for Researching Identity

As we explained earlier, Vygotsky argued that humans use tools and other cultural artefacts to mediate their relationship with the world around them, rather than acting upon the world directly. This concept of 'mediated activity' is central to sociocultural theory since it is through the internalisation of external (i.e., social) activity that we begin to regulate internal psychological functions. As Vygotsky (1981) himself put it, "all higher mental functions are internalized social relationships" (p. 164).

Within Vygotsky's own work, the focus remained on the relationship between the subject's use of tools and the development of higher mental functions, rather than an understanding of the nature of *activity* itself. It was not until later that Leontiev (1981) extended the concept further by shifting the unit of analysis away from the tool, to the activity within which the tool was being used. This is the basic principle of what we now understand as activity theory.

Within Leontiev's theory of activity, one's individual activity only has meaning in relation to its specific social context: "the human individual's activity is a system of social relations. *It does not exist without those social relations*" (Leontiev, 1981, pp. 46-47, emphasis added). The activity (i.e., social practice) of 'language teaching' – what languages teachers do and what, therefore, contributes to the formation of their teacher identity as the subject of that activity – does not exist 'out there' in its own right. Rather, it is defined by the context within which it occurs: its *community*, the *rules* which regulate that activity, and how roles and responsibilities are distributed within that community (i.e., *the division of labour*). Engeström (1987) conceptualises this set of relations to be that of an "activity system" (Figure 4.1):

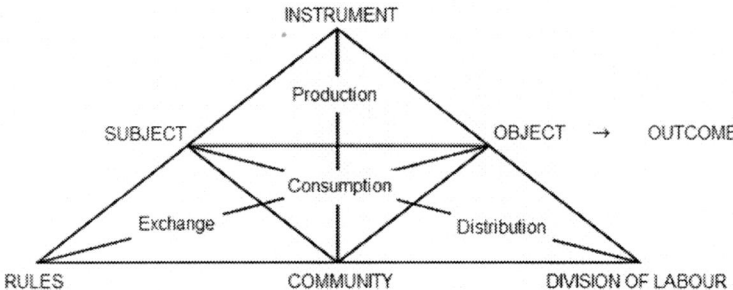

Figure 4.1. The structure of human activity as a system. (Engeström, 1987, p. 41)

Thus, an understanding of language teacher identity resides in an understanding of the activity the teacher is expected to perform – as the *subject* of that activity – within his or her wider system of social, cultural, and historic relations. In this sense, identity is again consonant with Hall's (1996) assertion that "identities are … points of temporary attachment to the subject positions which discursive practices construct for us ... They are the result of a successful articulation or 'chaining' of the subject into the flow of the discourse" (p. 6).

However, it must also be acknowledged that the constituent nodes of the system – the rules, community, division of labour, subject, object, and even the instruments themselves – have histories of their own. By bringing to the present system of activity these pre-existing histories, any activity we observe now, in the present, must be understood in relation to the wider social, cultural, and historic context from which it has emerged. Drawing on another concept central to Vygotskian sociocultural theory – genetic analysis – an understanding of activity also therefore requires an understanding of its 'genesis', or its social and cultural origins: "'behaviour can only be understood as the history of behaviour' (Blonsky). This idea is the cardinal principle of the whole method" (Vygotsky, 1994, p. 70).

Genetic Analysis: Linking Cultural-Historic Discourses to Individual Practice

Vygotsky's genetic framework consists of four interrelated levels of analysis – the phylogenetic, cultural-historic, ontogenetic, microgenetic – which are distinguished by the nature of human development in relation to physical time (Vygotsky & Luria, 1994). Cole and Engeström (1993) illustrate the nested relationship between each of the four domains in Figure 4.2 below, with the ellipse representing one specific event in time:

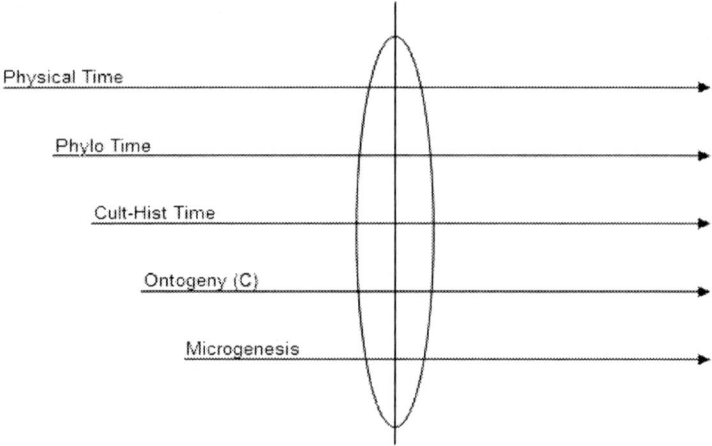

Figure 4.2. Sociocultural theoretical domains of genetic analysis.
(Cole & Engeström, 1993, p. 20)

In broad strokes, *phylogenetic* analysis concerns the nature of human development over the course of evolution as a 'natural' species (i.e., the biological basis for human development), while *cultural-historic* analysis is concerned with the development of the 'external' world within which human activity unfolds (the

56

social, cultural, and historic basis for development). *Ontogenetic* analysis shifts the focus from these two broader lines of development to the subject, as an individual, across their lifespan. Ontogenesis, itself, is the culmination of continuous and ongoing instances of *microgenetic* activity, or the moment-by-moment interactions the individual has with the world.

It is here at the microgenetic domain of development that the teacher's activity system occurs on an ongoing daily basis. From a sociocultural perspective, this is the basis for defining who the subject 'is' with respect to concrete, social practices (i.e., activity). To use Varghese et al.'s (2005) conceptions of identity, this alludes to 'identity-in-practice'.

However, as we explained earlier, microgenesis can only be properly understood when considered in relation to its own genesis. In other words, it is necessary not only to understand the present form of the concrete, observable activity, but also the social, cultural, and historic context from which that activity has emerged (the *cultural-historic* domain). This might, for example, be expressed through public policies on languages and teaching (the discursive construction of identity), whereas the microgenetic domain examines how that activity then unfolds in the immediate context of a specific system of social and cultural relations (the concrete, practical construction of identity).

Thus, by focusing on *activity* as the primary unit of analysis – 'identity-in-activity' – we have a framework to understand identity as a synthesis of practice (microgenetic development, or 'identity-in-practice') *with* discourse (cultural-historic development, 'identity-in-discourse'), rather than the suggestion (implied or otherwise) that the two are somehow separable or independent domains of analysis in their own right.

Up to this point, it might appear that we have neglected the issue of agency. However, given the dialectic nature of genetic development, agency is an inherent aspect of microgenesis. The participant, as the subject of that system of activity, brings to that activity his or her own experiences, history, and background (i.e., their ontogenesis) from which he or she makes sense of the system and, in turn, decisions on how to then act within it. While agency is therefore constrained, because of the limitations of the subject's own experiences and background, as well as the nature of the activity system itself (e.g., the tools available or the role the subject plays within the division of labour), this constraint is indicative of a notion of agency which is a dialectic between social structures and the self, with "neither subject (human agent) nor object ('society', or social institutions) ... having primacy [since] *each is constituted in and through recurrent practices* [i.e., activity]" (Giddens, 1982, p. 8, emphasis in original).

The remainder of this chapter illustrates the application of this framework language teacher identity using data from a larger study of language teaching in Australia (Cross, 2006). The teacher, whose classroom practice we draw on for microgenetic data, is a Japanese teacher in the middle years, Elle[2]. We begin, however, with a brief discussion of the cultural-historic domain for Elle's activity, by analysing the social, cultural, and historical context for teaching Japanese in the middle years in the state of Victoria, Australia.

THE ACTIVITY OF TEACHING JAPANESE
AS A FOREIGN LANGUAGE IN THE MIDDLE YEARS

Cultural-Historic Genetic Analysis

In the cultural-historic analysis we present here, the key sociocultural 'tool' we see as having landscaped the cultural-historic context for the genesis of Elle's individual classroom activity is *policy*. This is not to suggest that policy dictates Elle's practice. Rather, it reflects Vygotsky's dialectic thesis on the nature of tools and social activity, in that policies "carry with them both possibilities and constraints, contradictions and spaces. The reality of policy in practice depends upon the compromises and accommodations to these in particular settings" (Bowe, Ball & Gold, 1992, p. 15).

Gale's (1999) idea of "policy as ideology", which extends Ball's (1994) notion of policy as text and discourse, further clarifies the notion of policy as a cultural artefact of wider social and cultural practices. While acknowledging that policies are represented in certain ways as text, and interpreted in certain ways as practice, Gale's point is that "policies are 'ideological and political artefacts which have been constructed within a particular historical and political context' (Burton & Weiner, 1990, p. 205)" (p. 399).

In this chapter, we appreciate King's (1979) definition of education policies as those "whose implementation can reasonably affect the promotion of learning" (p. 60). As such, the two key areas of policy which we see as being relevant for the teaching of Japanese in this particular context are those concerning 'teaching Japanese as a foreign language', together with those on 'teaching in the Victorian middle years'.

Teaching Japanese as a foreign language. As one of the authors has discussed in more detail elsewhere (Cross, 2005), the ostensible goal of the Victorian curriculum for Japanese (i.e., a subject in which students learn "to *communicate* in the target language" (Victorian Board of Studies, 2000, p. 5, emphasis added)) seems to hold little relevance in the present social, cultural, political, and educational context for Australian schooling. Rather, the shift towards a focus on the 'basics' – literacy, numeracy, and critical thinking – has eroded the once assured place Japanese had as a subject with inherent value in its own right when languages were first introduced as a compulsory key learning area (KLA) in the mid 1990s.

While initiatives during the 1990s secured dedicated support from both state and federal governments which led to a decade of Japanese language teaching that Lo Bianco (1999) has dubbed the "tsunami" of Australian languages education, these same developments were also the cause of its eventual demise. Shifting from a moral and social rationale to one purely economic and material, the reformulation of the *National Policy on Languages* (Lo Bianco, 1987) to *Australia's Language* (Commonwealth Department of Employment, Education & Training, 1991) was censured by some as so narrow in its terms of reference that it become void of a balanced social and cultural argument that would continue to frame "language learning as a symbol of the way in which we understand our society" (Liddicoat, 1996, p. 7).

The result – a utilitarian relationship between LOTE ('Languages Other Than English', the curriculum for languages education as it is known in Australia) and partisan economic policy – left the status of languages education under a different political persuasion uncertain. Indeed, the orientation of the Howard Coalition government since replacing Labor in 1996 has seen a return to what Lo Bianco (2003) describes as "the primacy of English" (p. 25), and arguments for the development of communicative skills in Japanese (or any foreign language) in schools diminish. Rae (2003), for example, recently postured whether we should even "persevere with the concept of LOTE as a key learning area that demands every student's participation over most of the compulsory years of schooling?" (¶1). The basis for his argument is one oft-heard: LOTE has done little to increase cultural diversity, with few students only ever achieving more than the most rudimentary level of proficiency. In response, Mueller (2003) advances a number of reasons why LOTE should be maintained as a core learning area but, in contrast to the rhetoric described earlier in terms of the conventional goal of foreign language learning (i.e., 'to communicate'), she argues instead for a rationale based on the contribution LOTE makes to the development of higher-order skills (i.e., "sound study habits and a better understanding of how to learn" (¶10)), and its "benefit for student literacy in the first language" (¶10). In short, "the compelling reasons for learning languages reside in the intellectual enrichment of the individual learner" (Australian Literacy and Languages Council, 1996 cited in Mueller, 2003, ¶11).

This position reflects the general trend that has been observed by commentators on language education in Australia in recent years – despite curriculum rhetoric that languages be taught with communicative intent, the reality is that LOTE is now justified and defended on the basis of being "a useful support for other curriculum areas, most recently, literacy in English" (Liddicoat, 2002, p. 30). Such observations have been echoed by Lo Bianco (2003) and others in their analyses of globalisation and the effect of the primacy of English on languages education; namely, the tendency for advocates of languages education policy to "sharpen their justifications for mass language learning [by] advancing the interdependent effects of literacy in second languages with literacy in English" (Lo Bianco, 2003, p. 27), and a trend amongst schools to "[re-evaluate] the extent of their present commitment to languages in the context of the higher priority now devoted to increasing performance in English literacy assessments" (p. 27). One clear example of this in Victoria has been the *Linking LOTE to the Early Years Literacy Program* (Victorian Department of Education, Employment & Training, 2000), which states outright that LOTE has an important role to play in the curriculum given the contribution it makes to supporting the "literacy development of English" (p. 9).

While this alone provides some insight into the political systems at work for rethinking how the curriculum goals of Japanese might be realised in practice, there is also a need to consider policies that have further shaped the context for 'teaching in the middle years of a Victorian high school' itself.

Teaching in the middle years of a Victorian high school. The Victorian Department of Education began its Middle Years Reform and Development project (MYRAD) in the late 1990s, in line with national initiatives to counter student alienation and disengagement in the upper primary and early secondary years of schooling. A plan for state-wide reform was then announced in late 2000, concurrent with the State government targets for Education:

1. To reach or exceed national benchmarks levels for reading, writing and numeracy by 2005,
2. To have ninety percent of students to complete Year 12 (or its equivalent) by 2010, and
3. To increase students aged 15-19 in rural and regional Victoria by six percent by 2005.
    (Victorian Department of Education, Employment & Training, 2001, p. 3)

The strategy for school reform advocated by MYRAD was a whole school approach that involved changes to the three interrelated areas of curriculum, pedagogy, and school organisation, with the central focus being a thinking-oriented, rather that subject-based, approach to teaching and learning. In particular, the focus was to be on the development of key cognitive skills (e.g., Bloom, 1956) and fundamental generic competencies (such as literacy, numeracy, problem solving, and critical thinking) *through* a variety of curriculum areas, rather than focusing on the content of the subject-matter itself.

Following from, and consistent with, the thinking-oriented curriculum, the Department similarly argued that teaching in the middle school embrace thinking-centred pedagogies, as exemplified in the following extract from a professional development module for teachers in the middle years:

It is important to use [thinking-based] strategies that cater simultaneously for the range of learners. These include: mind-mapping (which uses both left and right brain processes), open-ended tasks or inquiry learning (which promote constructivism, and allow students to function at the level and in the manner specific to himself/herself as a learner), or strategies that provide choice. One successful approach to providing choice is the learning centre, a very successful version of which utilizes both Bloom's *Taxonomy of Cognitive Processes* (Dalton & Smith, 1986) and *Multiple Intelligence Theory* (Gardner, 1983) as organizing principles, and presents a wide variety of activities, of which students complete only a selection, chosen in negotiation with the teacher. This structure caters for the highly varied interests and levels of development of young adolescents, provides room for student choice and input, and fosters independent learning. (Victorian Department of Education & Training, 2002a, ¶2)

The (re)organisation of schools was also identified as an important aspect of the middle years reform initiative if innovations in curriculum and pedagogy were expected to be successful in practice. The Department encourages, for example, interdisciplinary team teaching to reduce the number of teachers students have contact with, so that both teachers and students have opportunities to develop a more personal knowledge of each other (Victorian Department of Education & Training, 2002b). Similarly, subject teachers have had to rethink their own teaching areas in relation to other subjects to ensure that thinking skills and learning strategies are now integrated across the curriculum as a coherent whole (Victorian Department of Education & Training, 2002c). Likewise, another significant aspect of school organisational reform has been the need for schools to identify and foster productive partnerships in relation to the needs of their immediate community to enable students to see the relevance of what is taught in schools with their own lives (Victorian Department of Education & Training, 2003).

Microgenetic Analysis

Having considered the social, cultural, and historic context within which Elle's activity as a Japanese teacher in the middle years of a Victorian high school takes place – with its emphasis on the primacy of English literacy (and thus a diminished emphasis on languages *other* than English), and the development of core, generic competences (over an emphasis on discipline-specific competencies and outcomes) – it is interesting to reveal that the microgenetic analysis indicated a teaching style that seemed inconsistent with how *language* teacher practice is theorised in the language teacher education literature. This was despite the fact that Elle was a recent graduate of a language teacher education program and had been employed at her school to be a (Japanese) language teacher.

While it is difficult to offer a concise set of methodological principles as to what constitutes good, language teaching given that we have moved into what some now describe as a postmethod condition (Kumaravadivelu, 1994), it is generally acknowledged that language teaching is considered to be most effective when teachers assume a 'communicative' orientation. That is, language teaching approaches in which teachers emphasise:

– opportunities for target-language use for meaningful purposes;
– expressing meaning rather than accuracy of form;
– the ability to use language rather than knowledge about language;
– the use of (seemingly) authentic material, contexts and tasks.

(Pachler, 2005, pp. 11-12)

However, Elle's classroom activity at the microgenetic level of analysis seemed entirely inconsistent with these general principles for language teacher practice. Instead, and in almost direct contrast to the conceptualisation of 'good' language teaching summarised above, Elle typically:

– used very little target language for genuine classroom communication
– concentrated on target language form and structure, over meaning or the use of a

whole-language communicative approach
- taught about the target language (i.e., a focus on analysis over use)
- relied on repetition and practice as a strategies for language learning
- used few authentic materials, contexts, and tasks.

However, although Elle's classroom practice appears inconsistent with how language teaching is understood from a theoretical perspective as to what constitutes good practice, it must be remembered that for her – as the subject of her own contextually specific system of activity – this approach to language teaching was 'the right approach' in this context. That is, and we emphasise that we are not suggesting that Elle's approach was necessarily an appropriate method of teaching language, Elle's teaching style *did* satisfy the particular activity system within which she practised as a 'language teacher'.

To give one brief example, Elle explained that by teaching Japanese in this way, she felt she was then able to fulfil certain obligations that she had towards her wider (school) *community*. She spoke, for example, of the importance of contributing towards a "whole school" approach to discipline, since she saw discipline and classroom management as being "everybody's responsibility" (Interview 2). By teaching Japanese in this way – without an emphasis on the use of target language to develop communicative competence – Elle was able to manage most of the classroom activity in English. At this point, it might seem reasonable to argue that the classroom discipline could have been administered in Japanese since this is a technique that seems to work well in contexts such as immersion classrooms. However, when Elle's activity system is examined as a whole, it also became clear that local community and parental attitudes towards having students develop communicative competence in Japanese was not especially strong, either: both at the microgenetic level (i.e., Elle's immediate context for practice), as well as at a broader societal level from which Elle's activity has emerged (see the earlier discussion of the cultural-historic domain). When asked to reflect on a lesson she had just been observed teaching, for instance, Elle explains:

> E: I don't think we've got the community completely on side. We've still got a lot of people out there in the community who will say to their kids, "Don't worry about German and Japanese"; that they're not relevant. So there's only Maths, your English, or your Science. So we're fighting against that to some degree, that they're not able to value LOTE. And try as we might to articulate the benefits of learning LOTE, and we're going to do that much more actively next year, it's been very difficult for us to reach some families. And so a lot of kids will be sitting there going, well … and I have a classic example in another class of a boy who, from the beginning of second semester, every single lesson, kept saying to me, "Why am I doing this? Why am I having to learn LOTE?", and I was going over the same ground over and over again, which got very tedious.
>
> R: And that came through from parents, you're saying?

E: I think that came through from parents. You know: "My dad or my mum doesn't see any value in me learning Japanese".

R: Okay.

E: So that's one thing which is really quite detrimental to what we're trying to do, and this is why I think a lot of these kids- why it's difficult to get them to do any homework. They're … it's not just Japanese homework, but it's other homework, it's actually that culture of bettering themselves that doesn't necessarily exist amongst … it certainly doesn't exist amongst every single family from where these students come. These are people who aren't terribly well educated themselves, and they don't value education in the way that you and I do. And so language is seen as a very elitist academic type of thing, and they just don't see it as important. (Interview 2)

In other words, the local community within which Elle's teacher activity takes place (that is, the community which the objects of her activity (her students) are from and live their day-to-day lives), as well as the attitude of the students' parents themselves, further influenced how Elle chose to use (or, in this case, avoid) the target language as a mediatory tool for her own classroom activity. Moreover, as intimated in the extract above, the influence of the community and the attitudes of these parents contributed to what Elle described as a sense of "resistance" her students had to "learning Japanese" (Interviews 1 & 3), which was yet another reason she gave for choosing English as her primary tool to mediate classroom activity over Japanese, even though she is, ostensibly, a Japanese language teacher.

Another brief but instructive example was the nature of the division of labour that existed within the activity system that Elle had been positioned in as subject. In short, the planning processes at her school necessitated an integrated and collaborative whole school approach (which also reflected the cultural-historic context from which this activity system emerged, as we discussed earlier with respect to middle school reforms). This meant Elle was often expected to plan and develop units of work for Japanese with teachers of other Key Learning Areas who had little or no experience in language teaching. As a result, the language lessons Elle taught tended to be very 'generic' in nature. In contrast to language lessons with discipline-specific objectives to develop students' Japanese communicative competence, for example, the objectives which formed the basis of Elle's language lessons often focused on skills for 'thinking' and 'learning', as a means of developing students' more general skills in (English) literacy and learning behaviours.

IDENTITY-IN-ACTIVITY: MAKING SENSE OF THE SUBJECT
WITHIN THE ACTIVITY OF 'BEING A LANGUAGE TEACHER'

By approaching the study of identity formation through the lens of sociocultural activity, we have been able to explore both the 'discursive' construction of identity in terms of the broader social, cultural, and historic domain (through policy), together with how that cultural-historic expectation has then been realised in 'practice' at the microgenetic level of concrete activity. Teacher identity resides in how teachers, as subjects of their activity systems (i.e., of 'teaching'), have made sense of their role within their systems, and how they then choose to act within it.

Surprisingly, the analysis revealed that Elle's activity, as a language teacher, was markedly different to how language teaching is conceptualised within the second and foreign language teacher education literature (i.e., a focus on the development of students' communicative competence in the target language (see, for example, Macaro, 1997; Nunan, 1991, 1999; Savignon, 2002)). In contrast, Elle's explanations of her activity lacked any significant reference to communicative goals or outcomes. To the contrary, there were numerous examples of English being used to establish and maintain classroom order, Japanese being broken down into structural components to be studied, analysed, and used in various activities for the development of thinking, group work and learning skills, and grammatical points and other stylistic features of Japanese being explained and compared with English in an effort to enhance the students' competence in first language literacy.

However, as we argued earlier, this is not to suggest that Elle was doing something 'wrong'. Rather, the analysis revealed that the discursive construction of her activity, together with ongoing instances of microgenetic activity that unfolded within the specific system of social and cultural relations within which Elle was positioned as a classroom teacher, created a completely different type of activity and outcome she was expected to satisfy as a 'language teacher'. In short, the activity Elle performed was what was expected of her within that particular system – what she understood to be right and most appropriate in the context that she found herself. By teaching Japanese the way that she does – that is, by using high amounts of the non-target language and attempting to develop her students' competencies in literacy, numeracy, and thinking skills, rather than focusing on the development of communicative competence in Japanese – Elle was satisfying the system of activity she found herself positioned within in this particular context.

Interestingly, despite having been trained as a language teacher and employed at her school to teach language, when asked about how she sees her own role within her activity system as a teacher of Japanese, Elle stated emphatically that, "I don't see myself as a Japanese teacher" (Interview 1). Rather, Elle sees her role as being "a middle years teacher", and assumes, with that, the associated notions of what she believes it means to be a teacher in the middle school; namely, "teaching the students [generic thinking and learning] skills, rather than lots of [Japanese] content".

IDENTITY-IN-ACTIVITY AND IMPLICATIONS FOR PROFESSIONAL LEARNING

While we have not foregrounded the issue of professional learning in this chapter so that we could focus on the matter of teacher identity, we would like to move towards our conclusion by briefly returning to comments made in our introduction: that there is still much to know of language teachers and their work, "what they do, how they think, what they know, and how they learn" (Freeman & Richards, 1996, p. 1).

This study has revealed that what the literature often holds to be 'good practice' (and what, therefore, constitutes the basis for teachers' professional learning), may not necessarily resonate with the reality of teaching as a sociocultural activity. That is, this study has demonstrated that teachers' activity unfolds within a very real social and cultural context at both a cultural-historic level (in terms of the discursive construction of that activity), as well as the microgenetic level of immediate school and classroom practices. This has a significant effect on how teachers, in turn, understand their own roles which leads them to ascribe certain identities while rejecting others (e.g., 'a middle years generalist' cf. 'Japanese language specialist').

We would therefore argue the importance of producing and disseminating knowledge intended for teachers' professional learning – whether pre-service or in-service – that remains mindful of the very real contexts within which that knowledge is to be applied. Without doing so, the knowledge base of teachers' professional learning runs the risk of losing relevance to teachers who otherwise fail to identify its relevance to their own contexts for activity.

NOTES

[1] Our thanks to Alex Kostogriz for his comments on a draft version of this chapter and, in particular, this ingenious play on words. Here, we also acknowledge a parallel with Lave and Wegner's (1991) earlier notion of "persons-in-activity" (p. 51), a concept expanded upon in Lemke's (1997) work on the ecosocial relationship between the biological organism, the social subject, and personal identity, which bears some overlap with our discussion in this chapter. In proposing the concept of 'identity-in-activity', however, our attention is directed towards how activity might be conceived of and used as a unit of analysis for understanding the relationship between activity and the formation of identity.

[2] Pseudonyms have been used throughout the chapter to refer to the teacher, her school, and her students to protect anonymity.

REFERENCES

Ball, S. (1994). *Education reform: A critical and post-structural approach*. Buckingham, UK: Open University Press.

Bowe, R., Ball, S. J., & Gold, A. (1992). *Reforming education and changing schools: Case studies in policy sociology*. London: Routledge.

Butler, J. P. (1990). *Gender trouble: Feminism and the subversion of identity*. New York: Routledge.

Buzzelli, C. A., & Johnston, B. (2002). *The moral dimensions of teaching: Language, power, and culture in classroom interaction*. New York: Routledge Falmer.

Cole, M., & Engeström, Y. (1993). A cultural-historical approach to distributed cognition. In G. Salomon (Ed.), *Distributed cognitions: Psychological and educational considerations* (pp. 1-46). Cambridge: Cambridge University Press.

Commonwealth Department of Employment, Education & Training. (1991). *Australia's language: The Australian language and literacy policy. Information paper*. Canberra, ACT: Australian Government Publishing Service.

Cross, R. (2005). *LOTE teachers' work*. Paper presented at the Australian Association for Research in Education Annual Conference – Creative Dissent: Constructive Solutions, Sydney, NSW.

Cross, R. (2006). *Language teaching as activity: A sociocultural perspective on second language teacher practice*. Unpublished PhD thesis, Monash University, Melbourne, Victoria.

Engeström, Y. (1987). Learning by expanding: An activity-theoretical approach to developmental research. Retrieved September 23, 2003, from http://communication.ucsd.edu/MCA/Paper/Engeström/expanding/toc.htm

Freeman, D., & Richards, J. C. (Eds.). (1996). *Teacher learning in language teaching.* New York: Cambridge University Press.

Gale, T. (1999). Policy trajectories: Treading the discursive path of policy analysis. *Discourse: Studies in the cultural politics of education, 20*(3), 393-407.

Gee, J. P. (1996). *Social linguistics and literacies: Ideology in discourses* (2nd ed.). London: Taylor & Francis.

Giddens, A. (1982). *Profiles and critiques in social theory.* London: Macmillan.

Hall, S. (1996). Who needs identity? In S. Hall & P. Du Gay (Eds.), *Questions of cultural identity* (pp. 1-17). London: Sage.

King, R. B. (1979). Education and educational policies. *Educational Theory, 29*(1), 53-66.

Kumaravadivelu, B. (1994). The postmethod condition: (E)merging strategies for second/foreign language teaching. TESOL Quarterly, 28(1), 27-48

Lave, J., & Wenger, E. (1991). *Situated learning: Legitimate peripheral participation.* Cambridge: Cambridge University Press.

Lemke, J. L. (1997). Cognition, context, and learning: A social semiotic perspective. In D. Kirschner & J. A. Whitson (Eds.), *Situated cognition: Social, semiotic, and psychological perspectives* (pp. 37-55). Mahwah, NJ: Erlbaum.

Leontiev, A. N. (1981). The problem of activity in psychology (J. V. Wertsch, Trans.). In J. V. Wertsch (Ed.), *The concept of activity in Soviet psychology* (pp. 37-71). New York: M. E. Sharpe.

Liddicoat, A. (1996). The moving focus: Australia's changing language policy. *Babel, 31*(1), 4-7, 33.

Lo Bianco, J. (1987). *National policy on languages.* Canberra, ACT: Australian Government Publishing Service.

Lo Bianco, J. (1999, June). *After the tsunami, some dilemmas: Japanese language studies in multicultural Australia.* Paper presented at the International Symposium on Japanese Language Studies and Japanese Language Education, Nagoya University of Foreign Studies.

Lo Bianco, J. (2003). *A site for debate, negotiation, and contest of national identity: Language policy in Australia.* Strasbourg, Alsace: Council of Europe.

Macaro, E. (1997). *Target language, collaborative learning, and autonomy.* Clevedon, Avon: Multilingual Matters.

Mueller, F. (2003). Learning languages in Australia: Too much like hard work? *Curriculum Leadership, 1*(4). Retrieved March 15, 2005, from http://cmslive.curriculum.edu.au/leader/default.asp?issueID=9691&id=4711

Norton, B., & Toohey, K. (2002). Identity and language learning. In R. B. Kaplan (Ed.), *The Oxford handbook of applied linguistics* (pp. 115-123). Oxford: Oxford University Press.

Nunan, D. (1991). *Language teaching methodology.* London: Prentice-Hall.

Nunan, D. (1999). *Second language teaching and learning.* Boston: Heinle & Heinle.

Pachler, N. (2005). Who are our students and what do they bring from previous experience? In J. A. Coleman & J. Klapper (Eds.), *Effective learning and teaching in modern languages* (pp. 10-16). Abingdon, Oxon: Routledge.

Penuel, W. R., & Wertsch, J. V. (1995). Vygotsky and identity formation: A sociocultural approach. *Educational Psychologist, 30*(2), 83-92.

Rae, L. (2003). Languages: Where next? *Curriculum Leadership 1*(3). Retrieved March 3, 2005, from http://cmslive.curriculum.edu.au/leader/default.asp?issueID=9691&id=4719

Ricento, T. (2005). Considerations of identity in L2 learning. In E. Hinkel (Ed.), *Handbook of research in second language teaching and learning* (pp. 895-910). Mahwah, NJ: Lawrence Erlbaum.

Roth, W.-M. (2004). Culture and identity. *Forum: Qualitative Social Research, 4*(1), Retrieved July 7, 2006, from http://www.qualitative-research.net/fqs-texte/1-03/1-03review-roth-e.htm

Savignon, S. J. (2002). Communicative language teaching: Linguistic theory and classroom practice. In S. J. Savignon (Ed.), *Interpreting communicative language teaching* (pp. 1-27). New Haven, CT: Yale University Press.

Savignon, S. J. (2005). Communicative language teaching: Strategies and goals. In E. Hinkel (Ed.), *Handbook of research in second language teaching and learning* (pp. 635-652). Mahwah, NJ: Lawrence Erlbaum.

Varfolomeeva, T., & Gearon, M. (2006, March). *The role of the native speaking Russian teacher in constructing identity through early age literacy practices in community language schools.* Paper presented at the "The Natives are Restless" Symposium: Shifting Boundaries of Language and Identity, Melbourne, Victoria.

Varghese, M., Morgan, B., Johnston, B., & Johnson, K. A. (2005). Theorizing language teacher identity: Three perspectives and beyond. *Journal of Language, Identity, and Education, 4*(1), 21-44.

Vélez-Rendón, G. (2002). Second language teacher education: A review of the literature. *Foreign Language Annals, 35*(4), 457-467.

Victorian Board of Studies. (2000). *Curriculum and standards framework II: Languages other than English.* Carlton, Victoria: Author.

Victorian Department of Education, Employment & Training. (2000). *Linking LOTE to the early years: Linking languages other than English to the early years literacy program.* Melbourne, Victoria: Author.

Victorian Department of Education, Employment & Training. (2001). *Middle years matters: Change for all in the middle years.* Melbourne, Victoria: Author.

Victorian Department of Education & Training. (2002a). *The middle years of schooling: Middle years reform program.* Retrieved March 14, 2005, from http://www.sofweb.vic.edu.au/mys/innovationandexcellence/MYRP/index.htm

Victorian Department of Education & Training. (2002b). *The middle years of schooling: The nature of adolescence.* Retrieved April 1, 2005, from http://www.sofweb.vic.edu.au/mys/MYonlinePD/pdf/MYPresentation1.pdf

Victorian Department of Education & Training. (2002c). The *middle years of schooling on-line PD Session 3: Curriculum for the middle years.* Retrieved April 1, 2005, from http://www.sofweb.vic.edu.au/mys/MYonlinePD/3/Index.htm

Victorian Department of Education & Training. (2003). *Middle years matters: School organisation.* Melbourne, Victoria: Author.

Vygotsky, L. S. (1978). In M. Cole, V. John-Steiner, S. Scribner & E. Souberman (Eds.), *Mind in society.* Cambridge, MA: Harvard University Press.

Vygotsky, L. S. (1981). The genesis of higher mental functions (J. V. Wertsch, Trans.). In J. V. Wertsch (Ed.), *The concept of activity in Soviet psychology* (pp. 144-188). New York: M. E. Sharpe.

Vygotsky, L. S. (1987). *The collected works of L. S. Vygotsky* (Vol. 1). New York: Plenum Press.

Vygotsky, L. S. (1994). The problem of the cultural development of the child. In R. van der Veer & J. Valsiner (Eds.), *The Vygotsky reader* (pp. 57-72). Oxford: Blackwell.

Vygotsky, L. S., & Luria, A. R. (1993). *Studies on the history of behavior: Ape, primitive, and child* (V. I. Golod & J. E. Knox, Trans.). Hillsdale, NJ: Lawrence Erlbaum.

Russell Cross
Margaret Gearon

Faculty of Education
Monash University

67

COMMUNAL SITES AND DIMENSIONS OF PROFESSIONAL LEARNING PRACTICE

SECTION INTRODUCTION

This section offers four studies into the ways in which professional learning has been facilitated in practice through collaborative learning projects. Each chapter draws us into an account of professional learning practices, both the author's own and that of the educational professionals with whom they work. The authors in this section write of the approaches taken to nurturing learning among professional communities and of the impact of the learning for each community. While each contributor draws on, and from, a particular professional learning project, together these chapters shed light on the power of 'community' in advancing professional learning communities.

It is precisely the power of 'community' that is unpacked in this introduction, given the proliferation and popularity of communal and collaborative approaches to professional learning. While not always formally framed in each chapter, we can see how the learning amongst participants and groups in each may be conceived of as the construction and development of particular communities of practice. Lave and Wenger's work on communities of practice is useful in framing this section. They describe a community of practice as "... a set of relations among persons, activity and world, over time and in relation with other tangential and overlapping communities of practice" (Lave & Wenger, 2002, p. 115). In these forms, professionals participate "... in an activity system about which participants share understandings concerning what they are doing and what they mean in their lives and for their communities" (ibid, p. 115).

All of these chapters describe approaches to enhancing the learning of novice and experienced professionals in communities, for the purposes of developing, diversifying and strengthening practice. Joanne Deppeler's chapter opens the section (Chapter Five) and describes the way collaborative inquiry worked to assist a group of teachers to understand, articulate and change their practice. Deppeler analyses the approaches to, and impacts of, a collaborative professional learning community that grew from a university-school professional development partnership. Deppeler argues that professional learning is highly complex but appears to flourish with a combination of expert input supported by collaborative and evidence-informed investigation and critical discussion. In this study, collaboration took account of diversity by acknowledging and understanding difference among the team members and ultimately, strengthening relationships. Deppeler asserts that teachers require long-term opportunities to apply tools of inquiry to address complex problems, to build trust and collaborative skills and to

69

become engaged with theories and research-based practices.

Deborah Corrigan's chapter (Chapter Six) describes two mentoring programs for career change teachers – the first being for beginning teachers and the second, for aspiring principals. Essential to each of these programs was the value placed on relationship. For beginning teachers, the work of modelling through mentoring was perceived to carry much professional significance. Mentors and mentees in the aspiring principals program identified networking, learning, emotional support, assistance and advice with processes and procedures as the benefits of their professional learning. Corrigan concludes that, not withstanding the complexities inherent in mentoring, programs built on this model have much to contribute to professionals and professional communities. An effective environment for mentoring to flourish needs to take account of shared understandings and conceptions of mentoring and be aware of the positive and negative dimensions such relationships bring. Mentoring programs operate as effective for professional learning with the provision of suitable mentor training for participants, consideration of the selection of participants and appropriate evaluation.

Ian Mitchell (Chapter Seven) tells us of an organically driven and long-term professional learning project designed to develop teacher research through developing teachers' identities as researchers and supporting the generation and representation of teacher-knowledge. This chapter identifies the professional learning that occurs in long term teacher-research from the perspectives of the teacher-researchers and academics involved in the process and those who read, and have engaged with, the research generated. Mitchell reflects on data gathered over 21 years, that is, on his professional learning and makes a series of assertions about the ways communities of practice among teachers may operate to support and elicit the complexity of teacher knowledge. Woven into this chapter is an account of the professional learning of teachers and academics and, by implication, the nature of the intersection of their professional knowledges. Mitchell's work highlights the powerful ways in which collaboration fosters professional learning designed to build and extend teacher knowledge. By implication, it also points to the struggle in which sanctioned and more powerful forms of knowledge (academic knowledge) could more effectively make space for, and engage in dialogue with, what may be considered by some as, a less powerful genre of teacher-research.

Libby Tudball (Chapter Eight) takes up the theme of professional learning communities (PLC) and analyses the features of a successful PLC. Tudball's chapter explores the successful formation and impact of a professional learning community as an effective unit in transforming teacher and organisational practice. The PLC described in this chapter was formed to support teachers in one primary school to engage more fully with civics and citizenship education (CCE). Tudball suggests that some of the features which underpin the success of this PLC relate to work undertaken by the teachers to develop and live out a shared definition of their goals. Space and relationships factored as similarly important in shaping this PLC. The process of learning saw teachers collaborate in each other's classrooms and develop strong professional relationships, allowing for sustained observations, conversations and reflections related to teaching and student learning and an increasing tendency for 'risk taking'. Again, in this chapter, we read about the importance of time to the successful functioning of a collaborative model of professional learning. Overall, Tudball presents teachers' engagement in professional learning communities as an effective pathway to classroom change.

The chapters that comprise this section are then affirmation of 'community' and collaboration as a vehicle for professional learning. 'Community' is a term that has been called on in a range of contexts for the powerful associations it carries. "... [T]he vague yet generally affirming nurturing meaning attached to 'community' makes it one of the most ideologically appropriated metaphors in contemporary public discourse" (Smith, 1995, p.105).

Underneath the term lies a set of values that support the concept of community for its association with local responsiveness, local autonomy and collectivity as a strong counter to an increasing global tendency towards individualism that we read much about in Section 1 of this book. Yet, beneath the romance and relationship associated with community sits power and difference which easily 'threaten' the harmony and unity it may uncritically portray. Young's work (1990) has been instrumental in highlighting the work of community in disguising the effects of power. Viewing community from this perspective, we see how:

> the invocation of community is a claim of power, but to different forms of power. Thus the communitarian/ communal discussion is inescapably about power and the effort to ensure social cohesion. (Bounds, 1997, p. 6)

That is, it is possible to then understand how the term 'community' may act as a site of exclusion and disempowerment. The powerful rhetoric of community, or its sense of magical cohesion for 'the common good', tends to construct a dialogue around what is 'in common' and stifles the question of 'common to whom?' It is both these sorts of questions that should be addressed when we consider 'community'.

Reading critically into the term 'community', might then allow us to consider how it operates both as a form of cohesion and collaboration, at the same time as it might be considered a space in which the interests and power of 'insiders' and 'outsiders' may be accommodated or ignored in particular ways. While communities of practice are important spaces for professional learning, it is possible to view them through the lens of neo-liberal reform discussed in the first section of book and understand them as the management of compliant relationships, or as Hennon (2000) describes, as a " 'micro point of management' of a variety of overlapping networks ..." (p. 254). It is possible to view in them, too, the work they do in professional reproduction and identity formation, the latter which is taken up in the third section of this book.

Explicit and implicit in these chapters is the recognition of power in its various forms. Deppeler describes the way in which the professional learning community she led encouraged teachers to identify and challenge the assumptions they held about student learning. Corrigan considers the ways in which mandated mentoring programs tended to contradict the nature of relationships between mentors and mentees. Mitchell reflects on the place of, and hierarchical relationship between, teacher-knowledge and academic knowledge in the academy as well as the roles of academics and teacher practitioners in a professional learning relationship. The professional learning communities written about by Corrigan and Deppeler were mandated and/or supported by bureaucratic systems. The learning communities described by Tudball and Mitchell are more organic and less formally connected to a larger 'system'. Drawing on Bauman, we see the inner paradox of the concept of community come to life. That is, the formation of community is borne of "… a desire to be part of it and is obliquely testament to not being part of it … Communities are then forms which come *after*, not *before* individual choice" (Bauman, 2000, p. 169, my emphasis).

The powerful and cohesive work of 'community' is evident within these chapters. We may read them with an eye on how individual, organisations and systemic interests are accommodated within professional learning communities and shape their formation, of the approaches taken within them and the learning that has been generated as a result of them. While each chapter presents powerful accounts of professional learning, they point to the need to situate the communities of practice within broader contexts and consider both the professional and political work they do.

REFERENCES

Bauman, Z. (2000). *Liquid modernity.* Cambridge: Polity Press.
Bounds, E. M. (1997). *Coming together/ coming apart: Religion, community and modernity.* New York: Routledge.
Hennon, L. (2000). The construction of discursive space as patterns of inclusion/ exclusion. Governmentality and urbanism in the US. In T. Popkewitz (Ed.), *Educational knowledge: Changing relationships between the state, civil society and the educational community* (pp. 243-265). Albany: University of New York Press.
Lave, J., & Wenger, E. (2002). Legitimate peripheral participation in communities of practice. In R. Harrison, F. Reeve, A. Hanson & J. Clarke (Eds.), *Supporting lifelong learning, Vol. 1: Perspectives on learning.* London: Routledge Falmer.
Smith, N. (1993). Homeless/global: Scaling places. In J. Bird, B. Curtis, T. Putnam, G. Robertson & L. Tickner (Eds.), *Mapping the futures: Local cultures, global change* (pp. 87-119). New York: Routledge.
Young, I. M. (1990). *Justice and the politics of difference.* Princeton: Princeton University Press.

Allie Clemans
Faculty of Education
Monash University

JOANNE DEPPELER

5. COLLABORATIVE INQUIRY FOR PROFESSIONAL LEARNING

INTRODUCTION

Inclusive education reform has challenged educators to develop policies and practices in schools that provide an effective education for *all* students. This chapter explores how collaborative inquiry was important for teachers' professional learning about improving inclusive practices in their schools. It draws on my work in a university-school professional development partnership, the Learning Improves in Networking Communities (LINC) project from 2001-2005[1]. The origins of the LINC project lie in a professional relationship built over ten years, with the director responsible for student support services for Catholic schools in Melbourne, Australia. Our experiences in previous professional development (PD) initiatives had highlighted the importance of contextual issues in attempting to transform practices in schools (Deppeler & Harvey, 2004). Within the changing policy environment of inclusive schooling in Australia, this project represented a conceptual and practical opportunity to take up the challenge to design a professional learning program that was both responsive to inclusive reform and generative of new practices. I use the term professional learning (Hoban, 2002) to distinguish from the episodic, one-size-fits-all professional development (PD) approach and to centre attention on teachers and their practices. We founded the program on our shared belief that transformation of practices can take place within a collaborative learning community in which teachers, alongside school leaders, inquire into their practice and participate in shared decision-making and conversation (Cochran-Smith & Lytle, 1999; Little, 2003). Growing evidence from research suggests that these same principles apply to learning communities when they are connected to a network of other learning communities, increasing professional interaction and learning across schools (Veugelers & O'Hair, 2005).

PROFESSIONAL LEARNING APPROACH

We view both collaboration and inquiry as central to professional learning and essential for the transformation of practices. Inquiry that is systematic, self-reflective and informed by evidence can be an effective tool for critically examining issues and influencing teachers' beliefs and learning about their practices (Cochran-Smith, 2005; Cochran-Smith & Lytle, 1993; Groundwater-Smith & Dadds, 2004; Timperley & Robinson, 2001). We recognise that teachers,

A. Berry, A. Clemans and A. Kostogriz (Eds.), Dimensions of Professional Learning: Professionalism, Practice and Identity, 73–87. © 2007 Sense Publishers. All rights reserved.

like all learners, learn through collaborating with others in articulating their ideas to construct knowledge and create solutions to the challenges situated within their context (Putnam & Borko, 2000; Vygotsky, 1987). Of importance is open communication so that members can collectively examine assumptions and engage productively in knowledge sharing and construction (Argyris & Schön, 1974). We adopted the term *collaborative inquiry* (CI) to describe our work. CI is one of several cyclical action research-based approaches that emphasise participation and democracy in the process of improving practice. (Bray, Lee, Smith & Yorks, 2000).

> Collaborative inquiry is a process consisting of repeated episodes of reflection and action through which a group of peers strives to answer a question of importance to them. (Bray et al., 2000, p. 6).

CI was new to us as researchers and also as a system approach to professional learning for our partners. We were therefore tentative about how our project might unfold. CI was not constrained by a specific set of methods (Bray et al., 2000). This flexibility would allow us to devise and modify processes as we collaborated with teachers in their schools and allow us to deal with the expected differences that would emerge from the inquiry process. We agreed on a number of precepts, consistent with our enactment of socio-cultural theories of learning to guide and frame the collaborative inquiry process:

Teacher investigations should:

- Address the stated school improvement foci of their team,
- Focus on student learning and participation
- Include observations of classrooms and students' voices
- Be consistent with principles of inclusive schooling

University researchers should:

- Participate as co-learners and not as experts transmitting knowledge
- Actively encourage and model dispositions consistent with our approach including: respect, open-mindedness, critical reflection of evidence and engagement with others and a sense of social justice

The program should:

- Respond flexibly and adapt to suit the context of each individual school
- Structure opportunities for learning content and pedagogical knowledge
- Provide scaffolded support to individual teachers for engaging in inquiry
- Structure opportunities to share knowledge
- Provide support to enhance discussion and dialogue amongst teachers

Our intention was to support teachers and leaders to collaborate in researching and improving practices that would enhance the participation and learning of *all* students in areas that were important to their school. While we expected that our approach would allow for different and alternative possibilities for inclusive practice within each of the schools, we also expected the process would contribute directly to improving those practices.

THE RESEARCH PROCESS

The professional learning program is school-based and teachers along with leaders work in teams, conduct inquiry and submit research reports and reflective journals at six-month intervals. Teams varied in size from five to twelve members. The program is delivered over two academic years and culminates in a postgraduate qualification in inclusive education at Monash University. At the start of the project, teams are given information on the principles underlying our CI approach and support for using tools of inquiry and conducting research. Teams begin with a self-evaluation process – collecting, analysing and discussing evidence about the beliefs, policies, and practices in their school (Deppeler, In press; Deppeler & Harvey, 2004). This process enabled teams to determine the improvement foci for their context and, at the same time, begin to use and understand the processes of CI. Teachers then address their team's priorities in different ways through individual investigations. Priorities are progressively refined for further investigation and improvement. Two other researchers and I collected data from multiple sources including: teachers' reflective journals, research reports, and presentations, emails occurring and between the participants and ourselves, surveys and audio recordings and field notes of meetings, observations, discussions, and interviews. Teachers monitored student learning and participation using observations, work portfolios, teacher assessment, and interviews. The multiple sources of triangulated data reflect an attempt to gain an in-depth understanding of the various perspectives during, and as a result of, the process of collaborative inquiry. The following account is based on extensive analyses of patterns with participants in two projects.[2] Representative talk is used to illustrate themes and to bring teachers' voices to the discussion of collaborative inquiry.

Teacher Beliefs

We emphasised teacher responsibility for collecting evidence to confirm or refute assumptions about student learning and participation. We also encouraged them to collaborate in examining each other's data and in making decisions about the foci for their initial investigations. We challenged teachers to reflect upon their explanations for student's disengagement and their expectations for these students. We reminded each other regularly that our stance was not to act as experts in advocating particular approaches but to prompt teachers to critically examine the beliefs they held about teaching and learning. We did not, however, allow teachers to uncritically reproduce deficit conversations about the students in their classrooms. We questioned their use of categorical labels of disability for determining instructional and assessment practices and attempted to focus their initial suggestions for inquiry on student learning and on what and how students' interpreted what was intended.

We expected that when teachers collected and then examined detailed observational evidence about levels of participation and learning, it would enable them to critically examine the impact of their practices on different students. This process, however, was not straightforward, and our early conversations revealed the beliefs and expectations teachers held about the more 'problematic' students in their classrooms. Teachers' varied with respect to their explanations for what they had observed in classrooms, their expectations for a student's capacity to learn and their beliefs about their capacity to teach these students. On the basis of their beliefs, teachers can be clustered into approximately three groups. At least one or two teachers in every team believed that lowered participation or performance resulted from specific disabilities and deficits inherent in the students themselves. They did not believe they had adequate knowledge or skills to teach these students and felt obligated to seek professional expertise. They expected that the academic performance of these students could be partially remedied by withdrawal and specialist instruction. For example, one secondary teacher requested that a member of our university team observe several boys 'that were having problems' in her classroom. She was observed dictating questions for students to write and then answer, for twenty minutes during a thirty-minute lesson. Later, in discussing why high levels of disruptive behaviour and non-completion of work had been observed, this teacher suggested that:

> The problem is the poor listening skills of these kids. Martin has a history of learning difficulties and is getting Special Ed (support). And I suspect Alex and James have got some auditory [processing] problems as well.

In a follow-up discussion, other teachers in her team confirmed the challenges they had encountered with these 'problematic' students. We prompted the team to consider what practices might facilitate increased participation. While some teachers agreed on the need to modify teaching, their initial suggestions for inquiry focused on investigating alternative interventions for training in skills that were thought to be deficit in these students. Team discussion:

> Ella: To be honest I don't think that anything we do is going to have much of an impact on some of these boys. For starters they're simply not interested. Cameron will tell you straight out that he is just waiting till he is old enough to leave school and get a job. If you challenge him with any work he just becomes aggressive. So one option is how do we change their attitudes?

> Rhonda: Ummm I don't know for some of these boys it's their learning disabilities that stop them from working and I know Jan [special education teacher] tries to help with that but the problems like auditory processing make it really hard to know... We just don't have the resources here. I think that if they were assessed or had the one-on-one they need. What can improve their auditory and listening skills?

> Kathy: If they [students] haven't got basic literacy when they get here then ... that's what's really stopping them from getting anywhere. I know that with this inclusion approach we're supposed to be dealing with all of the students well I mean we just don't have the time for individual teaching and there is only so much you can do in the classroom.

Michael: Well I don't have behaviour issues with Cameron and his mates in IT [Information Technology], for the most part they are pretty reasonable but realistically I agree their reading and writing skills are a real problem. I don't know whether it's auditory or learning disabilities or what but it's pretty obvious they have got problems and it's hard to know what we can do to support them. My question is: What strategies are going to help them cope with secondary [schooling]?

When asked about their expectations for lower performing students, teachers in this group believed that if students had not acquired basic literacy competencies by the end of primary school, they did not expect much improvement would occur during secondary school.

Most teachers believed that students' behavioural and learning difficulties developed for a number of reasons other than 'disabilities'. Although unable to suggest what practices might increase students' participation, their initial suggestions for inquiry typically focused on investigating practices that would improve the behaviour of the more challenging students in their classrooms.

A minority of teachers including those with responsibilities for 'literacy coordination' believed they were particularly skilled in teaching literacy. Teachers in this group talked about curriculum and believed student's disengagement was due to inappropriate teaching for students' with literacy difficulties. Literacy was considered vital and these teachers were passionate about investigations focused on school-wide pedagogy that would result in all students experiencing positive literacy learning. While a number of these teachers noted that they did not feel confident to support the social development of students diagnosed with autism, they did not believe these students should be withdrawn from their classrooms.

In all schools, there was an important emphasis placed on the relationship between students' literacy competencies and their experiences of schooling. Literacy was viewed as a pivotal skill that enabled students to learn and to participate in school life. Teacher's concerns regarding the continued failure of many students related particularly to the impact writing skills had on enabling students to complete assigned work. Literacy coordinators voiced strong views regarding particular conceptualisations of literacy. Not wanting to contribute to a debate on literacy approaches but to honour our shared belief that all students are capable learners, we supported the teams' decision to invite a literacy educator to work with them in refining the focus for their investigations. We believe this event was crucial to teachers' subsequent professional learning for three reasons: 1) the contribution from the literacy educator was valued by teachers because it arose from their shared problem solving 2) was timed to occur in immediate response to their decision-making, and 3) the literacy workshop sessions provided the theoretical and pedagogical content to frame investigations which, in turn, prompted the development of a common language to engage with evidence about student learning and to construct knowledge.

Developing a Common Language to Understand Practices

The literacy expert conducted workshop sessions using the Freebody and Luke (1990) *Four Resources Model* and a genre approach to text type and supported teams in devising a number of joint investigations. Some members in each of the teams began by conducting an audit of all the work assigned to students, in the previous term, at a selected year level. Teachers collected the assigned tasks, along with the assessment criteria and examples of student work assessed as 'well done' and 'unacceptable'. Interviews were held with teachers to clarify what understandings they had of the various tasks and criteria. It soon became clear that not only did teachers use different criteria for similar assignments but they also had different understandings of what constituted a 'report' in science or history and what was meant by an 'essay'. The following is taken from discussion at session where teachers from several teams shared their findings of the audit process with Marie the literacy expert.

> Kath: One area of confusion we need to work through is what is meant by the term *essay*. It is used by different teachers for writing tasks that seem to describe many different types of writing – arguing, comparing and contrasting and describing.

> Marie: Yes the task specification is not clear enough. And some teachers are using mixed types like in this science assignment where the students are expected to use their understanding of the properties of an element and then to write a creative essay.

> Jenni: Yes, can I suggest we use the Write Ways[3] as a model of forms to classify these various types as a starting point – we can always go back and revise them to suit our individual purposes.

> Marie: Okay so let's work in groups and divide up the sample tasks and sort them into appropriate text types. You will not only need to examine the purpose for the writing but the precise structural and grammatical features.

> John: I don't know if we should separate into groups – we have already seen how different teachers are in their understanding of this – I think we should work on this together – I'm not sure I for one have as complete an understanding as Jenni (English teacher) of all this genre stuff.

> Kath: Yes we might think we are talking about the same thing but it's pretty obvious that we are not all on the same page. So maybe we should focus on one text type at a time and that way we can be consistent with one another.

Moving through Language to Assumptions and Practice

Using a common language, teachers were able talk to one another and engage with the audit evidence. These discussions allowed them to unravel understandings about what it meant to be literate and to consider the impact their various understandings had on students. It also allowed them to think about their assessment practices in new ways and focus attention on previously overlooked assumptions about student learning. A particularly powerful example in this respect involved the collaborative examination of students' writing. Teachers ranked four samples from the least to the most successful attempts at writing an argument and explained their ranking. Sample C was unanimously ranked the least successful because:

It's really difficult to read. You have to really concentrate to get the words.

It's just incoherent. It's very difficult.

Very poor. The spelling is a problem, the grammar a lot of the time is non-existent.

It's just a few, like ideas off the top of the head, like this is what I think and I'll write it down. No attempt to organise or develop anything and very hasty really, in the way its set out.

No conclusion just a list of thoughts. Spelling & grammar is so bad.

When teachers then re-examined the samples using explicit criteria, writing strengths previously unnoticed became apparent, allowing teachers to shift their ranking of the pieces. For example, teachers agreed that Sample C had achieved the overall purpose of the text which was to put forward or justify a point of view. The piece was generally structured in accordance with the expected stages for this text-type. While the response was short, it had a number of salient structural and language features which reflected an understanding of the text-type. For example, it was noted that the rhetorical device of refutation was used for the main argument. Although spelling was an area that would need attention, teachers agreed it was a far less important criterion. Teachers' comments after this activity and in reflective journals frequently mention the importance of this activity in changing the assumptions they made about students who experienced literacy learning difficulties. The following extracts are illustrative:

I realise how inconsistent we can be in assessing. When you get to look at this list of criteria and you start looking deeper into it, it exposes different flaws you wouldn't necessarily see. Whereas when you're reading quite a few essays the overall fluency factors in more highly than if you were going to get really stuck into looking at criteria. When I first marked I didn't see there was any understanding just the bad spelling and grammar, even though we only give 10% to spelling. This must happen a lot and they [the students] end up with the wrong message.

It's almost like a bias. Spelling on our marking criteria sheets is in a separate section. It's only a few points in actual fact. This way we are forced us to stick to the important criteria and they [the students] get more feedback on which bits they are good at and those they are not.

This shared analysis made it possible for teachers to reframe their assessment practices and to question how they provided feedback to students so it connected to learning. For example, teachers across teams agreed upon criteria for examining various writing genres and began to construct rubrics. Having common language also supported teachers in reading the theoretical and applied research literature and in designing collaborative projects focused on pedagogy. For example, one or two teachers in every team investigated student responses to various scaffolds to support writing in different subjects. Teachers talked frequently about the importance of connecting theory to their practice.

> I really try to think about what's behind my teaching now – to understand the theory. It's not just about the teaching like how to teach argument but it's understanding how students learn to write and what they think about my teaching.

The strong theoretical base for the pedagogical approaches investigated by the teachers increased the chance that there would be clear evidence of success. Student improvement was confirmed by literacy testing and linked to teachers' professional learning[4] (Deppeler, In press). As evidence regarding student participation and learning was also integral to the work of the teachers, any changes in student performance were readily apparent as part of the teaching learning process. One of the most important themes throughout teacher discussions of the evidence of student improvement was that teaching had influenced the learning of the lower performing students. This, in turn, allowed teachers to change their expectations for these students. The following quotes from conference presentations are typical of the many teachers who reported being surprised by student improvement:

> I was very pleased and surprised that through my initiatives the students wound up making far more articulate and well-considered comments during class discussions. Some had never volunteered much of anything before.

> After I had completed my first assignment and observed the students and collected samples and actually reflected on that [data] I was actually getting such a lot out of it ... and seeing things and changing things that I had not even contemplated before. I found out there is a better way to do things. I had never interviewed kids or found out what they thought about a particular piece of work, I just couldn't believe what they could achieve!

Reflected in these comments is a shift in focus to what students 'can do' rather than what they cannot and a valuing of the student's contribution as a source of data. Echoing Black & William's (1998) work, assessment practices that emphasised teacher-student interaction such as interviewing, questioning, feedback, sharing criteria and peer and self-assessment practices became common.

80

Collaboration for Learning

Collaboration was an important influence and catalyst for professional learning. While teachers' investigations were informed by literacy theory, they were reframed in light of the professional experience of each team and variations relevant to each context. For example, in every team, teachers constructed and investigated rubrics for assessing learning but their individual applications responded to the particular goals of their team, the assessment activities that had preceded them and were connected to the broader assessment approach in each school. Collaborative discussion not only influenced the specific direction of individual member's projects but it is through collaborative analysis of evidence to understand student learning that teachers constructed new knowledge for themselves. What becomes evident over time in analysing the transcripts of these discussions is that there is an increased tolerance for uncertainty among the teachers. In many instances teachers value what they don't know as an opportunity for further discovery. The following reflections are from a teacher in evaluating her first attempt at constructing and using a rubric for argumentative writing at Year 7. Her comments emphasise her preparedness to deal with ambiguity and to go beyond what is known and the importance of collaborating with colleagues and students in this endeavour.

> One of the most significant conclusions reached was the importance of a clearly defined rubric. The rubric I devised for the assessment task soon revealed its weaknesses and inadequacies. Sometimes the language used for the criteria descriptions was ambiguous and served only to confuse the students. Sometimes, not enough specific detail was apparent in a criteria description so obvious problems in a student's writing could not be addressed without swaying the criteria sheet. This presented an obvious problem as I had assured students that adhering to the rubric criteria was a recipe for success. To deviate from it when marking essays, therefore would have been extremely unfair. Evidently, the implementation of rubrics will involve much trial and error. Its success relies heavily on agreement between teachers and students about expectations. Communication is crucial.

One of the major benefits of collaboration was the increased opportunity for teachers to access information and alternative views not possible during the daily work of a teacher. This included engagement with peers and other professionals and the availability of research literature through the Monash University databases. This changed not only what teachers noticed but how they interpreted events. As success, was confirmed, teachers were quick to incorporate pedagogical knowledge into their everyday practice and share practices with colleagues at their school professional development days and with other participants at networked conferences. Teachers identified that the refinement of their investigations was enhanced because of the number of teachers working towards similar goals in CI teams in and across school sites.

> With most PD you go off and you might get excited at the time but when you get back to school – it never seems to go anywhere. Even with the best of intentions you just get caught up in other things. With LINC we've got a team to keep the momentum up and knowing it will benefit the school. We have our pride too. Knowing our work is going to be shared with the other schools.

Collaboration was not only important for enhancing professional learning but the extended opportunities to discuss professional issues was believed to have strengthened relationships and built a respect and understanding for differences among the team. As teachers collaborated in more than one investigation, they became increasingly more willing to observe and teach in one another's classrooms. Earlier concerns that observation would expose them to professional scrutiny were replaced with a focus on documenting student responses to pedagogy. Teachers discussed observations and examined videotapes of their classrooms and explored the uncertainties they had about what had and had not worked. Draft reports were discussed with colleagues to gain further understanding. Throughout these discussions, teachers frequently encouraged one another by asking questions and by sharing their practices and their reading and understandings from the research literature. While collaborative discussion supported learning so, too, did learning to collaborate support their collaborative discussion.

Conditions that Enhance Professional Learning

A number of conditions in our approach appear to have enhanced teachers' learning. Teachers unanimously agreed that the requirement that they submit work for assessment for university credit was essential for motivating their initial participation and maintaining the quality of their work. Teachers believed this fully funded opportunity provided an incentive and imposed an obligation and the responsibility to complete their collaborative investigations. Many teachers commented on the value of the writing process in enabling them to make sense of their findings. Our team's flexibility in making and legitimising a number of changes in response to teachers' requests was perceived to be critical in maintaining their participation and commitment. For example, our team was involved in modifying university schedules for submission of work and rescheduling meetings with teachers and teams at their request and at the school sites. School leaders increased opportunities for collaboration by modifying the timetable and providing teacher release and generally promoted the work of the team and a culture of inquiry throughout the school (Deppeler, In press). When leaders collaborate with teachers to create a culture of critical inquiry, they may face personal and professional challenges. Nathan a deputy principal reflects:

> To me, the compelling arguments for the development of school based action research teams in schools is becoming more self-evident all the time, however, for this approach to work; to bear fruit; it is important that I and

other leaders at my school understand this premise in all its nuance. As with many complex things, the more I read and journey into the complexity, the more I realise I have to find out. Coupled with this first point, but much more pertinent just to myself, is the need to have a knowledge of leading in this time of change. This is so important, for without developing greater knowledge of leadership it is impossible to develop greater capacity. To rely on my natural leadership style is to rely on too narrow a band of strategies and capabilities. My leadership capacity can be developed through knowledge … and a degree of self-awareness. I know that my natural inclination is to be persuasive, to argue with the resistors, or to quickly be dismissive. This is an area of my leadership that I need to work on. For a successful culture of collaborative inquiry to develop, staff must both share knowledge about the 'craft' of teaching, but also evidence about their own 'teacher generated' professional knowledge, and about their values and beliefs. For this to happen, LINC leaders must foster an atmosphere of trust and respect. In what way can I refine and establish the leadership structures within the group? In what ways can collaboration be structured and supported?

Nathan's insights may be exceptional to the extent that he collaborated with other leaders in these schools to investigate leadership practices that supported CI and the professional learning of teachers. It is possible that this activity not only enhanced his reflection but also stimulated leaders to make use of this knowledge within their context; enhancing the CI processes.

Autonomous Learners

Our social constructivist view of learning emphasised the importance of the teachers' role in supporting student learning and involved us in modelling this same approach in our support for teachers' learning of CI. We gave teachers very clear guidelines on what was expected of them and attempted to build upon their individual knowledge with a view to ultimately transferring responsibility for the CI process to the teacher. As teachers conducted their second round of investigations, they became increasingly less reliant on us to support the CI process. While a majority of their second investigations continued with a focus on pedagogy, several focused on alternatives to writing (e.g. student understanding of science and mathematical concepts). Overall teachers' research questions became increasingly more sophisticated and were reflected in the titles of their investigations. For example, *Scaffolding a science report* was refined in a subsequent investigation to: *Using joint construction & student rubrics for understanding of key terminology & its relevance to scientific report writing.* Teachers' discussion of proposals for a third round of investigations reflect clarity about what they intended to do and a confidence with the CI process. At a final conference, a teacher comments on the value of working with colleagues and using inquiry to solve practical problems:

> We used to get together and discuss what we were finding hard in the classroom and you would end up arguing about one program or another or waste hours talking about a student's problems. You just didn't know what to do so you would try anything. Now we work together to find a way forward. We ask each other about what we know and what we need to find out.

While pedagogy was still of interest, teachers' discussions of their third investigations can also be characterised by increased references to the thinking of the student (e.g. What can I understand about this student's mathematical thinking?) What can be understood from the questions students asked, or from the language the student used or from how they participated in an activity?

Approximately one third of the teachers who completed the programs developed competencies in CI such that they could set new learning goals and monitor their personal and team's progress towards their achievement. Some of these teachers were in leadership positions in their schools and others were in their second or third year of teaching. Their comments contain frequent metacognitive and critical reflections on the value of CI for understanding the processes of teaching and learning.

> ... in the beginning and not really knowing anything about research I had too many opinions about what our school should be doing that were just based on intuition or the latest trend ... now I have learned to wait and examine the data before making a decision or forming opinions about students.

Janet enthusiastically reported at a conference that her research was informed by theory but "it was not taken from the research literature. I am breaking new ground and have the evidence." Her comment illustrates a confidence in her own authority to advance practices.

While most teachers benefited from scaffolding and collaborative discussion to become autonomous learners, one or two teachers in each of the teams remained reliant upon their colleagues and us for support. These teachers were active members of their teams and could confidently implement the advocated pedagogy into their classrooms but failed to adopt a critical researcher stance. They remained reliant on explicit models for using procedures at each stage of the inquiry process. It is not clear whether these teachers needed more time to engage confidently and independently with the inquiry process. In follow-up interviews they indicated they would never have participated in postgraduate research had it not been for their school's involvement in our project and that support from our team and their colleagues was crucial for maintaining their participation. Our emphasis on collaboration meant that it was often difficult to determine the boundary between their individual and their colleagues' contribution to their analysis and presentation of their findings. This created challenges for those of us with the academic responsibility for ensuring that teachers' submitted work was original and met academic requirements. Attempting to purposefully and actively connect with the diversity of teachers in these cohorts created challenges in negotiating the tension between collaboration and individual submission of work and in rethinking what structures might best reward and support professional learning.

DISCUSSION

In this chapter, I set out to look constructively at our experiences with collaborative inquiry as a professional learning initiative in relation to the inclusive education agenda. Teachers in these schools have begun to deal with students previously conceived as 'problematic' as if they were no different from other students. After an initial period of uncertainty, teachers were able to move to more collaborative and systematic approaches to reshape and generate new practices. Professional learning is highly complex but appears to flourish with a combination of expert input supported by collaborative and evidence-informed investigation and critical discussion. Central to these activities was the development of a common language that enabled professional conversations and was key to advancing teachers' understanding and inquiries. It also appears that teachers' understanding of student learning and diversity cannot be easily separated from their understanding of pedagogy. Discussion about student learning and teaching practices occurred along with discussion about theories of literacy. Similarly, in collecting and engaging with evidence in order to analyse their literacy practices, teachers questioned the beliefs and assumptions about students which underpinned them. As teachers became more capable in using inquiry, they became more capable and confident in developing pedagogy in teaching literacy and in reframing assessment practices. One important finding from our work is that teachers' learning in relation to inquiry and collaboration develops over time. Teachers therefore require long-term opportunities to apply tools of inquiry to complex problems, to build trust and collaborative skills and to become engaged with theories and research-based practices. This process appears to be enhanced by simultaneous attention to conditions that provide opportunities for collaboration, access to resources and incentives and that emphasise teacher responsibility for enacting and completing research. Concurrent attention to the motivation, knowledge and skills of individual teachers themselves is necessary to understand teachers' diverse learning responses to the CI process.

Our experiences of exploring CI, using the practices described above, has promoted teachers professional learning across a range of primary and secondary contexts and subject areas. In each context, some adaptation was required and therefore our findings do not imply that these practices will apply across all situations. Future research may need to explore the tensions between fidelity and adaptation in implementing CI with teachers in multiple sites. Our particular approach to CI is undoubtedly demanding in terms of time and financial resources and therefore may be impractical in other contexts. More fundamentally our findings generate questions about the role of universities in supporting teachers' continuing professional learning. Consistent with previous research, our initial precepts appear to be well founded. A contextualised approach that actively involves teachers and academics as partners in CI can promote teacher and student learning. This is in contrast to the 'expert' approach in which academics deliver short-term sequences of pre-determined content to teachers as passive recipients. The remaining challenge is how to structure academic practices so that they support collaborative discussions and inquiry about teaching and research as a long-term goal and as part of university culture.

NOTES

[1] The Learning in Networking Communities (LINC) project is a research and professional development partnership between the Catholic Education Office, Melbourne and Monash University (2001-2005). The study was partially supported by the Australian Research Council of Research Strategic Partnership Industry Research Training (ARC-SPIRT) scheme (2001-2003). The Catholic Education Office, Victoria (CECV) provided funding in support of the research in their role as the industry partner in the ARC-SPIRT scheme. The CECV also provided the funding to support the teachers participation in postgraduate studies at Monash University, which has made this project possible (2001-2005).

[2] Project 1 (2001-2003) 45 teachers in eight primary and secondary schools.
Project 2 (2004-2005): 45 teachers in five secondary schools.

[3] Wing Jan, L. (2001). *Write ways: Modelling writing forms* (2nd Ed.). South Melbourne, Australia: Oxford University Press.

[4] ACER conducted an evaluation of LINC in 2002-2003 as part of the Australian Government Quality Teacher Progamme (AGQTP), a strategic national project involving a major research study of ten professional development activities, and entitled *Investigating the links between professional development and student learning outcomes*. See ACER (In press) for a more detailed account and Project D, in Ingvarson, L., Meiers, M. & Beavis, A. (2005). Factors affecting the impact of professional development programs on teachers' knowledge, practice, student outcomes and efficacy, *Education Policy Analysis Archives, 13*(10), 1-28.

REFERENCES

Argyris, C., & Schön, D. (1974). *Theory in practice: Increasing professional effectiveness.* San Francisco: Jossey-Bass.

Australian Council for Educational Research (ACER). (In press). *Investigating the links between teacher professional development and student learning outcomes: Vol. 1: Commonwealth Department of Education, Science and Training, Quality Teacher Program 2001-2003.* Melbourne, Australia: ACER.

Black, P. & William, D. (1998). *Inside the black box.* London: NFER Nelson).

Bray, J., Lee, J., Smith, L., & Yorks, L. (2000). *Collaborative inquiry in practice: Action, reflection, and making meaning.* Thousand Oaks: Sage Publications.

Cochran-Smith, M. (2005). Teaching for social change: Towards a grounded theory of teacher education. In M. Fullan (Ed.), *Fundamental change: International Handbook of Educational Change* (pp. 246-281). Dordrecht: Springer.

Cochran-Smith, M., & Lytle, S. (Eds.). (1993). *Inside/outside: Teacher research and knowledge.* New York: Teachers College Press.

Cochran-Smith, M., & Lytle, S. (1999). Relationships of knowledge and practice: Teacher learning in community. In the series *Review of Research in Education, 24*, 249-305. Washington, DC: American Educational Research Association.

Deppeler, J. (In press). Improving inclusive practices in Australian schools: Creating conditions for university-school collaboration in inquiry. *European Journal of Psychology of Education.* [Special issue: Inclusive education ten years after Salamanca].

Deppeler, J. M., & Harvey, D. H. P. (2004). Validating the British index for inclusion for the Australian context: Stage one. *International Journal of Inclusive Education, 8*(2), 141-153 [Special issue: Working with the Index for Inclusion across diverse contexts].

Deppeler, J., Loreman, T., & Sharma, U. (2005). Improving inclusive practices in secondary schools: Moving from specialist support to supporting learning communities. *Australasian Journal of Special Education, 29*(2), 117-127.

Freebody, P., & Luke, A. (1990). Literacies programs: Debates and demands in cultural context. *Prospect: Australian Journal of TESOL, 5*(7), 7-16.

Groundwater-Smith, S., & Dadds, M. (2004). Critical practitioner inquiry: Towards responsible professional communities of practice. In C. Day & J. Sachs (Eds.), *International handbook on the continuing professional development of teachers* (pp. 238-263). Berkshire: Open University Press.

Hoban, G. F. (2002). *Teacher learning for educational change: A systems thinking approach.* Philadelphia: Open University Press.

Little, J. W. (2003). Inside teacher community: Representations of classroom practice. *Teachers College Record, 105*(6), 913-945.

Putnam, R., & Borko, H. (2000). What do new views of knowledge and thinking have to say about research on teacher learning? *Educational Researcher, 29*(1), 4-15.

Timperley, H., & Robinson, V. (2001). Achieving school improvement through challenging and changing teachers' schema. *Journal of Educational Change, 2*, 281-300.

Veugelers, W., & O'Hair, M. J. (2005). *Network learning for educational change.* Berkshire: Open University Press.

Vygotsky, L. S. (1987). Thinking and speech. In R. Rieber & A. Carton, (Eds.), *Collected works* (Vol. 1, pp. 39-285). (N. Minick, Trans.). New York: Plenum.

Joanne Deppeler
Faculty of Education
Monash University

DEBORAH CORRIGAN

6. MENTORING AS A PROCESS FOR ENGAGING IN PROFESSIONAL LEARNING

INTRODUCTION

Originally in Greek mythology, Mentor was a loyal friend and adviser to Odysseus, King of Ithaca. Mentor helped raise Odysseus' son, Telemachus, while Odysseus was away fighting the Trojan War. Mentor became Telemachus' teacher, coach, counsellor and protector, building a relationship based on affection and trust.

While the origins of mentoring point to the fact that this idea is not new, it does appear that in more recent times mentoring has been used as a mechanism for developing successful relationships that build the professional wisdom of all those involved. In this chapter the workplace context used to describe mentoring relationships will be schools, however, the context could be any organization. Within the context of schools, two mentoring programs that are designed to assist professionals beginning a new career role will be discussed to highlight some of the strengths and weakness of such programs for their professional learning. This chapter will also make some brief evaluative comments on these programs based on data collected from participants. However, it is important to first explore the current ideas of mentoring, particularly as a process that engages people in professional relationships.

DEFINITIONS OF MENTORING

Modern day definitions of mentoring reflect much of the teacher, coach, counsellor and protector roles traditionally associated with the idea of mentoring, but also include descriptors such as parent figure, supporter, trouble-shooter, scaffolder, guide, role model, sponsor, trainer, developer of talent and door opener. A great deal of the literature and conversations around mentoring actually focus on what mentoring is not! It appears that this is a far easier task than to define what is meant by mentoring.

There have been attempts to define mentoring such as those made by Asburn et al. (1987) who describe mentoring as "... the establishment of a personal relationship for the purpose of professional instruction and guidance" (p. 2) or Crosby's (1999) definition of mentoring as a trusted and experienced supervisor or advisor who by mutual consent takes an active interest in the development and education of a younger, less experienced individual" (p. 13). However it is difficult to define mentoring as it is about the relationship between a mentor and a

A. Berry, A. Clemans and A. Kostogriz (Eds.), Dimensions of Professional Learning: Professionalism, Practice and Identity, 89–103. © 2007 Sense Publishers. All rights reserved.

mentoree. In fact there may be some dangers in defining mentoring because as Wildman et al. (1992) suggest

> … mentoring involves highly personal interactions, conducted under different circumstances in different schools, [but] the roles of mentoring cannot be rigidly specified. Therefore, it is a mistake to develop any external definition or conception of mentoring and impose it by means of political pressure or high-powered staff development activity. (p. 212)

Mentoring relationships are complex and involve not only the personalities of the mentor and mentoree, but also the interpersonal or psychosocial development, career and/or educational development, and socialization (Field, 1994, p. 65) of participants with different experience, expertise and orientations. More commonly mentoring is described as a process with models proposed for how the mentoring process occurs. These models are numerous (as would be expected) as no two relationships are identical due to the individuals involved in the mentoring process.

Some models of mentoring focus on how mentors approach the mentoring task. Such models include comprehensive lists of the different mentoring roles (for example, Abell et al., 1995), while others have developed this notion further and examined the particular orientations of individual mentors. For example, Saunders, Pettinger and Tomlinson (1995) suggested a loose typology of four orientations of teacher mentors:

1. Hands-off facilitator – where the mentor emphasizes discussion with the mentoree rather than team/shared teaching. This orientation is dependent on the view of mentorees as autonomous teachers developing their own potential.
2. Progressively collaborative – where the mentor works alongside the mentoree, building confidence and skills and offering advice.
3. Professional friend – where the mentor regards the mentoree as a member of the organization (school) and values the importance of the mentoree's classroom performance above such things as challenging or praising the mentoree.
4. Classical – where the mentor takes on a role of counsellor, listening to problems and giving feedback.

There is an acknowledgement in Saunders et al. (1995) that mentors have their own perspectives of what mentoring is and they bring these to the role.

Mertz (2004) has proposed a conceptual frame for "defining and distinguishing mentoring from related supportive relationships" (p. 543), and describes the mentor as role model, peer support and sponsor (see Figure 6.1). The conceptual model she proposes is a work in progress and begins to unravel the confusion that exists around mentoring. It is also aimed to facilitate dialogue around the ideas of mentoring that have been limited in the past through a lack of shared understanding of the distinction between mentoring and other supportive relationships. While she proposes what appears to be a hierarchical model, I propose that both mentors and mentorees find themselves moving between different points and dimensions of supportive relationships, depending on the perceived need at the time. So while the model presented in Figure 6.1 begins to represent the complexity of mentoring relationships, the hierarchical structure, in my opinion, does not accommodate the flow of mentoring relationships at particular times.

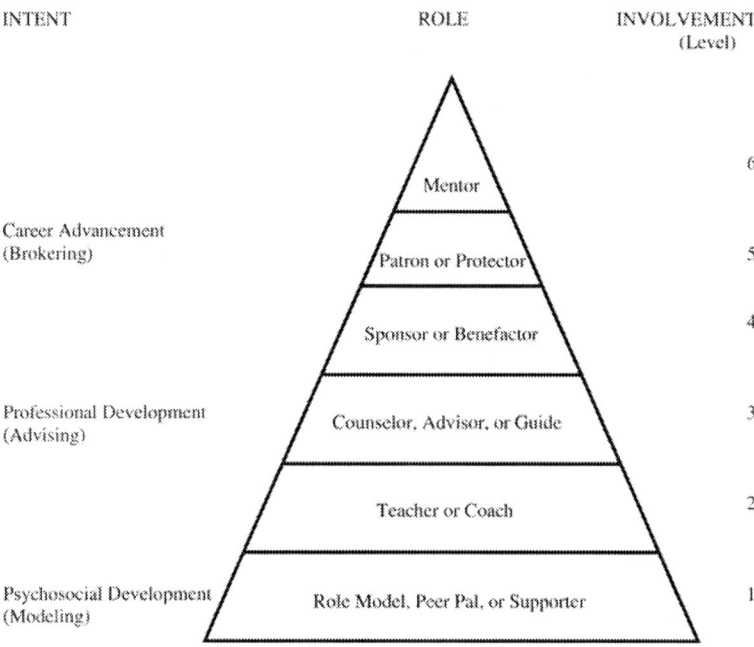

INTENT   ROLE   INVOLVEMENT (Level)

Mentor   6

Career Advancement (Brokering)   Patron or Protector   5

Sponsor or Benefactor   4

Professional Development (Advising)   Counselor, Advisor, or Guide   3

Teacher or Coach   2

Psychosocial Development (Modeling)   Role Model, Peer Pal, or Supporter   1

Figure 6.1. Supportive work relationship arranged hierarchically in terms of primary intent and level of involvement (Mertz, 2004, p. 551)

Mertz's model relies on the twin concepts of **intent**, the perceived purpose of the activity and whether that intent is sought or valued, and **involvement**, the amount of time and effort required to realize the intent (p. 547). The model identifies three categories of intent and ties them to different supportive relationships:

1. psychosocial development (modeling),
2. professional development (advising), and
3. career advancement (brokering).

This model distinguishes psychosocial functions of mentoring ("those aspects of a relationship that enhance an individuals' sense of competence, identity and effectiveness" (Kram, 1985, p. 31)) from career functions of mentoring ("those aspects of a relationship that enhance advancement in an organization" (Kram, 1985, p. 24)). Kram's career functions can be further subdivided into professional development ("activities designed to help individuals grow and develop professionally" (Mertz, 2004, p. 549)) and career advancement ("activities designed to help individuals advance professionally" (Mertz, 2004, p. 549)). Such a distinction assists in distinguishing kinds of activities and roles in terms of intent and involvement (Mertz, 2004), and while professional development certainly contributes to career advancement, the distinction is a useful one as it is possible to promote one (e.g. professional development) without attending to the other (e.g. career advancement) and vice versa.

Within this conceptual frame, the primary intent of the relationship at each stage is the important focus. For example, the primary intent at the modeling stage is a focus on the person. The relationship provides a person who may give social and emotional support and affirmation. At the advising stage, the primary intent is professional development, where the advisor is focused on the present and within this context, maximizing success and potential. In the final brokering stage, the primary intent is to focus on what the mentoree needs to do to get ahead within the professional context and it has a future orientation.

Involvement within this conceptual frame focuses on the critical elements of time and intensity of the involvement. From Figure 6.1 above, Levels 1 (Role model, Peer pal or Supporter) and 2 (Teacher or Coach) demand lower levels of involvement in terms of time and intensity. At Levels 3 and 4, the time and intensity of the involvement increase as there is an obligation for advice to be received and acted upon, and consequently, the level of trust has increased from that required at Levels 1 and 2. In Levels 5 and 6, there is a comparatively high level of involvement as the partners within the relationship are linked together in a common purpose – the advancement of the mentoree. The mentor invests in this success by using their own networks and reputation to support and promote the mentoree, there is a sharing of power and influence within the process, a sharing of ideals, dreams and understandings, and they will be highly exposed before each other. Such involvement requires a high level of trust, time and intensity.

These final levels (Levels 5 and 6) start to highlight the commonly understood notions that mentoring is not for the emotionally fragile or socially challenged, for those who are uncomfortable facing their own limitations and learning, or for those with diminished enthusiasm, lacking wisdom, judgement and generosity. Mentoring is not about cloning or acquiring a disciple, or an opportunity to prove your capacity or to create a power base. It is about those who are committed to excellence and high standards as expectations of the profession.

Mertz's conceptual frame becomes useful as the roles she describes will probably come into play within any mentoring relationship. As stated previously, individuals come to a mentoring relationship with preconceived ideas of what such a relationship includes. This conceptual frame accounts for the myriad of ideas individuals may have about mentoring while, at the same time, building and extending on those ideas to develop different conceptions of mentoring. Different mentoring relationships can be classified into particular types, despite the highly individual nature of each mentoring relationship.

TYPES OF MENTORING

As individuals have preconceived ideas of what they bring to any mentoring relationship, there is no set process followed as these relationships progress. While four loose typologies were highlighted above, these typologies focused on what the mentor might bring to the relationship, rather than on the type of relationship that might develop. It is therefore helpful to explore the particular types of mentoring relationships that commonly occur:

- Guiding mentoring – mentors make suggestions or demonstrate necessary skills, persuade and coach to apply suggestions, probe and draw out ideas and confront mentorees to understand the impact of what they are doing.
- Informational mentoring – mentors act as a role model and describe step by step procedures, provide wise counsel or advice based on their experiences in similar situations, teach and praise and arrange for the mentoree to access other resources, and often involves one-way communication.
- Collaborative mentoring – mentors set up joint problem solving and decision making, open discussions, brainstorming, mutual agreement on working together and alternate leadership roles. It requires a proactive mentoree.
- Confirming mentoring – mentors are empathic listeners and encourage mentorees to take charge, they expect initiative, act as a sounding board, wait to be consulted and confirm the mentoree's direction and goals.
- Developmental mentoring – individuals are guided in their assumption of new roles, new job identities, and organizational expectations (socialization). It is also an effective approach to acquire new knowledge, skills and behaviours needed to achieve career success and personal development. The pitfall of this approach is that this form of mentoring can be a form of torch passing from the experienced to the less experienced.

Mentoring can be detrimental to growth if those being mentored develop too great a reliance on mentors, who are often expected to provide answers to all possible questions. While these types of mentoring relationships can all involve the dimensions of intent and involvement highlighted as critical components of any mentoring relationship by Mertz (2004), they vary in the levels of intent and involvement required. For example, informational mentoring requires quite low levels of intent and involvement, while collaborative mentoring requires quite high levels of both these dimensions.

Below are two accounts of mentoring projects that currently exist for professionals in the school education sector. The first program is an induction and mentoring program designed for beginning teachers in the teaching profession, while the second is similar in career progression as it represents mentoring for first time principals. Both of these programs are part of a state government education department program for professional development and career development for staff within Australia (the first project is also conducted in conjunction with the Victorian Institute of Teaching (VIT) and is a requirement for all beginning teachers who are provisionally registered as teachers until they apply and fulfill the obligations of full registration).

MENTORING BEGINNING TEACHERS

Mentoring of teachers beginning in the profession has become a widely used, and an often-mandated practice throughout many Western countries. Within Australia, there is a growing demand for the accreditation of teachers against defined standards. For beginning teachers (or provisionally registered teachers) to become fully registered in Victoria (a state within Australia) a mentoring program assists this process.

The mentoring program involves training sessions for mentors and information sessions for provisionally registered teachers about the process of gaining full registration. The mentors undertake two days of training to highlight the important characteristics of mentoring and how they can assist their mentorees through this accreditation process. There are three distinct phases to the mentoring program – (i) induction for orientation, (ii) induction for professional learning and (iii) documenting professional practice. Mentors assist provisionally registered teachers to compile "evidence of practice" that involves an analysis of their teaching and learning, a selective record of collegial teaching activities they have undertaken and commentaries of professional activities. The process culminates in the presentation of evidence before a panel of peers at the school level and an application and recommendation for full registration.

The aims of this mentoring process are outlined below:

> Mentoring is a key strategy of effective induction. Mentors work closely with new teachers, providing peer support and collegial advice to assist them in reflecting on their work and improving their practice. This allows the individual needs of the new teacher to be met in a timely and relevant manner and guides their progress to demonstrate the Standards of Professional Practice for Full Registration. Mentoring promotes the mutual and ongoing benefits of collegial activity and engages the professional community of the school, not just teachers new to the profession. Mentoring should be seen to be separate from performance assessment arrangements. This will protect the integrity of each role and foster trust and transparency in the mentoring relationship. (VIT, 2006. Supporting provisional registered teachers, p. 1)

In 2005 a number of beginning teachers ($n = 548$) and their mentors ($n = 336$) were surveyed[1] about their mentoring experience throughout the year. The survey focused on five main aspects of mentoring; personal attributes that the participants need for constructive dialogue, the requirements of the system such as support from the school leadership or curriculum initiatives, modeling of effective teaching practices, competent pedagogical knowledge for articulating effective practices and feedback for the purposes of self-reflection in order to improve practices (Hudson, 2004).

In this survey, the means have been generated from the number of responses to 35 short items based on a 5-point Likert scale. In a comparison of mentors and mentorees the mean scores for each group were calculated based on the two groups' responses. These are represented below in Figure 6.2. The highest possible score is 5.00 and the five dimensions measured within this survey are personal attributes, modeling, pedagogical knowledge, the requirements of the (school) system and feedback.

As can be seen from Figure 6.2, the means from mentors are consistently higher than those for mentorees. However, analysis of the survey data indicates that mentorees are highly supportive of the mentoring process. The highest means score possible is 5.00 and the lowest mean in any category is 3.65 (for mentorees in the area of feedback). The dimensions of mentoring that were most highly valued by both mentors and mentorees were personal attributes (which include being supportive, attentive, comfortable talking about teaching practices, instilling positive attitudes and confidence, and assisting in reflection on practice) and modeling (which includes the following attributes; enthusiasm, teaching, effective teaching, rapport with students, hand-on lesson, well designed lessons, classroom management and syllabus language). In the remaining dimensions, mentors valued mentoring around pedagogical knowledge, system requirements (which involves quality control through curriculum provision and in reforming education such as through mentors involvement in preservice education, understanding of key practices that includes the aims for teaching, specific curriculum, school policies) and the provision of feedback. Mentorees, on the other hand, valued feedback next, then mentoring around pedagogical knowledge and system requirements. The importance of feedback was values by mentorees and least valued by mentors.

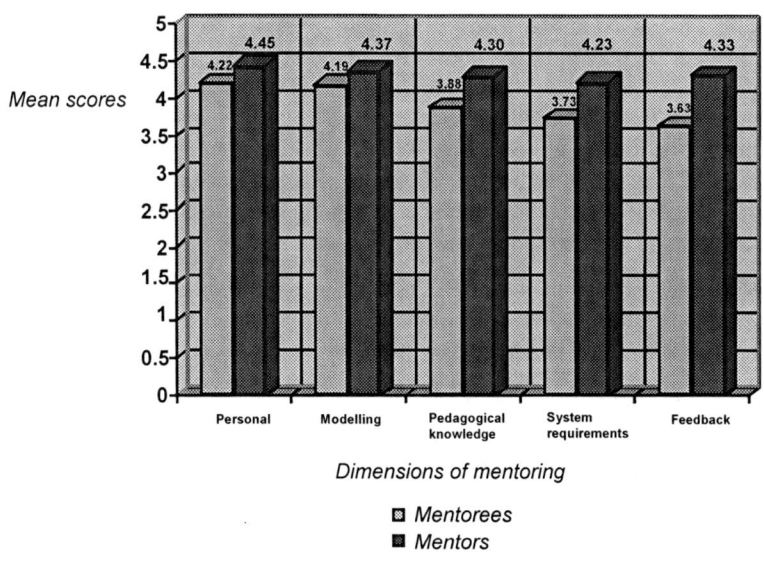

Figure 6.2. Summary of means from mentoring survey

Clearly personal attributes, those personal dimensions that support professional dialogue, and effective role modeling are important aspects of the mentoring process. This is not surprising given that mentoring is a professional relationship that requires personal effort or intent. In Mertz's model described above, intent is an essential part of mentoring as it is an important component of the psychosocial development of the mentorees. However, in this model (see Figure 6.1), psychosocial development requires low levels of both intent and involvement. Consequently, mentoring of this type as quite limited in terms of the possible benefits from such a mentoring relationship.

Mentoring around pedagogical knowledge and system requirements and the provision of feedback are all elements that have a higher level of intent due to their orientation towards professional development. In Mertz' model, the mentor adopts an advisory role and this relationship requires higher levels of involvement from all participants. It appears that these elements were less valued in the mentoring program for beginning teachers and that the mentoring relationship is therefore operating at quite low levels due to its emphasis on personal rather than systemic elements.

The low level of mentoring may be realistic (and understandable) given that this program was aimed to induct new teachers into the profession through their participation in an accreditation process. However, it is important to note that this mentoring process is a mandatory one for mentorees and the criteria for selection of mentors is not defined. Mentors' reasons for participating in this program range from their beliefs about being highly effective and committed professionals who are motivated to share their knowledge to senior staff who are required by their school to undertake such roles.

To build on the survey responses of these mentors and mentorees, another research project[2] exploring the mentoring of beginning teachers has followed up these same participants with interviews to gain further insights into the mentoring relationships that have been established.

As stated previously by Saunders et al. (2005), mentors bring their own perspectives of mentoring to the role of mentor. Subsequent interviews of mentors highlight a range of views about mentoring remain, despite the fact that mentors have undergone the same training program:

> … mentoring for me is then – once a teacher is comfortable with the way the school runs then the mentoring is monitoring their everyday kind of role as a teacher so that's … my understanding. (ML – a mentor)

> Mentoring is having someone in the school who you can talk to professionally about where you are going and how you are going to get there. Rather than just having a buddy who might be someone you can just dump on. The mentor is someone who is interested in your progress that's got some experience or values for you that can help you figure out where you want to go or how you can get there … It's more about professional development, perhaps career path, student management, how you go about the job that you do – all the issues that can impact negatively on your experience. It's not

personal life. For some this may be about styles of learning but for others its not. (CP – a mentor)

Mentoring is the curriculum planning and getting the lessons right. (SG – a mentor)

Interviews from mentorees also showed a range of understanding about mentoring:

My mentoring experience was brilliant. It made me feel so positive about what I was doing and in the classroom. I had a lot of reassurance from my mentor that what I was doing in the classroom was great teaching. I had a lot of constructive feedback … I didn't feel threatened by what she did. We had a great relationship from the start. She's young like me and a great teacher and I admired what she was doing in the classroom from the start. There was something about the way that she came about our relationship. We became really good friends, so our conversations were just like two friends sitting down and chatting together ... Mentoring is a very close personal relationship. (SH – a mentoree)

Well mentoring is a year-long process whereas induction is very separate. Your mentor looks after your teaching skills and your adjustment to school life, in terms of, not so much the school per se, but being a teacher in that school. Whereas induction introduces you to the way things are done in that school. (OT – a mentoree)

These quotes highlight the different ways mentorees perceive of the role of mentor and highlight the value they place on the personal relationship and attributes in the mentoring relationship.

Regardless of the quality of the mentoring relationship, the work of modelling was seen as critical. Despite having an almost non-existent mentoring experience, the following dialogue between the interviewer (KM) and the mentoree (BL) highlighted the positive role of modelling.

KM: What about … is your mentor a good model for you?

BK: Mmmm – he is – because he is a very professional – now even though I haven't had much personal contact with him in terms of, you know, of the whole mentoring process – he is actually a very professional teacher.

KM: So you respect and admire him?

BK: Yeah. And he's the sort of person you would look up to and say – Hey – I want to be like that.

KM: And that's important.

BK: Of course – of course … I suppose even though he hasn't spent much time with me, the fact that he is who he is as well – you know – helped in a way – even little things like how he deals with students – I remember the first time I got to school I was thinking how am I going to deal with these kids? – And I see him – and its like – Wow!

KM: That's how you do it

BK: That's how you do it and that's how I want to do it!

The importance of mentoring around pedagogy is perceived as more valuable by the mentors than the mentorees. One mentor has highlighted its importance below:

I think the new grads have more than an understanding of it [pedagogy] because it is taught more vigilantly as part of the Diploma of Education and that educational theory affects – like I know I go into my son's school and they're using the 'white hats, red hats' … within the classroom and I'm going "Uh, oh, I kind of know about it" … [I] know then that the teachers coming through university now know because it's part of it, but it wasn't there twenty years ago but I'm learning from what my mentorees are bringing in and I think they are very much aware of it in their own teaching … The teaching of it [pedagogy] is much more rigorous and look at what the new grads are bringing in with them and it just seems to be so much more what I ever had when I was a teacher – and being able to apply to their teaching. (ML – a mentor)

The importance of feedback to the mentoring relationship is often cited by participants and yet comments are limited in their scope. The most common theme about feedback is that it is always useful, that it is important to know about what you are doing well and the areas in which you could improve and that making time for it is always difficult. This comment made by a mentoree is a good example of the perspectives held by both mentors and mentorees.

I think you definitely need feedback in your first year out and I think it's something that schools could do a lot more of. In general, it is nice to know where your strengths and weaknesses are and to hear 'Yes you are doing this really well but you could improve doing that'. So I think feedback is really important. I did get feedback but not as much as I would have liked. People tend to tell you if you are doing a bad job, but they forget to tell you if you are doing a good job and sometimes you need to know that you are doing a good job. There are areas obviously in which you can improve. My mentor has only seen me teach sometimes (rarely). We didn't ever specifically set aside time for teaching. (EC – a mentoree)

The importance of the mentoring relationship to establish the mentoree's familiarity with system requirements has ranked in the area of least importance for both mentors and mentorees. Consistently, participants conclude that the 'system' devalue this knowledge, evidenced by the lack of time schools and the system are prepared to commit to the mentoring process. As stated by one of the mentors:

I do think this mentoring formal thing is a good thing but I do want it to be a bit more teacher friendly. I want it to be a mandatory thing that gives us extra time to work with these graduate teachers as I think this is invaluable. (MG – a mentor)

From the perspective of both mentors and mentorees, the value of mentoring in assisting in their professional learning process is well recognized.

I think mentoring certainly makes my teaching much more satisfactory – I learn a lot from the teachers that I work with, especially the new graduate teachers – they come in with fresh ideas. And as a mentor I am always looking to learn. (ML – a mentor)

Mentoring increased my professional capacity. I learnt so much – about the way to assess, the way I speak to children, the language I use, my questioning, about organization (SH – a mentoree)

MENTORING NEWLY APPOINTED PRINCIPALS

A mentoring career change program with newly appointed principals was implemented in government schools in Victoria over two years as an induction into their position. This mentoring program was designed as a professional development process over a period of 12 months in a formally mandated mentoring program.The developmental mentoring program was designed to encourage first time principals to become effective leaders through a process which socialized them into leadership, explored individual and organisational expectations and their new professional identities. It was designed on the assumption that mentoring would contribute to their effective acquisition of new knowledge, skills and behaviours needed to achieve career success.

In the two year time period, some 255 first time principals have been involved in the program as mentorees and some 250 experienced principals have acted as mentors. As there are approximately 1600 schools within the government system in Victoria, this represents a significant commitment to supporting the development of principals as leaders within the Victorian government school system and assisting them with their transition into a new career. The goals of this mentoring program have been to reduce the level of uncertainty felt by individuals as they move into a new career position. Through this mentoring program, opportunities have been provided for professionals to share experiences, establish contacts and networks that can aid in the identification, possible approaches and solutions to major issues facing principals and to provide opportunities for these professionals to reflect on their professional practice.

All new principals are required to participate in this program. The mentoring program consisted of three formal professional development days and on-going meetings arranged informally between mentoring pairs throughout a 6-9 month period. At the completion of the initial professional development days, both mentors and mentorees were asked to evaluate the program and indicate their goals for the mentoring relationship. After the follow-up day, mentorees were asked to evaluate the effectiveness of the mentoring program and partnership. The data presented below reflects the participants' comments.

It was an important part of the developmental mentoring process for mentorees to set goals for themselves as they undertook this process. The success of this goal setting has been moderate with only some 55% of mentorees actually setting goals for themselves. Feedback from the different groups indicated mixed reasons for this moderate response which included that there was little need to set goals as they were compelled to participate in this mentoring process as it was mandated. Many of the mentoree participants expressed they were unsure what the mentoring process involved. There is also a danger in this form of developmental mentoring process that it can be a form of 'torch passing' from the experienced to the less experienced and this sentiment was expressed by some of the mentorees. It was clear that mentorees and mentors brought their own perspectives of mentoring to the relationship. This is despite initial professional development activities designed to explore and develop understanding of mentoring among all participants.

The major areas in which mentors and mentorees set goals were around personnel, skill development and cultural change, school structures and the types of programs offered within schools. This range reflects one of the strengths of a developmental model of mentoring as one which allows mentorees to acquire new knowledge, skills and behaviours needed to achieve career success and personal development. Of those mentorees who set goals, 67% felt that they had achieved their goals to some extent, 27% had not achieved their goals to any significant level, with 8% not responding. The success of the goals setting approach can then be questioned and mentoring relationships of this kind can become like a balancing act between building professional knowledge and identity and 'torch passing' from the experienced to the less experienced.

In developing the mentoring relationship, mentoree participants were asked about the frequency of their meetings over the course of the year. While most respondents did not provide any indication of this (33%), 25% had between 0 and 2 meetings, 27% indicated they had participated in between 3 and 5 meetings, while 15% indicated they had met more than 6 times. It appears that the level of involvement of all but a small number of participants has been strong in this program. Qualitative comments indicated that while responses to this question of meeting frequency were based on meetings specifically for developing the mentoring relationships, there were other opportunities provided through their professional activities where mentoring partners met. Other participants felt that mentoring, by its very nature, meant that meetings were only necessary when the need arose. Significant impediments to the frequency of meeting were often noted, such as the lack of time or large geographic distances that existed between mentoring partners. Nevertheless participants all agreed that there was strong support (95%) for meetings due to their helpfulness. It does appear that there may be a mismatch here between the actual frequency of their meetings and their perceived value among participants.

When participants were asked what has been most worthwhile in their mentoring relationship, they identified networking, learning, emotional support, assistance and advice with processes and procedures as the benefits. The advantages for mentorees in the mentoring process are often cited as career advancement and psychosocial support such as encouragement, friendship, advice and feedback on performance. The experiences of the mentorees within this program support these notions, to some extent, although the career advancement notion is not strongly highlighted here. This may be because all of the participants involved are principals and therefore at the same level of the career structure, despite their differing levels of experience.

In addition mentoree participants were asked how their mentors had assisted them in specific areas such as developing problem-solving skills, building confidence for their new role, the opportunity to network with other principals, maintaining confidentiality, providing ideas to assist with change management within their school and assisting in helping them to meet their needs. Responses to a number of questions indicated high support in all of these areas, from response rates of between 78 and 93%. Despite some initial reservations about the mandatory nature of their participation, participants this program have found it to be beneficial to them as they enter their new position as principals. In the next section, I will highlight some of the implications mentoring programs have for participants as they engage in professional learning.

SOME IMPLICATIONS FOR MENTORING AS A PROCESS FOR ENGAGING IN PROFESSIONAL LEARNING.

Both of the programs outlined in this chapter ran for the duration of one year. In terms of a life long approach to learning, this time frame is relatively short, yet it nevertheless is substantial in comparison with many other professional development opportunities that education professionals engage in. It is therefore reasonable to conclude that mentoring is a long-term process rather than a quick fix. Indeed, it is the development of a professional relationship that is the fundamental cornerstone of mentoring as a means for engaging in professional learning.

Much of the uncertainty surrounding the development of a mentoring relationship rests with the preconceived ideas participants bring to such a relationship and the time needed to clarify the basis for a mentoring relationship. The conceptual framework proposed by Mertz, despite its hierarchical limitations, does begin to provide a framework that can assist participants in gaining a shared understanding of the scope of such a relationship. The ideas centred around intent and involvement are particularly helpful and highlight the need for investments of time and effort from participants as well as time and support from organizations for such relationships to have maximum benefit.

Given the fundamental dimensions of intent and involvement, it does seem appropriate to question the mandatory nature of both of these programs (even though participants have supported these programs and articulated many benefits). The mandated nature of participation in mentoring processes for mentorees can play a significant role in destabilising the development of such professional relationships. This was initially an issue in the principal program where all participants were at a similar career level, with the only difference being the amount of experience each possessed. If this enforced relationship building is undertaken, it becomes imperative that participants quickly realise the additional benefits that participation in such programs can provide.

The benefits of mentoring programs can be numerous and include the provision of personal and emotional support, career development and satisfaction. Mentorees also experience opportunities to develop competencies, skills and knowledge for improved performance while mentors have the opportunity to develop both professionally and personally. For all participants the benefits appear to be improved skills, access to new ideas and personal growth.

The development of any professional relationship as a generative means of professional learning is always a balancing act and mentoring is no different. This makes the development of a clear and shared understanding critical in these relationships. The principal program discussed above makes this clear.

In the Beginning Teachers mentoring program discussed above, key elements of mentoring, namely personal attributes, modelling, pedagogical knowledge, understanding system requirements and receiving feedback are not articulated to participants as necessary components of mentoring in this program's aims, however, the provision of feedback and familiarisation of system requirements are implied as important elements within the program as they are seen as acting as mechanisms for monitoring the health of such a professional relationship and defining what are the results from such a mentoring program.

Monitoring professional and personal growth and professional and personal learning within such relationships is a critical aspect of mentoring. It is this that frames mentoring as a positive professional learning activity. Mentoring provides a vehicle for mentors and mentorees, both alone and together, to reflect on their practice, reconsider what they are doing and why, and work towards improving their practice. Schon (1987) called this process "reflection-in-action" and considers this process a powerful mechanism for changing work practices and/or personal beliefs. Mentoring is a professional relationship that can engage two or more and bring benefits to both. As a mechanism for contributing to professional learning of communities in general, mentoring is an obvious attraction.

For a suitable environment for mentoring to flourish, it would need to take account of a shared understanding conceptions of mentoring, an awareness of the positives and negatives such relationships can offer; support for such programs particularly in terms of human, financial and system resources; the provision of appropriate mentor training for participants to aid in a shared understanding; consideration given to the selection of participants; and appropriate evaluation of the mentoring programs. While not without its complexities, mentoring has the potential to contribute much to the professional learning of participants and professional communities.

NOTES

[1] This survey was based on work undertaken by Hudson (2004).

[2] Australian Research Council Link Grant (2004-2007) – Evaluating professional experience and mentoring in the preparation and induction of teachers for the teaching profession.

REFERENCES

Abell, S. K., Dillon, D. R., Hopkins, C. J., McInerney, W. D., & O'Brien, D. G. (1995). Somebody to count on: Mentor/intern relationships in a beginning teacher internship program. *Teaching and Teacher Education, 11*(2), 173-188.

Asburn, C., Mann, M. & Purdue, P. A. (1987) *Teacher mentoring: ERIC Clearinghouse on teacher education.* Paper presented at the annual meeting of American Education Research Association, Washington, DC.

Crosby, F. J. (1999). The developing literature of developmental relationships. In A. J. Murrell, F. J. Crosby & R. J. Ely (Eds.), *Mentoring dilemmas: Developmental relationships within multicultural organizations* (pp. 3-20). Hillsdale, NJ: Lawrence Eribaum.

Field, B. (1994). The new role of the teacher: Mentoring. In B. Field & T. Field (Eds.), *Teachers as mentors: A practical guide* (pp. 63-77). London: Falmer.

Hudson, P. (2004, December). From generic to specific mentoring: A five-factor model for developing primary teaching practices. Paper presented at annual conference of *Australian Association for Educational Research*, Melbourne.

Kram, K. (1985). *Mentoring at work: Developmental relationships in organizational life.* Glenview, IL: Scott Foresman.

Mertz, N. (2004). What's a mentor, anyway? *Education Administration Quarterly, 40*(4), 541-560.

Saunders, S., Pettinger, K., & Tomlinson, P. (1995). Prospective mentors' views on partnership in secondary teacher training. *British Educational Research Journal, 21*(2), 199-218.

Schon, D. A. (1987). *Educating the reflective practitioner: Towards a new design for teaching and learning in the professions.* San Francisco: Jossey-Bass.

Wildman, T. M., Magliero, S. G., Niles, R. A., & Niles, J. A. (1992). Teacher mentoring: An analysis of roles, activities, and conditions. *Journal of Teacher Education, 43*, 205-213.

Deborah Corrigan
Faculty of Education
Monash University

IAN MITCHELL

7. PROFESSIONAL LEARNING

Moving from Professional Talk to Teacher Research

INTRODUCTION

Teacher research is an effective vehicle for professional learning at both the individual teacher and school level (Lytle & Cochran-Smith, 1992; Pring, 2000). In this chapter, I draw on 21 years of a self-funding teacher-research project that has involved teachers in many schools, at varying points on a journey from collaborative professional development, sharing of good practice to more formal aspects of research. I use these experiences to explore the professional learning that occurs in long-term teacher-research from the perspectives of both the teacher researchers and readers of accounts of this research.

Reflecting on, developing and refining new practice is risky and requires high levels of energy and effort. While all points on this journey should be valued, one finding has been that, over a period of several years' involvement in teacher research, the teachers need a sense of progress and development to sustain an on-going commitment. A second finding is that, over time, teacher-research can generate a great deal of practically sophisticated knowledge that fills a void in the current knowledge base of teaching. In this chapter, I look at professional learning in terms of the development in teachers' perceptions of themselves and in the knowledge that they generate that can occur over a period of several years. I also explore how this knowledge can be identified and represented usefully, the features of reporting that is accessible and credible to teachers, and how teachers can be supported in this journey.

CONTEXT

The Project for Enhancing Effective Learning (PEEL) began at one working-class high school in Melbourne, Australia in 1985. The original group consisted of the author, who taught part-time in the school and part-time at a university, two academics and a group of nine teachers, of six different subjects, who shared concerns about the prevalence of passive, dependent, unreflective learning in their classrooms. PEEL had, and continues to have, a focus on student learning. It built on several strands of research that had involved or influenced the academic participants. The most important of these strands was Baird's doctoral research into promoting metacognition (Baird, 1986). Baird's experiences in how he had engaged with a (supportive) teacher in his research, as well as other experiences

A. Berry, A. Clemans and A. Kostogriz (Eds.), Dimensions of Professional Learning: Professionalism, Practice and Identity, 105–119. © 2007 Sense Publishers. All rights reserved.

with teacher-academic collaboration meant that we began with a belief that only teacher researchers, who felt ownership over the research could develop the kinds of knowledge needed to achieve real change in how teachers teach and how students learn (Lytle & Cochran-Smith, 1992). Accordingly, in contrast to Baird's research, control over all aspects of the research, including research questions and design was shared among all members of the group. The teachers were entirely in charge of what they did in their classrooms. The project was not an initiative of any system or institution; it has received no significant external funding (it is now self-funding) and was not associated with study for any higher degree. There was no money for time release and the teachers donated one of their preparation periods most weeks when they agreed to meet with the academics for a period of two years. This structure of (mainly) school-based groups of teachers meeting in professional learning communities (Borko, 2004) to reflect on practice against ideas of learning remains central to the way PEEL operates. As the project has grown, there has been a greater emphasis on groups reporting some of their experiences for others and there is now a large body of documented outcomes and insights from teachers.

In spite of three very difficult initial months that included the failure of the initial strategies and a student reaction that was critical and even hostile to a classroom culture that emphasized thinking (Baird & Mitchell, 1997), the teachers persisted, learnt from their initial failures and began to achieve substantial classroom change (White & Mitchell, 1994; Baird & Northfield, 1995; Loughran, 1999). At the end of two years, the teachers found both the process and outcomes of involvement in PEEL so rewarding that they refused to allow the project to end. Although the two full-time academics were no longer able to attend, the project continued at its original school and then began to spread to other schools in Australia and then other countries as other teachers heard about it. There are now networks of PEEL groups in many schools in the states of Victoria and New South Wales, as well as groups in other Australian states and several other countries including an extensive network in Sweden.

Over the past 21 years, the PEEL project has involved thousands of teachers. Part of the context for this chapter is that there are many teachers who have been collaborating with academic friends over long periods of time, taking on increasingly sophisticated roles in knowledge generation.

DATA

PEEL was not intended to run past two years and we certainly did not plan a two decade systematic collection of data on long term change. Nevertheless, data was systematically collected on various aspects of the work after years one, six, twelve, thirteen, seventeen and eighteen of the project (Baird & Mitchell, 1997; Baird & Northfield, 1995; Dusting et al., 1996; Mitchell & Mitchell, 1997; Mitchell, et al., 2001; Loughran et al., 2002)[1]. Another major data source for this paper are my experiences of 21 years of leading and attending meetings of a range of types: of PEEL groups in schools, of convenors of PEEL groups – who meet regularly to share successes and difficulties from their groups, of PEEL teachers who have agreed to engage in more formal research (Northfield & Mitchell, 1995), and of cross-school PEEL days that have a particular theme (e.g. case writing or teaching English from a PEEL perspective) that are advertised to the PEEL network. Many of these meetings had minutes taken, many did not, but the largely unfunded[2], voluntary nature of PEEL means that it is essential that all of them are fruitful, hence all have included regular analysis after the meetings about how the meeting went, what sorts of discussion were and were not useful and whether and why they met the needs of the participants. Data of this type are real – in that what follows is grounded in very rich experience, but is not easy to present in a chapter such as this. Perhaps the strongest evidence is that PEEL, with no funding or system-level support, has continued and grown for 21 years – clearly something is providing payoffs for the teachers.

A further major data source that is documented is the writings of the PEEL teachers in 86 editions of *PEEL SEEDS*; the journal of the PEEL collective. PEEL has been characterised by a great deal of writing by many teachers. The seventh edition of the PEEL database (Mitchell et al., 2006.), which provides access to all of the *PEEL SEEDS* articles to the end of 2006, contains 1282 articles by 598 teachers[3].

In the remainder of this chapter, I draw on these very large data sources to argue for a series of assertions about the professional learning that occurs in long-term teacher-research in each of the areas mentioned in the introduction: developments in teachers' perceptions of their role and the knowledge they are generating, in identifying and sharing this knowledge in ways accessible to other teachers and in supporting teachers as they move from professional talk to teacher research. I use the device of arguing for assertions as a way of presenting ideas that have emerged, often gradually from experiences spread over many years. I do not mean to imply that these are incontestable, nor even that they are 'finished' from our perspectives. PEEL continues and our understandings evolve. The extent to which readers agree with the assertions will be dependent on the extent to which they help them make sense of their own experiences.

A final cautionary comment is that, while PEEL provides a rich context for what follows, it is only one context and is not presented as the only way of generating professional learning from teacher research.

ASSERTIONS ABOUT THE DEVELOPMENT OF TEACHER'S PERCEPTIONS OF
THEIR ROLE AND TEACHER KNOWLEDGE

As mentioned in the introduction, a sense of progress and development in both themselves and their work has proved essential for teachers to sustain energy and effort. Better understandings of the nature of this development have enhanced the ability of change agents to stimulate and support the journey.

Assertion 1: Teachers rarely undertake research to contribute to the knowledge base of education.

The academic literature is a foreign world for teachers; their reasons for beginning a process of collaborative action-research are for their own professional learning and to achieve change in their own classrooms. Some join because they value an opportunity for collaboration and sharing, some to extend their practice. All have issues in their classroom that they want to address. It takes a long time and a lot of affirmation for teachers to accept that they have generalizable contributions to make to a wider audience.

Assertion 2: Teachers come to perceive they are engaged in research some time after they have moved into this role.

Many teachers engage in forms of reflective practice. This does not mean that they will move to what could be called teacher-research. PEEL positions teachers as researchers; while this was in one sense accepted by the original group, it was at least three months before they genuinely perceived themselves in this role (Baird & Mitchell, 1997). Moreover, the regular presence of university friends in the original group (something not possible as the project grew) almost certainly accelerated this shift in perception.

There is no clear point on the journey when a teacher moves from reflective practice and collaborative professional learning to teacher-research. Any attempt to find even an approximate position will depend on the definition of research being used. If research is defined as the deliberate and (at least semi-) systematic development of new knowledge (Cochran-Smith & Lytle, 1993), then many PEEL teachers have begun to engage in research quite early in their involvement in the project. However it has taken much longer for them to perceive themselves in this role. The amount of personal interaction with academics the teacher has had is often important here – affirmation is crucial. While time must be allowed for this development, it is an important step as it typically leads to significant changes in the way teachers analyse and talk about their practice – they look for more generalizable patterns and insights.

Assertion 3: Teachers develop new dimensions of sense-making.

Baird (2003) argued that PEEL helped teachers make better sense of their practice. He defined sense-making as knowing both what needs to be done and why and what you are doing and why. Scheele et al. (2005) pointed out that this new sense-making changed the ways teachers talked to each other and with their students, they also articulated a range of new dimensions of sense-making. For many (non-PEEL) teachers, their practice makes sense if they are covering their curriculum, setting tasks that are feasible and appropriate for their students and minimizing problems of management. While teachers vary widely, that may be it.

As the PEEL teachers began to achieve real and substantial change in their classrooms, they found themselves accumulating wisdom in a wide range of interconnected areas: the nature of quality learning and of 'good learning behaviours' (White & Mitchell, 1994), teaching procedures that promote these, tactics for promoting a metacognitive awareness of learning (Mitchell, 2006), the risks associated with quality learning, the trusts that need to be developed, teacher behaviours that support risk taking, the role of student talk and student questions, the changes in students, and teachers' conceptions of and attitudes to learning and teaching that are needed for any changes in behaviours, how to promote quality learning in contexts such as library research, laboratory exercises, class discussions and the role of assessment in promoting student change is an incomplete list. Each of these can be regarded as a new dimension along which their practice developed and made sense. An important aspect of the professional learning from long term teacher research is that teachers develop the confidence and ability to frame their practice in such elaborated and multi-dimensional ways.

Assertion 4: The process of teacher-research changes the balance and relationship between science, craft and art knowledge of teaching.

Teaching has elements of a science, a craft and an art. By 'science' knowledge I mean generalizations and constructs grounded in research. This is often dismissed as irrelevant 'theory' by teachers who see teaching as a craft, learnt by practice. Craft knowledge is an important part of teachers' professional knowledge. Teachers new to PEEL tend to share concrete, subject-specific, craft tips about what they have tried. PEEL has, in part, aimed at developing professional knowledge that is more scientific (i.e. overtly linked to 'theory') than is common in school staffrooms. Recognition of the value of this is one part of the professional learning in long-term teacher-research; better integration of science and craft knowledge is a second.

PEEL was stimulated by ideas from the literature on learning: ideas about metacognition (Flavell, 1976) and Baird's notion of poor learning tendencies (Baird & White, 1982). The participants set out to develop new practice that was grounded in research, that linked learning and teaching and that would improve teachers' abilities to develop, explain and predict successful practice. Sharing and finding reasons for failures tends to shift the teacher talk into generalizations about issues of student learning and change. However, applying these pieces of 'theory' to practice has required the development of a large body of new craft knowledge that we have found must accompany more general insights if they are to have meaning and value. An important part of the journey of teacher research, that is reflected in the ways the teachers talk and write, is the shift from sharing context specific stories and ideas to a search for deeper causes and for generalisations about practice that allow ideas to be applied more widely

Science and craft knowledge can be mapped onto the theory-practice binary. However, there is a third form of teacher knowledge: teaching will always have aspects of an art, with teachers making rapid decisions in response to complex and sometimes unexpected stimuli, using equally complex but commonly tacit analytic frames. The term 'art knowledge' is intended to describe knowledge that has not been and is not readily codified – skilled teachers often cannot articulate what they do, let alone why. This is what Schon (1987) termed a junk category because it defies investigation. We have consistently found in PEEL that practice precedes understanding: that important elements of new practices developed by teachers begin as tacit 'art' knowledge. Another crucial part of the professional learning occurs as the process of collaborative reflection on practice allows teachers to identify and codify this hitherto unarticulated wisdom and hence move it into craft and science knowledge that can be both used by others and extended by the originator(s).

The following article (Mitchell, 2003, pp. 38-40) reports a good example of this. The (primary) teachers at this PEEL meeting were discussing, quite casually, the issue of whether or not colouring activities (assumed to be merely 'down time') could include some elements of metacognition; unexpectedly they identified and codified a major change in their practice that they had developed over the previous few years, but which had been tacit until this meeting.

Insights from a Primary PEEL Collective Meeting

PEELing Up Colouring Activities

Kerry reported how she and Amanda had been meeting with Jo and Sandra to produce a Primary version of *About PEEL*. At that meeting, Kerry and Amanda had both said that they thought that they could not, and were not "doing PEEL" all the time: their (young) students needed some 'down time' such as colouring activities. Jo had pushed them, arguing that there would be PEEL aspects to how they ran a colouring activity. This report stimulated a high powered brainstorm. Amanda said that, well yes, she did talk to the students about the concept of and need for 'down time' and how to use it effectively. So did Kerry, who also would discuss with her students the psychomotor skills they were learning (e.g. tracing along a line). Amanda then realised that she had removed the constraints that Prep teachers tend to put on colouring (e.g. use yellow for the sun and brown and/or black for dogs) and gave her students choice (which they then considered the consequences of) over colour. Kaylene said she sometimes put out scissors with colouring shapes and allowed her students to cut and rearrange them before colouring. Someone else (the ideas were flying faster than the pen) gave students choices over using texta, crayon or pencils; again with later consideration of consequences.

Jo had been right. The discussion brought out hitherto tacit knowledge about how completely PEEL perspectives (on learning) can pervade teaching.

Using a PEEL Language

Kaylene summed up the discussion on colouring with a brilliant insight: you may not be using PEEL procedures all the time but you are using PEEL language all the time … Six features of PEEL language were mentioned and a seventh was added by me later.

1. Discussion of why we are doing this.

Purposes and reasons for tasks and the big ideas and key skills associated with them are explicitly discussed. So often tasks are presented as just that – tasks.

2. Student Choice.

Primary teachers constantly make decisions for students about the 'best' (or only!) way to do tasks. This group has given students far more control over their work with real decisions to make.

3. Discussion of consequences of choice.

The benefits of giving students choice are enhanced by non-judgemental debriefs on the consequences of choices: Were coloured felt tip pens a good choice to use on a sheet with work on both sides?

4. Using labels for teaching procedures.

All the teachers built up a shared meaning with their students for a list of teaching procedures such as Venn Diagrams and Mind Maps that they select and use regularly. The students become familiar not only with the procedures, but their purposes in terms of learning. As Sandra stressed at one point – PEEL is about doing things with a purpose.

5. Thinking about thinking/learning about learning.

The teachers use words and phrases such as 'reflecting', 'linking' and 'down time' to talk about thinking and learning and to give students a vocabulary to do this.

6. Encouragement to take risks.

Many decisions involve safe options and risky options. Amanda argued for giving greater respect for students' intellectual capabilities and encouraging and trusting them to step outside conventional boundaries.

7. Highlight good learning behaviours.

The current (PEEL) list of good learning behaviours is at least the fifth draft of a list that was first developed in the second year of the project to list the sorts of behaviours that we felt reflected quality learning. ...One value for me of a list such as this is that it made me far more sensitive to these behaviours. This meant that when one occurred, I was much more likely to stop the class and briefly comment on what it was as well as how and why it was 'useful' to the class – a word I used a lot in my classes. I was particularly likely to do this early in the year; making comments such as 'Let's look at what Ken has just done; he has put forward a different explanation and argued for that by finding a link between what we are doing and home. Thanks Ken, that example was very helpful to the discussion.'... These comments allowed me firstly to raise students' awareness of (what I regard as) good learning behaviours and secondly, to give some positive feedback to students who were good orally (but who) were not necessarily strong performers on written tasks.

This article illustrates some aspects of how knowledge is co-constructed in PEEL. I was acting as the recorder (and not the chair) at a meeting where, as a person with no primary teaching experience, I was not seen as a source of important kinds of expertise. I do, however, sometimes make a more general comment that perhaps reframes something the teachers have said or links it to something other PEEL teachers have said or done and reflect it back for further discussion. On this occasion, I did not construct the key generalization about a 'PEEL language' – a teacher did; I did, however, in the written account bring in two aspects of earlier work in PEEL that I felt enriched the initial list. In this way I was moving back and forth between the position of novice and expert (Toohey & Waterstone, 2004). This meeting involved important professional learning by the participants (including me), however it had a significant impact on many other teachers who read the account or were exposed to it in subsequent meetings. The codification of what is now called a 'language for learning' stimulated what has become an important element of what PEEL means in many primary and secondary classrooms.

ASSERTIONS ABOUT THE IDENTIFICATION AND REPRESENTATION OF TEACHER KNOWLEDGE

One criticism of teacher-research is that it does not generalise. As 'language for learning' illustrates, a feature of PEEL has been the extent to which the findings and advice, if appropriately framed and represented, do generalise to a wide range of classrooms.

Assertion 5. Over time, reflective teacher talk needs to moves from discussion of activities to generic procedures to strategies.

The nature of the teacher talk in many PEEL groups has moved through three increasingly general levels of advice. This development seems to have been important in determining whether a group sustains its vitality in the medium term (2-3 years).

As discussed under Assertion 4, teachers are used to sharing content-specific activities (e.g. 'Here is a good way of introducing algebra in Year 7'). This has value, but it is not an efficient way of sharing good practice as most activities can only be used once per year with any one class. An important part of professional learning involves looking for the generic features of these activities, generating advice that crosses topic and subject boundaries; but the shift to increased levels of generalization that occurs over time does not end here. What we call generic procedures, such as mind mapping or role play are often referred to as strategies in the literature, however they are more tactical than strategic in that they refer to an approach that lasts for one or two lessons rather than the whole year. Labelling them as strategies is to frame teaching as a series of short-term actions without long-term guiding principles. Over time, genuinely strategic statements such as 'provide students with genuine choices' or 'promote student talk that is tentative hypothetical and exploratory' have emerged as frames to cluster large chunks of the teacher behaviours and teaching procedures that teachers involved in PEEL have found effective. Mitchell and Mitchell (1997) listed twelve such statements (see Table 7.1) in an analysis of cases written by experienced PEEL teachers. These statements are strategic in that they are enacted, in many ways, over the course of a whole year. They are not listed in any rank order; they are recurring themes in the articles reported in *PEEL SEEDS* (the PEEL journal) and collected on the PEEL database (Mitchell et al., 2006.). The two principles just listed, for example, select 299 and 190 articles respectively out of the 1282 on the 2006 database.

Table 7.1. Principles of teaching for quality learning

1	Share intellectual control with students.
2	Create occasions when students can work out part (or all) of the content or instructions.
3	Provide opportunities for choice and independent decision making.
4	Provide a diverse range of ways of experiencing success.
5	Promote talk that is exploratory, tentative and hypothetical.
6	Encourage students to learn from other students' questions and comments.
7	Build a classroom environment that supports risk-taking.
8	Use a wide variety of intellectually challenging teaching procedures.
9	Use teaching procedures that are designed to promote specific aspects of quality learning.
10	Develop students' awareness of the big picture: how the various activities fit together and link to the big ideas.
11	Regularly raise students' awareness of the nature of different aspects of quality learning.
12	Assess for different aspects of quality learning, not for rote learning.

Assertion 6: Thinking about learning helps teachers articulate their practice in complex ways.

While sound reasons are given in the academic literature for the complexity of teacher knowledge, actual descriptions of it do not reflect this complexity. There are certainly accounts that convey the complexity of teacher's work, but there is a lack of rich articulations of sophisticated teacher knowledge. One probable reason for this is that it is not easy to get teachers to describe the important elements of their practice, it may also be because searching for this type of knowledge is time consuming and not highly valued in academic publications. The focus on linking teaching to how students approach learning as well as the collaborative reflection illustrated earlier, have been important in tackling this problem in PEEL – thinking about learning helps teachers articulate their practice in new ways that reflect the new dimensions of sense-making discussed earlier. Related to this is the emphasis in PEEL in achieving (gradual) **change** in how students learn. Thinking about their year long agendas, for example getting students to offer and defend ideas, has also helped teachers articulate their practice.

Assertion 7: Two ways of unlocking tacit teacher knowledge are case writing and asking teachers to react to statements that have emerged to make sense of complex bodies of practice.

Unlocking the tacit art knowledge of good teachers requires a process of stimulated reflection. To date we have found two approaches that have been successful in helping teachers explicate subtle, but crucial, aspects of their practice. The first is the writing and sharing of drafts of cases that are based on critical incidents in their classrooms (Shulman & Colbert, 1989). Good case writing includes the thoughts and decision making of the teacher as s/he reacts to the incident. Asking teachers to include these in their cases helps them recall hitherto tacit aspects of what they did, and why.

A second approach has been to ask teachers if and how they implement each of the 12 Principles of Teaching for Quality Learning (Table 7.1). We make no claims that this list is definitive or complete. What it does do is provide frames for thinking about practice that helps teachers experienced in PEEL codify and communicate their existing practice (Loughran et al., 2004).

ASSERTIONS ABOUT REPORTING, WRITING AND SHARING TEACHER-RESEARCH

The range of dimensions along which long-term teacher researchers think about their practice causes serious problems when they try to codify and communicate it. There are real risks of intimidating and overwhelming the reader as well as of producing advice that seems formulaic and prescriptive. This is a serious problem for long-term teacher-research projects.

The wisdom that emerges from long-term teacher-research is much more than a set of practical tips. Identifying, exploring and findings ways of representing the knowledge is an important part of professional learning.

The interconnected and richly detailed nature of practically sophisticated knowledge means that it is not easy to report in ways that are accessible, credible and empowering for other teachers (Toohey & Waterstone, 2004). Posner (1982) said that, in order for new ideas to be adopted, they must be intelligible, plausible and fruitful. Gunstone & Northfield (1987) added that they needed to be feasible. In what follows, I use these four criteria to discuss reporting and sharing teacher research. Professional learning involves much more than just understanding new ideas, it involves trying and refining and adapting new ideas. Sharing of teacher research with teachers should stimulate, facilitate and support these processes.

Assertion 8: The best way into making new teacher knowledge intelligible for other teachers is via practice – both reading accounts of practice and trying new, albeit imperfectly understood, approaches in their own classroom.

We have found that when talking about a change in practice that involves new ways of thinking about teaching and learning and changes in what is valued and why, teachers need to experience (either first or second hand) examples of the new approach in order to begin to understand it. When we have presented to teachers generalisations that have been developed by other teachers as ways of representing important aspects of their practice, the generalisations have often appeared either meaningless or trivial until accompanied by rich accounts of the practice on which they are based. This is not to say that the general frames are then of little value; on the contrary, they often empower teachers to transfer ideas to their own contexts, but on their own, they carry little meaning.

The complexity of the knowledge associated with classroom change is illustrated in this following article from *PEEL SEEDS* Number 1. It is an account from a very early stage in the professional learning often associated with PEEL. I have used it dozens of times in in-service activities with teachers and it has consistently stimulated rich discussion and analysis.

Geography – Coastlines

In the past, I would have conducted this class by first showing a series of slides with different types of coastlines. During the slides, I would have given the students information about the different types of coastlines.

For this lesson however, I stood aside a little and simply wrote the heading "Coastlines" on the board. I then asked students to describe different coastlines and put their ideas on the board.

The students' early response was fairly typical; "What do you want us to say, sir?" After fifteen minutes waiting and thinking time however, I filled the board with their responses.

When this was finished, I showed the slides and was pleased with the lively discussion during and after. In fact, I was thrilled when, at the end of the lesson, I was talking to the class about estuaries and fjords and the students, not me, had taken the class there. The lesson ended where I would normally want, but not necessarily be.

(Rod Greer, Stawell Secondary College, *PEEL SEEDS*, No. 1, February, 1989, p. 10)

At the most obvious level, this describes a simple change in one teacher's lesson. However, teachers have always identified more profound changes than a mere switch in activity. They see a shift in intellectual control as the teacher abandons

115

the role of source of all information and works flexibly and reactively from the students' experiences and contributions (Principle 1 in Table 7.1). They identify the major changes in student and teacher talk associated with this shift (Principle 5). They list risks that the teacher took: Would the students have anything to say? Would they say anything? Would he be able to use what they said? They also identify the risks for the students in this new environment (Principle 7) and can build meaning for some of the issues of medium-term change for this class associated with this incident – the value of a debrief with the students on whether and how learning had occurred for example.

Assertion 9: In addition to being intelligible, new teacher-knowledge must be shared in ways that render it *plausible*, *fruitful* and *feasible*.

To be plausible means that teachers believe that the changes associated with new practices **could** occur in classrooms similar to their own: a reaction 'my students would/could never do that' is a failure of plausibility. One requirement for plausibility is sensitively written accounts of risky, stressful and often only partially successful practice that are crafted to link to and provide new insight into aspects of the reader's practice. Greer's case above has proved to have this sort of credibility. Video cases are proving even more effective in providing a 'vision of the possible'.

To be fruitful for a reader, research must offer some prospective improvement to current practice. In the case of PEEL, the focus on learning has meant that many problems of concern to teachers, such as low levels of student interest and high levels of off-task or disruptive behaviour are now seen as symptoms of student dissatisfaction with the learning and teaching transactions in their classroom. This reframing, that turns these problems into ones that teachers can more easily address has been an important reason for PEEL's longevity and spread. Fruitful accounts of research will take problems that matter to the teacher reader and frame them in ways that provide invitations to constructive action.

To be feasible, new ideas about learning and teaching must be accompanied by adequate classroom wisdom about how to apply them. As stated earlier, a particularly low status form of knowledge in the literature is the details of how and how not, as well as when and when not, to apply new ideas. Yet this scientific craft knowledge, with its intricate connections between theory and practice, is essential for any impact on the classroom and teacher readers recognize its value. A school teacher reader who identifies potential value in some research will generally ask 'OK, where/how can I start to use this'. We have found it important to provide multiple possibilities – different teachers are attracted to different entry points.

Assertion 10: When reporting teacher-research to academic audiences, we need new cannons of excellence for defining quality.

Professional learning applies to tertiary as well as school educators. The preceding assertions relate to what (school) teacher readers look for when being presented with new teacher knowledge. This knowledge is not generated in the same way as academic knowledge and should be judged by cannons of excellence that recognise teacher-research as a separate genre. That is not to say that all teacher-research should be regarded as good. As a starting point for discussion, I offer four criteria for quality in teacher-research when considering publications in the mainstream literature:

1. Good teacher-research will show evidence of the knowledge having emerged collaboratively, being tested against experiences of a number of classrooms (Northfield, Mitchell & Mitchell, 1997). One outcome of this is knowledge that is far more likely to generalise.
2. The research will show understanding of learning and change and will show evidence of a search for patterns and underlying causes in terms of ideas of learning and change. Good teacher-research will show an awareness of the complexity of classrooms and will not place it in one of Schon's inaccessible junk categories – too complex to unravel. Instead, reports of good teacher-research will include insights into the complexity that explain and support the reported outcomes and provide advice and predictions for future action.
3. The research will be reported in ways that do not disconnect the findings from practice, that include sensitively written accounts of practice that allow the reader to generate intelligibility, plausibility and fruitfulness.
4. The research findings provide invitations to action and enough classroom-tested advice to provide starting points for action.

While these criteria are not inconsistent with some of the criteria associated with academic research, they do reflect some differences in the research and in the reporting that we have found to be important. Teacher-research typically has a broad, rather than narrow focus, shows greater breadth (more classrooms) and length (often years) than academics who are researchers of classrooms can achieve, but commonly has less depth – intensive interviewing, for example, is not easy for teacher-researchers to fit into a working day. The type of reporting described above reflects the reality that, by themselves, generalizations, no matter how insightful, over-simplify practice. It also values craft knowledge as an essential component of the wisdom developed from teacher-research.

MY PROFESSIONAL LEARNING: HOW CAN I SUPPORT THE JOURNEY OF TEACHERS IN LONG-TERM TEACHER-RESEARCH?

The preceding discussion allows for some conclusions and advice on how to stimulate and support teachers in long-term projects such as PEEL (i.e. voluntary and with teachers not enrolled in higher degrees). Although PEEL has been teacher-led, with teachers entirely in charge of what they do in their classrooms, the role of academics has been crucial to its vitality and growth. Our experiences do not support the view that full-time teachers, alone in schools can sustain a research culture. Some conclusions drawn from my own professional learning as an academic supporting teachers, stepping between school and university contexts are:

– Choose problems that emerge from the teachers concerns and needs (which may

not be those of the system)
- Focus on issues of learning – they are at the heart of classroom practices
- Establish a culture of sharing, testing and extending ideas in a range of contexts and of searching for underlying causes and reasons
- Build processes to identify the tacit 'art' knowledge that is part of new practices
- Affirm the value and importance of the teachers' work, including their reflections and insights – it is much easier for an academic ('outsider') to see this than it is for teachers
- Over time (months), help teachers move from sharing context-specific, new teaching ideas to discussion of more generic and strategic features, purposes and outcomes
- Help teachers reframe their practice by mirroring it back to them from perspectives they may not have thought of. It is important that this is done in ways that leaves ownership with the teachers and which positions teachers and academic colleagues as having different, but equally important types of expertise
- Capitalize on the development that occurs in teachers over multiple years by planning long timelines and providing, as appropriate, increasingly sophisticated challenges. The wisdom that comes from teachers in their third or fourth year of teacher-research is qualitatively different from the wisdom that emerges in the first six months
- Document and share teacher research in ways that are intelligible, plausible, fruitful and feasible – with both visions of the possible and concrete advice.

NOTES

[1] All PEEL publications, as well as other details, are available at www.peelweb.org
[2] PEEL groups are unfunded. Sales of publications provide income for some teacher release for some of the theme meetings. Research grants have provided some support for the teachers engaged in more formal research.
[3] For a continuously updated online version see *PEEL in Practice* at www.peelweb.org

REFERENCES

Baird, J. R. (1986). Improved learning through enhanced metacognition: A classroom study. *European Journal of Science Education, 8,* 263-282.
Baird, J. R. (2003). Making sense of PEEL; Making sense with PEEL. In I. J. Mitchell, J. A. Mitchell, R. T. McKinnon, S. K. Scheele & D. Lumb (Eds.), *PEEL in practice: 1300 ideas for quality teaching* (7th ed.). Melbourne: PEEL Publishing. Accessible at http//www.peelweb.org
Baird, J. R., & Mitchell, I. J. (Eds.). (1997). *Improving the quality of teaching and learning.* Melbourne: PEEL Publishing.
Baird, J. R., & Northfield, J. R. (Eds.). (1995). *Learning from the PEEL experience.* Melbourne: PEEL Publishing.
Baird, J. R., & White, R. T., (1982). Promoting self-control of learning. *Instructional Science, 11,* 227-247. [The study of university students learning that resulted in PLTs]
Borko, H. (2004). Professional development and teacher learning: Mapping the terrain. *Educational Researcher, 33*(8), 3-15.
Cochran-Smith, M., & Lytle, S. (1993). *Inside/outside: Teacher research and knowledge.* New York: Teachers College Press.

Dusting, R., Pinnis, G., Rivers, R., & Sullivan, V. (Eds.). (1996). *Towards a thinking classroom.* Melbourne: PEEL Publishing.

Flavell, J. H. (Ed.). (1976). Metacognitive aspects of problem solving. In L. B. Resnick (Ed.), *The Nature of Intelligence.* Hillsdale, NJ: Erlbaum.

Gunstone, R. F., & Northfield, J. R. (1987). Learners-teachers-researchers: Consistency in implementing conceptual change. *Tijdschrift voor Didactic der Beta - Wetenschappen* (Journal for the Teaching of the Exact Sciences), *5,* 60-74.

Loughran, J. J. (1999). Professional development for teachers: A growing concern. *The Journal of In-Service Education, 25*(2), 261-72.

Loughran, J. J., Mitchell, I. J., & Mitchell. J. A., (Eds.). (2002). *Learning from teacher research.* New York: Teacher College Press.

Loughran, J. J., Mitchell, I. J., & Mitchell. J. A., (2004). Attempting to document teachers professional knowledge. *Qualitative Studies in Education, 16*(9), 1-21.

Lytle, S. L., & Cochran-Smith, M. J. (1992). Teacher research as a way of knowing. *Harvard Educational Review, 62*(4), 447-474.

Mitchell, I. J. (2003). Insights from a primary PEEL collective meeting. In J. Flack, S. Marinielle, J. Osler, A. Saffin, K. Strapp & I. J. Mitchell, *PEEL from a primary perspective* (pp. 38-43). Melbourne: PEEL Publishing.

Mitchell, I. J., (Ed.). (2006). *Teaching for effective learning: The complete book of PEEL teaching procedures.* Melbourne: PEEL Publishing.

Mitchell, I. J., & Mitchell, J. A. (Eds.). (1997). *Stories of reflective teaching: A book of PEEL cases.* Melbourne: PEEL Publishing.

Mitchell, I. J., Mitchell, J. A., McKinnon, R. T., Scheele, S. K., & Lumb, D. (2006.). *PEEL in practice: 1300 ideas for quality teaching* (7th ed.). Melbourne: PEEL Publishing. Accessible at http//www.peelweb.org

Mitchell, J. A., Loughran, J. J., & Mitchell, I. J. (2001). *Insights into PEEL practice: Invitations to action.* Melbourne: PEEL Publishing.

Northfield, J. R., & Mitchell, I. J. (1995, April). *Bringing a research focus into the teaching role.* Paper presented at the Annual Meeting of the American Educational Research Association, San Francisco, CA.

Posner, G. J., Strike, K. A., Hewson, P. W., & Gertzog, W. A. (1982). Accomodation of a scientific conception: Toward a theory of conceptual change. *Science Education, 66,* 211-227.

Pring, R. (2000). *Philosophy of educational research.* London: Continuum.

Scheele, S. K., Mitchell, J. A., & Mitchell, I. J. (2005). PEEL: Making more sense of teaching and learning. In I. J. Mitchell, J. A. Mitchell, R. T. McKinnon, S. K. Scheele & D. Lumb (Eds.), *PEEL in practice: 1300 ideas for quality teaching* (7th ed.). Melbourne: PEEL Publishing. Accessible at http//www.peelweb.org

Schon, D. A. (1987). *Educating the reflective practitioner.* San Francisco: Jossy-Bass.

Shulman, J. H., & Colbert, J. A. (1989). Cases as catalysts for cases: Inducing reflection in teacher education. *Action in teacher education* (Spring, 1989).

Toohey, K., & Waterstone, B. (2004). Negotiating expertise in an action research community. In B. Norton & K. Toohey (Eds.), *Critical pedagogies and language learning* (pp. 291-310). Cambridge: Cambridge University Press.

White, R. T., & Mitchell, I. J. (1994). Metacognition and the quality of learning. *Studies in Science Education 23,* 21-37.

Ian Mitchell
Faculty of Education
Monash University

LIBBY TUDBALL

8. 'PROFESSIONAL LEARNING COMMUNITIES'

Exploring Their Power and Influence in Teacher Professional Learning

INTRODUCTION: THE POWER OF PROFESSIONAL LEARNING COMMUNITIES

Achieving effective teacher professional learning can be influenced by a range of complex factors. Yet recently there has been increasing acceptance in the literature that when schools operate with the functions and characteristics of *professional learning communities* (PLCs), the process is more likely to be successful. PLCs have been the subject of substantial international academic research, and there has been ongoing interest in their role in improving teaching and learning. Since the early 1990s, many researchers in the fields of teacher professional learning and school reform have explored aspects of the functioning of PLCs. Newmann (1991) claimed that society in general, and education, in particular, could benefit substantially from efforts to transform impersonal, fragmented bureaucratic organisations, into places where participants share goals, and pursue a common agenda of activities through collaborative work that involves stable, personalised contact, that is sustained over a long term.

From their longitudinal study of sixteen high schools in California and Michigan, McLaughlin & Talbert (1993) reported that teachers' groups and professional communities "offer the most effective unit of intervention and powerful opportunity for reform" (p. 18), and "participation in a professional community supports the risk-taking and struggle entailed in transforming practice" (p. 15). In the PLCs, the teachers were provided with the support to consider educational goals and their meaning in terms of their classrooms, their students, and their subject area. The study found that teachers who made effective teaching adaptations that improved learning for their students had belonged to professional communities that encouraged and supported them in transforming their teaching. Through discussion with other teachers and leaders in the professional community, teachers' ideas of good classroom practice, and their own professional learning was developed.

Hargreaves (1994) noted that international studies of teachers working together found that true collaborative cultures need to be mounted not just for specific projects or events, but should be deep, personal, enduring, and absolutely central to teachers' daily work. In further research, Hargreaves (1994) also found that when teachers work closely with colleagues and share burdens, they give each other the moral support and collective strength to set priorities among all the demands they face in schools.

A. Berry, A. Clemans and A. Kostogriz (Eds.), Dimensions of Professional Learning: Professionalism, Practice and Identity, 121–135. © 2007 Sense Publishers. All rights reserved.

Kruse, Louis and Bryk (1994) argued that a PLC functions with each of these five dimensions: shared norms and values, collective focus on student learning, collaboration, deprivatized practice where teachers visit each others classrooms, and reflective dialogue. In the research presented in this chapter, these functions of a PLC are discussed.

In a more recent book on PLCs, Eaker, Dufour and Dufour (2002) also concluded that the PLC can become the organisational structure that hosts and scaffolds teachers' professional learning. They grouped the conceptual framework for PLCs around three major themes that can be evident in school practices, policies and programs: a solid foundation consisting of collaboratively developed and widely shared mission, vision, values and goals; collaborative teams that work to achieve common goals; and, a focus on results as evidenced by a commitment to continuous improvement.

McLaughlin's (1994) research also supported the potential influence of PLCs and she found that:

> Creating conditions for professional learning communities offers the most powerful opportunity for reform. The path to change in the classroom lies within and through teachers' professional communities. The best teacher professional development takes place not in a workshop or in discrete, bounded convocations, but in the context of professional communities – discourse communities, learning communities... Teachers can and do typically belong to multiple professional communities, each of which functions somewhat differently as a strategic site for professional growth. Thus the argument is made, that enabling professional growth, is, at root, about enabling professional community. (p. 31)

Two important studies, *Professionalism and community: Perspectives on reforming urban schools* (Louis, Kruse & Associates, 1995) and *Authentic achievement: Restructuring schools for intellectual quality* (Newmann & Associates, 1996), provided many answers to educators' questions about the power and influence of PLCs, and provided insights into the role of school structure and professional community in leading to improved student achievement. In these definitive works on the importance of PLCs in teacher professional learning, the researchers found that teachers' collective engagement in continuing efforts to improve practice can play a critical role. Newmann's (1996) research showed that "a sustained, school wide concentration on the intellectual quality of student learning, and a school wide professional community among the staff, were the keys to successful restructuring" (p. xiv). But studies such as these raise difficult questions: what characteristics do schools need in order to generate collaborative cultures; what structural and physical conditions need to exist; what is the role of leadership in this process; how is collegiality facilitated and enacted; and, how important are PLCs in relation to other factors that may be influential and powerful in achieving effective teacher professional learning?

In this chapter, each of these questions is discussed through an exploration of data and findings from case study research conducted in an Australian elementary school operating as a PLC. Kruse, Louis and Bryk's (1994) definition of PLCs is used as a conceptual framework to analyse and draw conclusions about the power and influence of the PLC in achieving professional learning.

METHODOLOGY

Since the mid-1990s, researchers have continued to explore the impact of PLCs mainly from what Kruse and O'Toole (2001) have described as a 'balcony view of what happens in schools, relying more on large-scale survey instruments than on the 'thick descriptions' characteristic of ethnographic studies' (p. 30). Westheimer (1999) argued that future studies should explore teacher collaboration within school contexts. This chapter draws on data from a four year longitudinal study of teachers engaged in professional learning at 'Chifley primary,' a five year old outer urban government school in the city of Melbourne, Australia (Tudball, 2004). Since this study was completed, the school has been recognised at the state and national level for providing an exemplary model of student engagement in civics and citizenship education (CCE). (The school and teachers' names are pseudonyms). The teacher participants in this study included Stewart, the school principal, Andrew, an experienced teacher leader, and classroom teachers Gaye, Cathy, Sally and Greg.

Since the intent of the case study research was to document and analyse an instance of the functioning of a 'successful' PLC, Chifley primary school was selected after I observed the team work and collaborative efforts of the teachers at a teacher professional development seminar. During the study I became a participant-observer researcher, where I watched and joined in, as the teachers worked together to improve student learning in CCE in their school. My research focus was on exploring what happened in day to day school practice, over time, as the team of teachers worked together to plan and deliver their CCE programs. I aimed to develop insights into how they developed successful strategies.

Excerpts from the teachers' views and researcher observations have been selected to explore and draw conclusions about the power of PLCs to influence professional learning. The data is drawn from interviews of teachers and school leaders, and observations of teacher meetings, classroom and whole school practice.

In May 1997, the Australian federal government demonstrated its strong support for a national program of CCE by introducing the *Discovering Democracy* program which aimed to:

> ... help students recognise the relevance of their political and legal institutions to everyday life, and to develop capacities to participate as informed, reflective citizens in their civic community. (Kemp, 1997, p. 4)

Achieving these goals provided considerable challenges for teachers and school communities where CCE had not been a priority in the past, and there was a clear need for professional learning to allow teachers to explore how they could develop CCE programs. In this chapter, the focus of the study is on how the PLC functioned to assist the professional learning of teachers at the year 5/6 level, as they worked to develop students' civic knowledge and understanding of democratic processes, and the rights and responsibilities of citizens, through their simulation of a functioning community in their classroom. The next section provides an analysis of how the various characteristics of the PLC operated at Chifley primary school.

COLLABORATION AS A KEY TO PROFESSIONAL LEARNING

In PLC models of teacher professional learning, there is a view that when teachers work together to set goals and develop a vision for student learning, and then decide what they have to do to accomplish that vision, there is more likely to be continuous learning for the staff, and benefits to student learning as well (Eaker, Dufour & Dufour, 2002). In the case study presented here, teachers demonstrated that a shared definition of what they wanted to achieve was viewed as critical by all participants in the study. Observations of teacher meetings revealed deep discussion of the key concepts, questioning about the scope and concept of CCE, and a willingness to admit the need for the group to develop new knowledge and pedagogies. All of the teachers admitted their need to develop and update their ideas about CCE.

The teachers also stressed the importance of shared leadership in the setting of goals. At Chifley primary, the principal, 'Stewart' expressed the view that:

> First you need to motivate staff to talk about what a new curriculum initiative might mean, and then get them to work out what they want the students to learn, and how can that happen. I am a great believer in getting staff working in teams, so they can learn from each other and collaborate in their efforts. Principals must recognize and use talent in their staff, and give them leadership opportunities.

Teachers commented that their professional learning is always a shared process, where input from all members of the group is 'expected and valued' in establishing the learning goals.

Eaker, Dufour and Dufour (2002) argued that:

> Schools that function as professional learning communities are *always* characterized by a collaborative culture. Teacher isolation is replaced with collaborative processes that are deeply embedded into the daily life of the school. Members of PLC are not "invited" to work with colleagues: they are called upon to be contributing members of a collective effort to improve the school's capacity to help all students learn at high levels. (p. 5)

Over five years of visits, classroom observations and teacher interviews at Chifley primary school, I discovered a wealth of evidence showing that collaboration was core to the whole operation of the school, and was the key strategy underpinning the development of teacher professional learning in CCE and all other areas of the curriculum. The principal said that:

The development of our CCE program began at first as a whole school collaborative process in a staff meeting, where we brainstormed what might be our overall school goals for CCE. Then we set up a team of staff to talk and further debate what might be the goals of the units, what teaching and learning strategies to include and so on. Our initial task was therefore to decide on our focus and then structure the time for a group to develop units of work.

By engaging the whole staff in discussions from the very start of the process, Stewart initiated a sharing of vision and goals, and strong collaboration; both seen to be key elements of the functioning of a PLC (Hord, 2004). The group of teachers agreed that they benefited greatly from the team approach, the sharing of ideas and strategies, and the daily, even hourly, conversations and reflections on how the classroom practice unfolded. The collaboration was both formal and informal, and the teachers continually looked back on goals they had set to evaluate what was being achieved. The study provided evidence of a scenario where teamwork in schools continuing over time helps teachers avoid what Huberman (1995) defined as the 'lone wolf scenario', and what Little (1999) described as a situation:

> ... in which teachers labour on their own to decide what instruction works, what standard of work is good enough, and what additional knowledge, skills or insights would best serve them and their students. (p. 234)

At Chifley, it was clear that there was shared responsibility for developing students' learning, and collective responsibility for students' success. This collaboration operated effectively within the school, for instance two teachers, Gaye and Greg, decided to team teach the year 5 and 6 classes so they could plan together and more actively support each other. The development of the CCE program was also enhanced by wider collaboration. Andrew, a key teacher leader, played a vital role in the teachers' professional learning, since he encouraged further collaboration through wider connections with the local CCE network and a state-wide 'Grants to Schools' program. Andrew saw that encouraging the teachers to develop their knowledge and experience was a vital ingredient in their ongoing professional learning, but he did not want to 'develop a hot house culture where the teachers can only see each others' point of view'. He encouraged various members of the team to attend meetings and professional learning sessions where their ideas could be stimulated by wider contact.

COLLECTIVE AND CONTINUOUS FOCUS ON STUDENT LEARNING AND RESULTS

Eaker, Dufour and Dufour (2002) stressed that a successful PLC begins through definition of the learning goals. Teacher professional learning is then designed around the achievement of these goals. Chifley primary school staff continually set new goals for the improvement of the school and the students' learning in CCE and other areas. In 2001, the school became one of the pilot schools in the *Business Excellence Australia, Quality in Schools Program,* which encourages schools to establish a culture of continuous improvement, leading to improvement in learning outcomes for all staff and students through a careful process of strategic planning and collaboration. The school began to use the *Tool Time Program* (Langford, 1999), which provided a structure for staff to use in planning and reflection. The approach integrated an improvement focus across all dimensions of the school's operation, and involved the principal, teachers, parents, and support staff in the process. There were clear links between the aims of this strategy, and the focus on supportive structures and continuous learning in a PLC. In observations of staff meetings, I recognised an easy acceptance of these structures. One teacher commented:

> I have worked in other schools where there is no clarity about what we are trying to achieve. Here we work out what we want to do, and then have the processes in place to make sure it happens.

Cathy commented that: "there was a systematic plan in place to ensure that the school had the best possible access to ideas about CCE, and both internal and external processes to ensure that the goals for CCE were achieved". The principal, associate-principal and senior management team then worked with the committee to begin to write the school policy on CCE. Stewart felt that writing a formal policy on CCE would ensure that the area would have a long-term future as a key element in school programs. Andrew was sure that:

> The principal's role at this stage was so important, because he kept saying "you tell me what you want the students to learn, let's think about what we need to do to ensure the teachers can meet these goals, and then how we can assess that the learning has happened".

STRUCTURAL AND PHYSICAL CONDITIONS

Louis and Kruse (1995) argued that for learning communities to function productively, the physical or structural conditions and the human capacities of the people involved must be optimal. It was clear that at Chifley, the school leaders' awareness of these factors assisted in the successful development of CCE across the school. Boyd (1992) presented a list of physical factors that can result in an environment conducive to school change and improvement: the availability of resources; schedules and structures that reduce isolation; policies that encourage greater autonomy, foster collaboration, enhance effective communication, and provide for staff development.

Physical isolation can be a real barrier to building PLC, especially in larger schools. In schools where classrooms are close together and 'open door' policies are supported, teachers find it easier to work together and to gain new insight into their own practices (Louis & Kruse, 1995). When teachers are physically close, occasions for sustained observations and conversations related to teaching and student learning increase. It was easy for Sally and Greg to observe each other and discuss their teaching, since they worked together continually during the Chifley

CCE community program. Andrew was also frequently available during class time and after school. Andrew commented that at Chifley:

> there are common workspaces, such as team planning rooms, which provide relief from classroom isolation and encourage conversation and sharing. As a new school, the design of the place lends itself well to team teaching, open classroom activities and risk taking. It's not like lots of schools that are basically walled classrooms in style, where the walls don't come apart and it is difficult to fit double classes.

SOCIAL AND HUMAN RESOURCES

As important as they are, structural conditions are insufficient to support and enact improvement in learning. Social and human resources must be evident for the enhancement and operation of a PLC (Louis & Kruse, 1995; Sparks, 2002). At Chifley, there was openness to improvement that characterizes schools with a focus on learning (Sparks, 2002). Stewart and Andrew gave total support to Greg and Sally and teachers at other levels who were implementing the CCE units. The teachers commented that there is always encouragement for teachers who want to take risks and try new techniques and ideas. Greg commented that:

> Stewart totally supported us when our team decided to combine two classes and run a simulated community where the children would apply for jobs, run businesses, a bank, shops, newspaper, law court and even a parliament. These strategies really helped the kids to develop real life skills, but there were times when we really needed support in the development of the programs.

Andrew had prior experience in teaching CCE, so he appreciated the fact that as the vital human resource base, teachers need to have the appropriate cognitive and skills base to implement CCE. He provided the teachers with books, kits and practical ideas to implement in the simulated community, and he was given time release from other duties to support the classroom teachers. Sparks (2002) argued that: "professional community is based on effective teaching, which in turn is based on an expertise in the knowledge and skills of teaching" (p. 32).

Shaughnessy (1998) created a list of "people capacities" (p. 19) believed to be necessary for fostering improvement of learning in a PLC. He argued that teachers need to "acknowledge their inadequacies, pose problems, take risks, hold on to humour, collaborate with other learners, and have a moral purpose" (p. 19). These capacities were evident among the staff teaching the year 5/6 simulation at Chifley. Greg was willing to admit that at first he knew little about CCE, but his knowledge and ideas grew as he collaborated and learned from his peers. Andrew had knowledge of CCE, but was still keen to collaborate with other educators who had broader ideas to contribute. For example, after attending a network meeting on student participation, Andrew was inspired by an expert from a Youth Research centre, to focus more on developing democratic practice in the school.

Both Sally and Greg were willing to take the risk of putting over fifty young people into a large space, and virtually let them learn through play, in order to implement authentic learning about community functions and citizenship. The whole staff team struggled at first to develop the scope and sequence planning for CCE classroom strategies, and to decide directions, but after auditing curriculum documents, gathering resources and sharing ideas, they found solutions to their problems. It was extraordinary to watch the active engagement of the children learning about the day to day social, economic and political operations of a civic community, through diverse teaching and learning activities.

SHARED PERSONAL PRACTICE AND REFLECTIVE DIALOGUE

Louis and Kruse (1995) and Hord (2004) agreed that a further core element of the successful functioning of a PLC is that teachers should share ideas through team teaching or through the visitation and review of each other's classroom practice. They gain help, support and trust as a result of developing warm and open relationships with each other. They have a willingness to accept feedback and to work toward improvement in a collegial team. While this was evident at Chifley primary, there are many instances in other schools where teachers would actively avoid this process. An obvious feature of the success of the CCE program at Chifley was the willingness of the whole staff, the group of seven teachers who did the initial planning and Greg, Sally and Andrew in the year 5/6 community simulation to share their practice. Elmore (2002) argued that:

> The design of work in schools is fundamentally incompatible with the practice of improvement … It provides almost no opportunity for teachers to engage in continuous and sustained learning about their practice in the setting in which they work, observing and being observed by their colleagues in their own classrooms, and in the classrooms of other teachers confronting similar problems of practice. (p. 29)

Through observations at Chifley primary school, I discerned that the teachers were comfortable exchanging ideas and having support staff move in and out of their classrooms as participant observers and critical friends. While the practice of observation of each other's work was not formally structured as an evaluative process, it was clearly an integral part of the way that CCE in the school was developed. The teachers valued the opportunity to share views on their needs as teachers, and the learning needs of children in their classrooms. In the Chifley *School Charter Goals*, the expectation that there would be continuous sharing and reflection was embedded into the published staff values statement.

The literature on PLCs also stresses the importance of trust amongst staff as a key ingredient in successful collaboration. Westbrook (2002) argued that: "trust promotes risk taking, honest communication and deep commitment to school initiatives. Conscious efforts to build trust characterize efforts to create PLCs" (p. 3). If teachers do not have trust, then it is very difficult for genuine community to be achieved.

TEMPORAL CONDITIONS

Time is frequently cited in the literature as a key element in the functioning of PLCs and in effective teacher professional learning, since time, or more particularly the lack of it, is one of the most difficult problems faced by schools using PLCs as vehicles for professional learning (Fullan, 2001; Watts & Castle, 1993; Peterson, 1999; Stokes, 2001). Stewart was clearly aware of the need for the teachers to have time to plan and talk. He was willing to fund teacher time release during school hours, and in addition there was a cultural expectation in the school that teachers would be available for meetings after school. Fullan (2003) recommended a "redesign [of] the workplace so that innovation and improvement could be built into the daily activities of teachers" (p. 353). As previous discussion has shown, this worked in practice at Chifley. Greg said that:

> When you are implementing something new into the school, and you are trying to encourage all the staff, you must have the support of the Principal or it will just flounder. His decision to write a formal policy, and his willingness to be there at the table to listen and contribute ideas, meant a lot to the team. We were trying to develop a view of how we could develop engaging programs for each year level, and Stewart was part of initiating that vision.

Fullan (2001) argued that the process of vision building occurs as people talk, try things, and re-try jointly, so skills increase, ideas become clearer, and shared commitment becomes stronger over time. The CCE writing team at Chifley knew that while the policy would establish broad goals, the program would be developed in detail at all levels through day-to-day practice over time.

In the first two years of the development of CCE, the teachers were therefore involved in multi-layered professional learning. As a planning team, the initial group of seven teachers worked together to share existing subject matter knowledge and ideas, strategies and resources for CCE. Andrew and Sally attended three *Grants to Schools* professional learning sessions, and then reported back to the staff. These days provided further support and gentle pressure as well, since there was an expectation that all of the schools would research their practice, and keep a journal of progress to be shared with state-wide colleagues from other schools. Each school knew they would be expected to provide a reflective report to be published at the end of the year long grants period. Sally commented that the teachers: 'appreciated that the program wasn't being developed in a rush, and there was time to try and develop the new ideas'.

LEADERSHIP

In the literature, it is seen to be important that shared and supportive leadership must be in place (Hord, 2004; Louis & Kruse, 1995; Rosenholtz, 1989; Senge, 1990) for PLCs to succeed. Stewart and Andrew's leadership was clearly of vital importance in establishing the culture, structures and support necessary for the school to function as a PLC, and to develop varied and innovative approaches to student learning in CCE. There was a great deal of evidence in Stewart's interview responses, and the views of the staff, that he had a strong focus on distributed leadership. Hord (2004) argued that:

> The collegial and facilitative participation of the principal, who shares leadership – and thus, power and authority – through inviting, expecting and valuing staff input to develop vision, plan, make and enact decisions is a core element of a PLC. (p.12)

Other researchers share the view that strong and effective leaders who appreciate and utilise their teachers' leadership abilities, and strongly focus on improving learning, have a powerful role in the positive development of PLCs (Newmann & Wehlage, 1995; Sergiovanni, 2001; Sparks, 2002). Stewart did not see himself as an administrator who provided top down directives for the staff to implement. He saw himself as a "leader of leaders" and he encouraged the teachers to share leadership. At Chifley primary school, Greg commented:

> I was an inexperienced teacher being asked to implement something new in the school, but Stewart's support ensured gentle pressure and encouragement. The fact that he formalized commitment by asking us to develop school policy on CCE meant we knew our work would be recognized. Andrew provided another kind of leadership. He had a lot of knowledge to share that really helped in our planning of classroom practice.

FACTORS BEYOND THE PLC IN ACHIEVING SUCCESS

The case study explored here demonstrates that a school functioning with the characteristics of a PLC can provide powerful support in teacher professional learning. The study affirms much of the literature around PLCs and their claims about PLCs as a vehicle for professional learning. However, teacher interviews and school observation revealed other factors which also contributed to the successful development of CCE at Chifley primary.

First, the passion and commitment of the teachers, and their willingness to implement change, was evident throughout the study. Several members of the team were 'teacher champions' who showed an extraordinary capacity to attempt innovative classroom practice. Andrew was a teacher leader with a passion for CCE, so he grabbed every PD opportunity possible to develop his understanding of the area. Andrew was well acquainted with debates that had been occurring in the education community about the concept and scope of CCE. He had attended numerous conferences on CCE and was also an active committee member of the Victorian Association of Social Studies Teachers (VASST) who provided professional development sessions with a CCE focus. Andrew was therefore immersed in conversations and literature about CCE, and provides a classic case of a teacher involved in "multiple discourse communities" (McLaughlin, 1994). It was Andrew who wrote the application seeking a grant for funding to implement CCE in the school. He knew that without money for time release, it would be difficult for the teachers to plan and act on their ideas. He joined a local area network of teachers interested in CCE, and encouraged the team of teachers at Chifley to also extend their knowledge. This study showed that a "teacher champion" like Andrew can provide substantial motivation for staff to implement new ideas.

Second, Stewart recognised a further influential factor in teacher professional learning: 'that it is fundamental for teachers to have subject matter knowledge, and an understanding of the curriculum area, if they are to develop and implement a new program". Stewart encouraged strategies that would lead to the development of new knowledge amongst his staff, and was prepared to fund teachers to attend professional development seminars and network meetings.

EXTERNAL SUPPORT AND PARTNERSHIPS

Chifley school leaders also recognised the importance of support and resources outside the school community in their project to develop CCE. Their involvement with the *Police in Schools Program* was evidence of what McLaughlin (1994) described as "teachers working in multiple professional communities, each of which functions somewhat differently as a strategic site for professional growth" (p. 31). The Chifley teachers gained new knowledge and ideas for teaching and learning strategies through their work with the police officers, and the children experienced positive interaction with law enforcers and developed an understanding of their role. Greg particularly appreciated his contact with teachers from local schools since, as a less experienced teacher, he was keen to develop his repertoire of skills and knowledge through sharing ideas.

Liebermann and Grolnick (1999) agreed that:

> The effects of wide collaboration extend in many directions. Working actively with others strengthens the investment participants have in the network; the work becomes quite literally their own. Connecting with other members across schools, institutions, roles, and geography enables participants to develop more complex views of the issues they are concerned about and encourages them to take different perspectives and different ways of knowing into account. (p. 19)

Little (1999) reinforces the way partnerships within and outside the school strengthen a learning community:

> Teacher learning arises out of close involvement with students and their work, shared responsibility for student progress, sensibly organised time and space, access to the expertise of colleagues inside and outside the school, focused feedback on one's own work, and an overall ethos in which teacher learning is valued. (p. 238)

CONCLUSIONS AND THE WAY AHEAD

The findings from the case study of Chifley primary school as a PLC were congruent with researchers' views that professional learning should involve teachers in identification of what they need to learn, and in the development of learning experiences that will be connected to, and situated within, their day-to-day practice (NPEAT, 2000; Sparks, 2002). At Chifley, Stewart affirmed this view by ensuring there was a thorough process of establishing and meeting the teachers' needs in the development of CCE. In the literature on teacher professional learning, it has also been recommended that professional learning "should be continuous and on-going, involving follow-up and support for further learning – including support from sources external to the school, that can provide necessary resources and new perspectives" (NPEAT 2000, p. 1). This was evident at Chifley, where the collaborative team worked over the whole period of time trying new ideas and strategies gathered from varied sources, as the CCE program was developed and enacted. Cochran-Smith and Lytle (2001) added that:

> The general orientation of the new approach to professional development is more constructivist than transmission-orientated – the recognition that both prospective and experienced teachers bring prior knowledge and experience to all new learning situations (p. 27).

This view is connected to the idea that professional development needs to be situated in the teachers' domains, so that they inquire into, and learn from, their own practice, have a focus on academic content and subject matter knowledge, as well as process, opportunities for hands on work, and clear connections to student learning outcomes (Ball & Cohen, 1999; Little, 1993, Sparks, 2002; Stokes, 2001). These ideas were an integral part of the development of CCE at Chifley.

The Chifley study found that when the structures and characteristics of a PLC are connected with clear goals for teacher professional learning, improvement in teaching and learning programs can occur. The findings were consistent with Kruse, Louis and Bryk's (1994) conclusions that a number of outcomes for both staff and students can been improved through PLCs: reduction in the isolation of teachers, increase in their commitment to the mission and goals of the school, shared responsibility for the total development of students, and collective responsibility for students' success. At Chifley primary school, the teachers became involved in powerful learning to define good teaching and classroom practice for CCE. They created new knowledge and beliefs about teaching and learning in this area that have since been widely disseminated to teachers across Australia, involved in improving practice in the development of civic knowledge and active citizenship. Cathy was sure that she would not have taken the risks she did in experimenting with classroom strategies if she had been working alone on her classroom. Greg valued the opportunity the team approach gave him to develop his understanding of both content and pedagogy. All of the teachers expressed views demonstrating that they felt professionally renewed and inspired through their collaborative efforts.

The study also showed that a wide conception of a PLC, encompassing external support and connection with wider professional partnerships, can add to the success of programs. The teachers showed a commitment to ongoing professional learning. They recognised that while the CCE program developed in the period of this study achieved their stated goals to develop the children's understanding of their local community, and their rights and responsibilities as citizens, there was scope for the further development of CCE in the school to encompass student participation and learning for global citizenship.

Fullan (2003) stressed that teacher professional learning should be ongoing, and while it is critical that it should be linked to classroom practice, it is also vital that teachers have opportunities for exposure to broader ideas and expertise in their fields of endeavour. He argued that for PLCs to operate successfully there needs to be far more intensive professional learning in schools, within a culture of continuous and open deliberation. He suggested that schools' performance should be continually tested by external ideas or standards about best practices. Outside curriculum ideas and student assessment information helps ensure that the process is not too insular. At Chifley, this process was ongoing in a range of ways. As this study drew to a close, Cathy explained that the school was involved in a *Triennial School Review* that all government schools undertake, and a series of assessment strategies were being utilised to assess student-learning outcomes in a range of key learning areas including CCE. The focus on continuous learning was therefore formalized through government policies, and through the school's decision to monitor its own quality. In addition, the leaders were continuing to encourage active student and staff involvement in the wider community, and professional learning was continuing within the school and through involvement in external programs.

In this chapter, it has been shown that the teacher team at Chifley collaborated in the PLC to generate innovative whole school and classroom approaches to CCE. They assumed that the school community provided a rich context for learning where teachers could build on their collective expertise in the course of critical reflection (Little, 1999). It was clear that the teachers worked together to "mobilize and focus the teachers' energies on a collective and improved vision of students' education and, along with it, a situated vision of and support for their own learning" (Darling-Hammond & McLaughlin, 1999, p. 389).

The example provided by Chifley primary school of teacher collaboration and innovation to improve student learning in CCE, is an exemplary demonstration of a successfully operating PLC. Achieving positive teacher professional learning and improving students' learning is a process requiring long-term commitment and funding, but the Chifley case shows that where the learning is situated in the day to day practice within the PLC, the learning can indeed be positive. I am sure the teachers at Chifley primary schools would agree with McLaughlin and Talbert's (1993) view that:

> Professional learning communities provide the context for sustained learning and developing the profession ... Effecting and enabling the teacher learning required by systemic reform cannot be accomplished through traditional staff

development models – episodic, de-contextualised injections of knowledge and technique. The path to change in the classroom lies within and through teachers' professional learning communities. (p. 18)

REFERENCES

Ball, D. L., & Cohen, D. K. (1999). Developing practice, developing practitioners: Towards a practice-based theory of professional education. In L. Darling-Hammond & G. Sykes (Eds.), *Teaching as the learning profession: Handbook of policy and practice* (pp. 3-32). San Fransisco: Jossey-Bass.

Boyd, V. (1992). *School context: Bridge or barrier to change?* Austin, Texas: Southwest Educational Development Laboratory.

Cochran-Smith, M., & Lytle, S.L. (2001). Beyond certainty: Taking an inquiry stance on practice. In A. Liebermann & L. Miller. (Eds.), *Teachers caught in the action: Professional development that matters* (pp. 84-87). New York: Teachers College Press.

Darling-Hammond, L., & McLaughlin, M. W. (1995 April). Policies that support professional development in an era of reform. *Phi Delta Kappan 76*(8), 597-604.

Eaker, R., Dufour, R., & Dufour, R. (2002). *Getting started: Reculturing schools to become professional learning communities.* Bloomington, Indiana: National Education Service.

Elmore, R. (2002) *Bridging the gap between standards and achievement.* Washington, DC: Albert Shanker Institute.

Fullan, M. (2001). *The New Meaning of Educational Change* (3rd ed.). New York: Teachers College Press.

Fullan, M. (2003). *Change forces with a vengeance.* London & New York: Routledge Falmer.

Hargreaves, A. M. (1994). *Changing teachers, changing times.* London: Cassell.

Hord, S. M. (2004). Professional learning communities: An overview. In S. M Hord (Ed.), *Learning together, leading together: Changing schools through professional learning communities.* New York: Teachers College Press.

Huberman, M. (1995) *Professional careers and professional development: Some intersections in professional development in education.* New York: Teachers College Press

Kemp, D. (1997). *Discovering democracy: Civics and citizenship education. A Ministerial statement.* Canberra, Australia: AGS.

Kruse, S., Louis, S. L., & Bryk, A. (1994). *Building professional community in schools* Madison, WI: Center on Organization and Restructuring of Schools, University Of Wisconsin-Madison.

Langford, D. (2003). *Tool time and education: Choosing and implementing quality improvement tools.* Montana: Langord International.

Liebermann, A., & Miller, L. (1999). *Teachers transforming their world and their work.* New York: Teachers College Press, in conjunction with ASCD.

Little, J. W. (1993). Teachers' professional development in a climate of educational reform. *Educational Evaluation and Policy Analysis, 15* (2), 129-151.

Little, J. W. (1999). Organising schools for teacher learning. In L. Darling-Hammond & G. Sykes (Eds.), *Teaching as the learning profession: Handbook of Teaching and Policy* (pp. 268-284). San Fransisco: Jossey-Bass.

Louis, K. S., & Kruse, S. D. (1995). *Professionalism and community: Perspectives on reforming urban schools.* Thousand Oaks, California: Corwin Press.

McLaughlin, M.W., & Talbert, J.E. (1993). *Contexts that matter for teaching and learning.* Stanford: Center for Research on the Context of Secondary School Teaching, Stanford University.

McLaughlin, M. (1994). Strategic sites for teachers' professional development. In P. Grimmet and J. Neufeld (Eds.), *Teacher development and the struggle for authenticity: Professional growth and restructuring in the context of change* (pp. 31-51). New York: Teachers College Press.

National Partnership for Excellence and Accountability in Teaching (NPEAT). (2000). *Professional development: Learning from the best.* North Central Regional Educational Laboratory. Retrieved from http://www.ncrel.org/pd/toolkit.htm

Newman, F., (1991). Linking restructuring to authentic student achievement. *Phi Delta Kappan, 72,* 6.

Newmann, F., & Associates (1996). *Authentic achievement: Restructuring schools for intellectual quality*. San Fransisco: Jossey-Bass.

Peterson, R. (1999). Time use flows from school culture, *Journal of Staff Development, 18*(1), 16-19.

Rosenholtz, S. (1989). *Teacher's workplace: The social organization of schools.* New York: Longman.

Shaughnessy, J. (1998). *Initial guidelines on becoming a learning community.* OERI Event No. 36. Portland, OR: Northwest Regional Educational Lab. ED 442174.

Sparks, D. (2002). *Designing powerful professional development for teachers and principals.* Oxford, OH: National Staff Development Council.

Stokes, L. (2001). Lessons from an inquiring school: Forms of inquiry and conditions for teacher learning. In A. Liebermann & L. Miller (Eds.), *Teachers caught in the action: Professional development that matters* (pp. 295-297). New York: Teachers College Press.

Tudball, E. (2004). *Improving student learning in civics and citizenship education through professional learning communities.* Unpublished PhD thesis, Monash University, Melbourne.

Watts, G. D., & Castle, S. (1993). The time dilemma in school restructuring. *Phi Delta Kappan, 75*(3), 306-310.

Westbrook, J., & Hord, S. (2002). *Reflections on the creation of professional learning communities: Multiple mirrors.* Austin: TX: Southwest Educational Development Laboratories.

Westheimer, J. (1999). Communities and consequences: An inquiry into ideology and practice in teachers' professional work. *Educational Administration Quarterly, 35*(1), 71.

Libby Tudball
Faculty of Education
Monash University

DIMENSIONS OF SELF, IDENTITY AND THE SHAPING OF PRACTICE

SECTION INTRODUCTION

The previous parts of this book have focused on political dimensions of teacher professionalism and professional learning (Section One), and communal sites and the practice of professional learning (Section Two). In this Section, we turn the focus inwards, to consider the personal aspects of professional learning. The six chapters that comprise this section explore dimensions of self, identity and the practice context as interacting elements that shape professional learning. The authors of these chapters are concerned with the influence of 'self' in the development of teachers' professional knowledge and with the particular contexts in which 'self' is expressed and understood.

Research into teachers' professional identity is an emerging area, particularly in the last decade (Beijaard et al, 2004). Based on a review of research on teachers' professional identity, Beijaard and his colleagues identified four "essential features" that relate to identity formation. These features offer a helpful framework for previewing the chapters in this section. They are:

1. Professional identity formation is an ongoing process of interpretation and re-interpretation of experience.
2. Professional identity implies both person and context.
3. A teacher's professional identity consists of multiple sub-identities (or 'selves') that more or less harmonize. The more central a sub-identity is, the more costly it is to change or lose that identity.
4. Agency is an important element of professional identity, meaning that teachers have to be active in their processes of professional learning.

Viewed in this way, professional identity formation necessarily draws on, and is shaped by, knowledge from a range of different sources. One important source of influence is the "professional landscapes" (Connelly & Clandinin, 1996) or institutional settings, in which teachers conduct their work.

Teachers' professional identities are constructed in, and from, experiences in their professional contexts and exist as repositories of knowledge about self/ves. Such knowledge is often represented in the form of stories; a means used by teachers to make sense of these multiple 'selves'. Stories shape both teachers and teaching; they are not only selected and managed by the tellers, but also are expressions of cultural values, norms, and structures. In this way, stories reflect the range of influences within teachers' "professional landscapes".

Three of the six chapters in this section focus on the professional identity formation of pre-service teachers (Williams, Watt et al., Viete and Peeler). The remaining three chapters present studies of the professional identities of educators across a range of settings including: teacher-librarians (Winter), teacher educators (Berry and Scheele) and educators in a vocational education setting (Clemans).

When does teachers' professional learning begin? In Chapter 9, Judy Williams explores the nature of professional learning before, and during, teacher education. Her research suggests that the professional learning of career change individuals often begins well before they enrol in teacher education programs. Williams raises the idea that mature aged teacher education students bring qualities, experiences and skills that are not often acknowledged or built upon in their teacher education programs. The chapter represents teachers' professional identity development as a continuing process that is socially constructed and enhanced by reflection on past and present experience, thus highlighting the first three of Beijaard et al.'s "essential features". Williams advises that teacher educators need to be aware of the diverse backgrounds and rich experiences of prospective teachers and work to support them in the process of reconsidering and reconstructing their views of teaching in order to "form new visions and understandings of learners and learning". The importance of accepting, respecting and building upon what individuals bring to their teacher education is an aspect that is also highlighted in the chapters by Rosemary Viete and Eleanor Peeler, and Amanda Berry and Sam Scheele.

Helen Watt, Paul Richardson and Nicole Tysvaer (Chapter 10) report research from their large scale, multidimensional study about the professional engagement and career development aspirations of recent teacher education graduates at three Australian universities. Their research considers several different facets of professional identity that teacher education students bring to their studies and changes that occur for these individuals over the period of their teacher education, in terms of engagement and career aspiration. Through their research, Watt, Richardson and Tysvaer identify three distinct profiles, or 'clusters', of beginning teachers: "highly engaged persisters" (Cluster 1), "highly engaged switchers", (Cluster 2) and "lower engaged desisters" (Cluster 3). Considerable variation was found to exist between cluster groups in their predicted persistence in the profession. These authors' work provides insight into how experiences shape identity, both those that prospective teachers bring and those that are experienced during their teacher preparation. In an interesting comparison with William's chapter, Watt et al identify from their research that an individual's previous career did not impact on their membership of a particular cluster.

In Chapter 11, Rosemary Viete and Eleanor Peeler identify conditions essential for the identity formation of pre-service teachers. They describe the effects of exclusion from participation in identity construction practices through the 'unknowing' cultural practices enacted within teacher preparation programs. Viete and Peeler propose a set of attitudes required from those working with prospective teachers for facilitating their effective identity growth. The expression of these attitudes, i.e., respect, attentiveness and responsiveness, then facilitates learning because, as they state, "[b]eing recognized and responded to as a knower is central to learning". Through their work, Viete and Peeler describe a pathway towards more effective professional learning and hence professional identity formation, for pre-service teachers. These authors talk about the importance of explicitly valuing and drawing on what all participants bring to their teacher education. In this way, notions of professional identity as an ongoing and active process are highlighted, as well as interconnections between person and context.

Working in ways that acknowledge and build on the multiple perspectives of all participants in the learning to teach process is the focus of Amanda Berry and Sam Scheele's research (Chapter 12). These two teacher educators document their professional learning journey as they seek to develop more comprehensive understandings of their practice. Through a self-study approach, they explore prospective teachers' perspectives of their practice and use insights from this research to reconsider their teaching and their students' learning about teaching. Berry and Scheele's work highlights the active role that individuals must take in professional identity formation, as well as some of the tensions associated with learning to manage conflicts between different selves. Their work demonstrates the important role of practitioner research for evolving one's identity as a teacher educator.

Allie Clemans explores the professional identity processes of two tertiary music educators through their stories of moving between the learning spaces of higher education and vocational education (Chapter 13). The complex, multifaceted nature of professional identity becomes apparent through Clemans' research as each music educator learns to identify, and deal with, tensions created by the different discourse emerging through personal, professional and institutional voices. Different dimensions of their professional identities emerge in connection with the professional knowledge landscape in which they work. Clemans identifies that drawing on multiple selves in the course of their work enables each educator to flow between different learning spaces, although it is their identities as working artists that serve as the basis from which to successfully negotiate these transitions. In this way, Beijaard et al.'s feature of "harmonising" identities is brought forward through Clemans' research.

The influence of the professional knowledge landscape is a key element influencing the professional identity formation of teacher librarians described by Rosamund Winter (Chapter 14). Winter describes features of this rapidly changing landscape as they have shaped the identity of teacher librarians since the 1980's in Australia. She draws on themes and issues from the professional association journals of teacher librarians as a means of tracing their influences on identity (re)formation and to illustrate the ways in which the professional discourse of this group seems to have been increasingly colonized from the outside (Stronach et al., 2000). One consequence of this rapid change process is that the profession has undervalued and understated the key pedagogical role of teacher librarians. Winter exhorts those within the profession to take a more active role in their professional identity processes, in particular, to 're-story' their identity for its important relationship to student achievement.

Collectively, these chapters draw attention to professional learning around self and identity and how these aspects shape professional practice. They invite us to consider a rich collection of issues associated with understanding professional identity as "inner diversity" (Stronach et al., 2000) and a "view of the professional self as a situated aggregation of mini-narratives, deployed in the construction of a professional story" (ibid, p. 127).

These chapters also advance our understanding about professional learning insofar as it contributes toward professional identity formation. Together they elaborate the conditions that nurture and sustain educators' professional identities, as well as those which suppress, distort and silence them.

REFERENCES

Beijaard, D., Meijer, P. C., & Verloop, N. (2004). Reconsidering research on teachers' professional identity. *Teaching and Teacher Education, 20*, 107-128.

Clandinin, D. J. F., & Connelly, M. (1996). Teachers' professional knowledge landscapes: Teacher stories. Stories of teachers. School stories. Stories of schools. *Educational Researcher, 25*(3), pp. 24-30.

Stronach, I., Corbin, B., McNamara, O., Stark, S., & Warne, T. (2002). Towards an uncertain politics of professionalism: Teacher and nurse identities in flux. *Journal of Educational Policy, 17*(1), 109-138.

Amanda Berry
Faculty of Education
Monash University

JUDY WILLIAMS

9. BECOMING A TEACHER

The Professional Learning Journey of Career Change Students in Teacher Education

INTRODUCTION

The teaching profession has been under increasing scrutiny in recent years, as educators and governments search for ways in which to improve the quality of education that is necessary to meet the demands of an increasingly complex and interconnected global community of the 21st century (Connell & Skilbeck, 2004; DEST, 2000; OECD, 2001). It has been argued that one of the keys to achieving social and economic progress is the quality of education delivered to students in classrooms, and that is, to a large extent, dependent upon the quality of the teaching, and the capacity of teachers to make a difference to students' lives (OECD, 2004). In Australia, there have been many government reviews, at both national and state levels, into the quality of teaching and teacher education (DEST, 2004; ETC, 2005). Several of the reports emanating from these reviews have suggested that more mature-aged or career change professionals were needed in teaching to take advantage of the many skills and experiences which they would bring to the classroom. In the foreword of one such report, the then Federal Minister for Education Brendan Nelson claimed that:

> attracting the best people into teaching as a career means reaching out not only to people at the start of their working life but also to people with experience in other occupations and professions. The experience that a former business person, scientist, landscaper or doctor could bring into the classroom can greatly enrich students' learning. (DEST, 2004, p. 3)

Although research has suggested that mature-aged or career change teachers can bring many qualities to teaching (Crow, Levine & Nager, 1990; Priyadharshini & Robinson-Pant, 2003; Richardson & Watt, 2005), these skills and experiences do not appear to have been examined extensively in the literature. This raises the questions: what life and work experiences do these people bring in to teaching? How relevant are these previous experiences to their teaching career? What are the experiences of career change students in the institutional context of teacher education? The research on which this chapter is based has attempted to answer these questions, and to provide teacher educators with a better understanding of the professional learning of students who are in the process of making a career change

A. Berry, A. Clemans and A. Kostogriz (Eds.), Dimensions of Professional Learning: Professionalism, Practice and Identity, 141–154. © 2007 Sense Publishers. All rights reserved.

into teaching. It is generally agreed in the teaching profession that to effectively educate students, teachers need to understand as much as possible about the 'whole person' in the teaching and learning situation. Just as importantly, teacher educators need to understand the diversity and complexity of their own students' lives in order to help realise the potential of each one of these future teachers.

CONCEPTUALISING TEACHER PROFESSIONAL LEARNING

The literature on teacher professional learning is varied and extensive. It has provided many different perspectives on what it actually means to become a teacher, with various researchers examining the contexts in which this learning occurs, and the social, intellectual and institutional influences on teachers' professional learning. Several key ideas have emerged from the literature, and many of these concepts are readily identifiable in the data obtained from the career change students in this study.

Broad conceptualizations of professional learning have highlighted the transformative nature of teacher education. Rather than learning *how* to teach, students are challenged with ideas and experiences that help them to learn *about* learning and teaching. Putnam and Borko (2000) argued that the process of becoming a teacher was 'situated learning,' a complex process that could not be separated from the social and institutional contexts in which it occurred. Similarly, Britzman (2003) argued that learning to be a teacher was a socially negotiated process

> rather than an individual problem of behaviour. This dynamic is essential to a humanising explanation of the work of teachers. Teaching concerns coming to terms with one's intentions and values, as well as one's views of knowing, being, and acting in a setting characterized by contradictory realities, negotiation, and dependency and struggle. (p. 31)

This view is supported by Bullough and Gitlin (1995) who argued that learning to teach was a process of gaining socially constructed knowledge, grounded in students' biography and life experiences. The importance of biography and narrative to teacher professional learning has been argued by many researchers, including Featherstone, Munby and Russell (1997) who maintained that learning to teach was a unique and personal journey, guided by others, and mediated by interactions within social and institutional contexts. Beattie's (2000) research focussed on narratives of professional learning, and highlighted the significance of "... personal biographies, family histories and experiences of growing up in different cultural environments" (p. 3).

Reflective practice, self-directed learning and self-awareness have also been highlighted in the literature as being essential to teacher professional learning (Knowles & Cole, 1994; Korthagen, 2001; Loughran, 1996). So too has the relationship between the prior experiences and beliefs of beginning teachers and their subsequent teaching practices (Grundy & Hatton, 1996). Feiman-Nemser (2001) believed that central to the task of learning in pre-service teacher education programs was the need to analyse existing beliefs and to form new visions and understandings of learners and learning. Research has therefore found that the journey to becoming a teacher is not simply about learning a set of practices that work in the classroom, but rather, it is a process of constant reflection and reconstruction of beliefs, values and practices that contribute to the education of students and teachers alike.

In addition to broad conceptualisations of teacher professional learning, there are also more specific skills and knowledge that research has shown to be inherent in the development of teacher professionalism. Jeans and Forth (1995) outlined what they believed to be four stages in the process of learning to be a teacher: *knowledge* of curriculum content, *confidence* to apply known skills to new situations, *competence* in engaging students in their learning in a systematic and purposeful way, and the development of a *professional identity,* which they described as "... a professional self image using information provided by significant others ... To this extent, professional identity is a social construction" (p. 3). Research has also suggested that relationships with students, peers and others whose perceptions were valued, were an integral part of a teacher's developing professionalism and sense of professional identity (Beijaard, Verloop & Vermunt, 2000; Mockler, Normanhurst & Sachs, 2002). Important also was the notion of collegiality, collaboration and mentoring, and of learning within communities of practice. Autonomous, reflective and self-directed learning appeared to epitomise the professional learning of teachers at all stages of their career (Sachs, 1999; Wenzlaff & Wieseman, 2004).

PROFESSIONAL LEARNING IN THE CONTEXT OF PREVIOUS CAREERS

Previous research in teacher education has shown that professional learning is a complex process that occurs in many different contexts. The research presented in this chapter provides some evidence that professional learning for teachers can occur in the context of their previous careers, and that this has a subsequent impact on these students' learning in teacher education. Such learning involves the development of skills, understandings and beliefs about teaching and learning, and the development of a professional identity in which the individual sees him or herself as a competent member of the teaching profession. The following section will consider data collected from an on-line survey of 375 career change students at two Victorian universities and from an interview with one of the respondents. It will examine the professional experiences of career change students, and align these with theories of teacher professional learning found in the literature.

Experiences That Career Change Professionals Bring To Teaching

In the survey, respondents were asked to identify the skills and experiences that they believed people from other careers brought into teaching. There were 326 responses to this question, and a quantitative analysis of the data revealed four broad categories of attributes:

- *Workplace competency,* including professional attitudes/professionalism, awareness of stress and pressure, ethical attitudes, goal orientation, communication and management skills, ability to work in teams, and subject/content knowledge;
- *Broad life experiences*, including maturity and wisdom, breadth of knowledge, different perspectives on life, and parenting;
- *Personal qualities* such as high levels of enthusiasm, commitment and motivation, communication and social skills, self-knowledge and confidence;
- *Beliefs about teaching and learning*, including teaching/training experience, practical application of theory and linking the curriculum to real world contexts, and relationships with the education community through involvement with schools or in coaching roles.

Many of these skills and experiences from previous careers align quite closely with the conceptions of teacher professional learning found in the literature, so it could be argued that for these students, the process of learning to be a teacher actually began in the context of their previous career. The data indicated that career change students had a high degree of confidence and competence in their previous work, but also high levels of motivation and commitment to teaching as a career. Many students indicated a strong commitment to personal and professional development, and appeared to be continuously striving for new learning, and for intellectual and emotional growth. A high level of communication skills and the ability to work with others was mentioned by many students, which indicated that collegiality and collaboration were characteristics of their work. Many students also expressed beliefs about teaching and learning, developed throughout their working lives, that they brought with them into teacher education.

Although the survey data provided a broad view of the professional learning of students in their previous careers, it still did not give a detailed picture of exactly what terms such as 'maturity' 'work experience' and 'people skills' really meant in the day to day experience of these students. Nor did it give a detailed understanding of how these experiences contributed to the students' journey towards becoming a teacher. We will now turn to one of the interviewees, Patrick, to gain an insight into the realities of one career changer's previous work experiences, and the extent to which these supported his professional learning as a teacher.

Professional Learning Profile: Patrick

Before enrolling in teacher education, Patrick had been a technician and project manager with a major Australian telecommunications company for nearly 20 years, and was in his late 30s when he decided to change his career to teaching. At the time of the interview Patrick was studying a Bachelor of Education (Primary) full time, and was in the second year of his course. During the interview Patrick revealed a broad range of experiences that he had gained in his previous career, and he detailed how his journey towards teaching had evolved. During the course of the interview, several themes emerged regarding the professional learning that had taken place in Patrick's previous career and how these experiences enabled him to grow and develop, and contributed to his eventual career change into teaching.

Autonomous, self-directed, professional development and reflective practice.

Patrick had worked for the same organisation for nearly 20 years, but he "really had a new job every four or five years" as he took on new challenges and levels of responsibility, working his way up through the ranks of the company. He began as an apprentice telecommunications technician after leaving school in Year 10, and then progressed on to the programming of telephone exchanges, project management, involving "multi-million dollar projects in the big corporate environment" and finally to staff management. Patrick gained skills in a variety of work roles, and undertook training provided by the company to further develop his expertise. He embraced the changing nature of his work roles and responsibilities, stating that he "… liked going through the different stages."

It appeared that Patrick's journey into teaching may have began about 10 years prior to his actual career change, although teaching was not a conscious career choice until the year before he actually enrolled in teacher education. During his early years in management Patrick's interests in personal and professional development lead him to undertake a course entitled 'Investment in Excellence' which proved to be a life changing learning experience for him. In Patrick's own words "… it [was] about investing in yourself. I was … a pretty introverted, shy person, and having done that course [I] started to believe in [myself] and that [I] could do things that [I] wanted to do." As a result of his new found confidence and knowledge, Patrick applied for and was successful in gaining a series of higher management positions in the organisation. However, after several years working at senior levels, Patrick started to question his commitment to working in the telecommunications industry, and began to realise that a change was on the horizon:

> My career path for the next five to 10 years had all been mapped out … and then I finally realised that this wasn't the ladder I wanted. I didn't want to do this for the next 30 years. I didn't know what I wanted to do but I knew that wasn't where I wanted to be and it wasn't my path.

The next stage in his journey of professional and personal growth set Patrick on the course that would eventually lead him into teaching. After resigning from the telecommunications industry, and spending a year of 'quality time' with his four daughters, which involved volunteer work at their school and going on school camp, Patrick continued to reflect on his personal values and goals in life, and it was during that year that he decided that a career in teaching was the right path for him.

Relationships with others: collegiality, collaboration and mentoring.

During his time in management and then his involvement in the educational community of his daughters' school, Patrick found that the experience of working with others, and their perceptions of his competence in the teaching role, greatly impacted on the development of his professional identity. Patrick believed that collegiality, collaboration in the work environment and the mentoring process for both mentor and mentee, were essential to his professional development and career progression. Before his move into management in telecommunications he had met a mentor who encouraged his continued progression within the organisation, a relationship that continued during his transition into teaching.

While he was working with his mentors and applying the principles that he learned in the 'Investment in Excellence' program, Patrick began to see himself not only as the mentee but as a mentor himself to his own staff:

> [My mentor] offered me my first management position, after I had gone through a journey to get me to a certain point, to get me the expertise ... And then I realised I'd been able to do this for myself, so I'd really like to do it for my staff as well. So I managed the business as we had to manage, but my side thing was also encouraging people to explore what they wanted to do and reach for things that they thought that they couldn't do but wanted to do.

The experience of being mentored and encouraged by others helped to develop Patrick's own capacity to mentor others in turn, and to bring out the best in his staff. He reflected on the processes and relationships inherent in his work environment, and questioned why people behaved in particular ways. He began to develop an interest in the ways in which people functioned in work situations, such as in boardrooms and group environments. "I kept thinking, how did people end up being ... this destructive with relationships ... I wonder[ed] what they were like as kids, and if they were lucky to hear about believing in yourself and making different choices ..." As a mentor himself, Patrick encouraged his staff to work in more harmonious ways, such as using different words to avoid conflict and to think about problems in such a way so as there were no losers, only winners. Patrick acknowledged the enormous amount that he had learned from his mentor, and from other colleagues. "I ended up having a few mentees as well as having [my own mentor]. There's always something you can learn from someone else. You really have two roles – you're being mentored and someone's mentoring you ... I learned heaps."

While he was volunteering at his daughters' school Patrick began to see himself in a teaching role, and when he mentioned this to the school staff he found that their perceptions mirrored his own:

> I spoke to the principal there, she was very supportive, and [she] started saying what I was thinking. She thought it would be great with someone with my expertise and my enthusiasm and my energy ... I'd be fantastic at it. That was encouraging, so I spoke to a few more teachers, and decided that it was the thing I wanted to do.

Beliefs about learning and teaching.

Throughout his career in telecommunications and during his year of volunteering at his daughters' school, Patrick's experiences helped him to develop beliefs about learning and teaching, and to reflect on his role in other people's learning. Patrick had developed a personal philosophy that included the need to value oneself and to invest in one's own growth and development, and in the growth and development of others. His mentoring of staff encouraged them to be confident enough to strive for their own goals, just as Patrick himself had done, and to explore more effective ways of collaborating and working together. The desire to contribute to others' lives was further developed during the time spent at his daughters' primary school, and it was at this time that he began to seriously consider the possibilities of a teaching career. When asked why he chose primary teaching rather than secondary teaching or adult education Patrick explained that

> at primary school they're younger so that there's more likelihood of being able to maybe spark something off earlier so they have more chance ... I know that you're not going to touch everybody's life and you're not going to change everything, but it would be great if you could just help that one or two along the way.

As the above excepts suggest, the interview with Patrick revealed that the learning in his previous career had many parallels with his professional learning as a teacher. He regularly looked for opportunities to further his professional knowledge, and significantly contributed to, and benefited from, a range of relationships that enhanced his professional capacity and career identity. For this reason it could be argued that career change professionals like Patrick are not beginners when they enrol in teacher education, but are in fact competent professionals who possess a high level of skills, experience and personal qualities that can lay the foundation for further learning in teacher education. It appeared that Patrick had made important steps on the way to becoming a teacher throughout his 20 year career experience in telecommunications, and that when he finally reached the formal teacher education stage he was already competent and confident in this ability to become a 'real' teacher. He appeared to be in control of his own professional learning, was able to develop positive relationships with others that facilitated his learning, and he held beliefs and values that would influence his approach to teaching and the construction of an individual identity as a teacher.

Professional learning in teacher education

Considering the range of professional experiences that students in this research had in their previous careers, what then were their experiences when they commenced the formal process of becoming a teacher? Did their teacher education programs enhance and build upon their existing learning? Survey data revealed that 16.6% of career change students were satisfied with their decision to enrol in teacher education; 34.8% were very satisfied and 42.2% were extremely satisfied. Only

5.3% were not very satisfied, and 1.1% were very unsatisfied. Although most students appeared to be very happy with their career choice, this did not mean that the process of becoming a teacher was always a positive one. The survey revealed that for career change students there were both significant challenges as well as rewards in teacher education.

Challenges in Teacher Education

A total of 292 students responded to the question concerning the challenges they faced in teacher education. Many students (198) made references to course related matters, such as dissatisfaction with some aspects of the course, difficulties in coming to terms with technology, and the perception that the course was geared towards younger students while career changers' experiences were not valued or acknowledged. One student wrote:

> Probably my biggest challenge is coping with the odd tutor who insists on running their class as if it is full of high school students who cannot possibly operate without their direct intervention and who have no understanding of any subject until they [the lecturers] have taught it. At 40 I don't appreciate being treated as if I am 14. However, as I said these tutors are definitely in the minority.

Some students commented that it was difficult to adjust to the expectations and demands of university study, and that being older than most other students presented some difficulties for them. Many students (106) experienced difficulties with the practicum, particularly with the requirement of combining full time placements in schools with existing work and family commitments. Another difficulty related to studying on-line or by distance mode, with particular concerned expressed about the lack of communication with and support from staff. Several students believed that there was a lack of understanding on the part of staff about the conflicting demands placed on distance education students. Data revealed that for many career change students the financial difficulties associated with tertiary study also presented a serious challenge. Reduced income and the need to combine full or part time work with their studies appeared to place significant strain on personal relationships, family finances and on their own health and well-being.

REWARDS IN TEACHER EDUCATION

Despite the difficulties encountered by many of the respondents, there also appeared to be many rewards in being a career change student in teacher education. A total of 294 students offered their views on the positive aspects of being in teacher education, the most significant of which were the opportunities for personal growth and development (mentioned 115 times), and the ability to apply their previous experiences to teaching (82). Many commented on the satisfaction they gained from developing their intellectual skills (45), while others stated that the very high levels of motivation and commitment to achieving their goal of becoming a teacher was a reward in itself (42). The development of personal qualities, greater awareness of their own potential and achieving self-knowledge were also significant rewards for many students:

> … as a mature aged student I believe that I am on my course because I truly want to be, and have made a conscious decision to be [a teacher]. This is reflected in my commitment and in my results. I feel confident to approach staff members on practicum and [to] converse [and] ask for help. Being of a similar age to many teachers is also possibly advantageous. This confidence is also useful in tutorials, being able to articulate questions, needs etc. Developing fresh ideas about and for myself. A mature attitude to study.

Many students commented that the opportunity to interact with others in academic and in social contexts was highly valued. Despite being older than most other students, several career change students commented that this was actually of benefit to both themselves and to the younger students. They enjoyed studying and socialising with younger people, and with like-minded mature aged peers, and believed that the range of perspectives was an advantage rather than a disadvantage. Interactions with students and teachers on practicum were also highly valued by most students. "First practicum was fantastic. I feel like teachers are valued, and you can really make a difference to kids' lives, even if small. I felt replaceable before [in my previous career] …" It seems apparent from this data that career change students brought into teacher education a commitment to collegiality and team work that enhanced their learning and enjoyment of the experience. To examine this process in more detail, we will again turn to Patrick's story to explore the rewards and challenges of his experience in teacher education.

Professional Learning Profile: Patrick

In his survey responses Patrick indicated that he was extremely satisfied with his decision to enrol in teacher education, and that he "… enjoyed the theory and the practical side of the course and still feels like this was the right choice." During the interview he elaborated on his experiences, and indicated that the learning process was continuing, mostly in a positive way, and that his previous experiences provided a solid basis from which to develop further as a teacher. Although not all experiences were positive, Patrick found that he could 'filter' the learning experiences in teacher education and take from each one those aspects that would help him to become a better teacher. As with his professional learning in the telecommunications industry, Patrick appeared to be in control of his professional growth as a teacher which, in collaboration with others, further developed his beliefs about teaching and learning and his competence and confidence in the classroom.

Autonomous, self-directed, professional development and reflective practice.

Patrick claimed that he enjoyed the coursework component in teacher education, and that he looked at everything he did at university in terms of how it would help him in the classroom. He acknowledged the diverse range of views amongst the teaching staff and the students, and that "…just listening to all the different views, you tend to then be able to say, 'that will work for me, that won't work for me,' and you start building your idea of how you're going to be as a teacher." Patrick believed that if he had come straight into teaching from school, without having had his other career experiences, he would have been more likely to merely accept what was presented in lectures and tutorials without considering alternative points of view. He believed, however, that his previous career experiences were not always recognised or valued by others, and that much of the university teaching tended to be 'transmissive' and one way.

As far as his teacher education experiences were concerned, the most enjoyable part for Patrick was always the practicum. In this context he was able to incorporate his previous career experiences, and the ideas presented in his teacher education course, into the realities of the school environment. Here he was able to draw upon his previous learning to help him reflect on situations that he encountered. As Patrick mused, "I find it interesting in the staffroom listening to the talk. It's amazing how the two environments [teaching and industry] are so different yet the problems are all the same." The classroom context also assisted him to reflect on theories and concepts presented in lectures, and on the advice he gained from his supervising teachers. Patrick also found that the teaching role enabled him to utilise his project management skills, developed over many years. He had to prioritise demands within a classroom environment of limited resources, just as he had done in his management roles. He would reflect on what was most important in his teaching, and the best ways in which to achieve his goals, given the limitations placed upon him as a teacher. "As a manager you are often doing that. You have all these things you need to do and you only have this budget: how are you going to manage it so that you get the maximum benefit?"

One of the most confronting experiences that Patrick had encountered on his practicum was a situation in which he made the decision to exclude a child from an activity due to the child's uncooperative behaviour. Patrick initially felt that he had 'failed' in his teaching role, but after discussions with his supervising teacher, who thought that it was in fact a successful lesson, Patrick was able to salvage the situation and to draw upon his management and communication skills to talk about the incident with the student, and to eventually develop a positive relationship with the child. On Patrick's last day at the school the student said to him "I'm glad you're around because if you weren't around I wouldn't have done half the work." This incident provided a significant learning experience for Patrick, as he was able to reflect on the situation, and draw on his previous experiences, the theories from his course about student engagement and his own beliefs about learning and teaching to negotiate a difficult situation.

150

Relationships with others: collegiality, mentoring and the perceptions of others.

Patrick's professional learning in teacher education had been greatly influenced by his relationships with others, just as his success in his previous career was nurtured by his mentor, other peers and his own staff. Patrick had found support from his fellow students, both career changers and non-career changers, and in particular from his relationship with teachers in his practicum schools. Networking with other mature aged students was important to Patrick, and he especially valued being able to discuss personal and academic issues with people in a similar situation to his own. Patrick believed that it was important that career change students not be segregated from younger students because he felt that "... those conversations are just as enlightening as the other ones ...," but circumstances such as combining study and work with managing a household provided common ground for the development of support networks among older students. In discussions about improving the experience of career change students in teacher education, Patrick suggested that perhaps greater effort could be made by the university to encourage increased social and academic networking amongst mature aged students to help provide this much needed peer support.

Patrick's practicum experiences provided many opportunities for his professional learning, and enhanced the perception of others that he was highly suited to and competent in the teaching role. The principal of one school encouraged Patrick to try his skills in a more demanding grade than that in which he had previously been placed, as she believed that he "... would benefit from having more challenges," while a classroom teacher commented that "it's amazing how quickly you fitted in, it's like you'd been here for so long." Staff in schools had also acknowledged Patrick's previous management experience, and on one occasion he had a long discussion with the principal about how to manage people who consistently underperformed and who lacked motivation. In this instance Patrick felt that "... my previous skills and experiences were indeed valued." Such perceptions helped Patrick to develop his sense of self as a teacher. He commented that he was able to benefit from the advice and practice of others, and that as he did at university; he was able to 'filter' his experiences and take from the staff and the students the knowledge that would suit him best as a teacher. Interaction with other professionals, and with students at university and in schools, was vital to Patrick in the development of his professional identity as a teacher.

Beliefs about learning and teaching.

Experiences that Patrick had in teacher education contributed to the continued development of his beliefs about learning and teaching. He already had a very strong belief that teachers and mentors could enhance the learning of others by developing positive relationships and by developing people's self-esteem and confidence in their own ability. This was evident in his previous career, and appeared to be a characteristic of his experiences in teacher education. During his practicum Patrick endeavoured to forge positive relationships with students and staff, drawing on relationship-building techniques that he used in project management. Following his difficult encounter with the student referred to above, rather than let the issue end as a negative experience of punishment and exclusion of the child, Patrick made a point of discussing the issue with the student and eventually establishing a positive relationship with him. "I think having dealt with very difficult male people in my previous industry has helped [to] give me different strategies to deal with younger males that might be difficult too." While Patrick was only in his second year of a four year degree at the time of the interview, it was apparent that his attitude to teaching was firmly grounded in the beliefs that he brought to the profession from his previous career and from his broader life experiences. The concepts that Patrick encountered in his teacher education course generally concurred with his own beliefs, but as indicated above, they were subject to filtering and debate when they did not fit comfortably within his own conceptualisations of learning and teaching.

No doubt these beliefs and values will be challenged, defended, modified or changed over the duration of his teaching career, but it appeared that at this relatively early stage in his formal journey to becoming a teacher, Patrick had begun to forge his unique professional identity through his commitment to personal and intellectual growth, and in his relationships with others.

CONCLUSION

The research discussed in this chapter has attempted to explore the meaning of teacher professional learning in the context of career change into teaching. It has looked beyond the labels of 'mature aged student' or 'career change student,' and beyond career titles, to examine the real life experiences of such students both before and during teacher education. While each student's experiences are unique and therefore cannot be generalised, the research has opened up the possibilities of what becoming a teacher might mean for those in the process of a career change into teaching. It is likely that they will bring a rich and diverse range of work and life experiences into teaching, and that they will already have well developed beliefs and values about learning and teaching. It may be argued that previous career experiences, just like other aspects of a person's life history, provide an important context for professional learning as teachers, and that perhaps the term 'career progression' is a more accurate description of their journey than 'career change'. The data has suggested that for career change students their professional learning in teacher education is a complex interplay between intellectual, social, personal and logistical demands. It involves a continuous interaction between their previous career experiences, their current employment commitments, their intellectual and emotional growth, the constant redefining of values and beliefs, negotiation of relationships with peers, mentors, students, and with families, and the often onerous emotional and financial costs of being a student. It appeared that for many career change students, becoming a teacher was not simply a matter of changing jobs, but was in fact, the realisation of a long-held ambition. It was a high-stakes venture, and was as much an emotional and spiritual journey as an intellectual one. As one of the students in this research proclaimed, "as mature students, we are not playing games!"

The presence of career change students in teacher education courses provides significant challenges for teacher educators as they encounter an increasingly diverse and experienced student body. Making teacher education relevant for all students is both a challenge and an opportunity for teacher educators, and indeed for the teaching profession as a whole. Development of policies and programs that enhance the learning of future teachers may involve, for example, greater flexibility in entry requirements, new perspectives on curriculum, and alternative assessment and practicum arrangements. It may also involve a more explicit acknowledgement on the part of the teaching profession that learning to become a teacher does not only occur within the confines of the institutional structures of schools and universities, but also in a range of other life and work contexts. Career change professionals provide a great untapped resource that can enhance the quality of classroom teaching and school leadership, to the benefit of the nation's students and to the teaching profession itself.

REFERENCES

Beattie, M. (2000). Narratives of professional learning: Becoming a teacher and learning to teach. *Journal of Educational Enquiry, 1*(2), 1-22.

Beijaard, D., Verloop, N., & Vermunt, J. (2000). Teachers' perceptions of professional identity: An exploratory study from a personal knowledge perspective. *Teaching and Teacher Education, 16*(7), 749-764.

Britzman, D. P. (2003). *Practice makes practice: A critical study of learning to teach.* New York: State University of New York Press.

Bullough, R. V., & Gitlin, A. (1995). *Becoming a student of teaching.* New York: Garland.

Connell, H., & Skilbeck, M. (2004). *Attracting, developing and retaining effective teachers: Update of country background report for Australia.* Canberra: Commonwealth Department of Education, Science and Training.

Crow, G., Levine, L., & Nager, N. (1990). No more business as usual: Career changers who become teachers. *American Journal of Education, 98*(3), 197-223.

DEST. (2000). *Teachers for the 21st century - Making the difference.* Retrieved July 20, 2004, from http:/www.dest.gov.au/schools/Publications/2000.htm

DEST. (2004). *Taking schools to the next level: The national education framework for schools.* Canberra: Department of Education, Science and Training.

ETC. (2005). *Step up, step in, step out: Report on the inquiry into the suitability of pre-service teacher training in Victoria.* Melbourne: Education and Training Committee, Victorian Parliament.

Featherstone, D., Munby, H., & Russell, T. (Eds.). (1997). *Finding a voice while learning to teach.* London: The Falmer Press.

Feiman-Nemser, S. (2001). From preparation to practice: Designing a continuum to strengthen and sustain teaching. *Teachers College Record, 103*(6), 1013-1055.

Grundy, S., & Hatton, E. (1996). *Teacher educators, student teachers and biography.* Paper presented at the Australian Association for Research in Education Conference, Singapore.

Jeans, B., & Forth, P. (1995). *The development of professional identity.* Paper presented at the Australian Association for Research in Education, Hobart.

Knowles, J. G., & Cole, A. L. (1994). *Through preservice teachers' eyes.* New Jersey: Merrill.

Korthagen, F. A. J. (2001). *Linking practice and theory: The pedagogy of realistic teacher education.* New Jersey: Lawrence Erlbaum Associates.

Loughran, J. (1996). *Developing reflective practice: Learning about teaching and learning through modelling.* London: Falmer Press.

Mockler, N., Normanhurst, L., & Sachs, J. (2002). *A crisis of identity? Teacher professional identity and the role of evidence based practice.* Paper presented at the Australian Association for Educational Research, University of Queensland.

OECD. (2001). *Teachers for tomorrow's schools.* Paris: OECD.

OECD. (2004). *The quality of the teaching workforce.* Paris: OECD.

Priyadharshini, E., & Robinson-Pant, A. (2003). The attractions of teaching: An investigation into why people change careers to teach. *Journal of Education for Teaching, 29*(2), 95-112.

Richardson, P., & Watt, H. (2005). 'I've decided to become a teacher': Influences on career change. *Teaching and Teacher Education, 21*(5), 475-489.

Sachs, J. (1999). *Teacher professional identity: Competing discourses, competing outcomes.* Paper presented at the Australian Association for Research in Education, Melbourne.

Wenzlaff, T., & Wieseman, K. (2004). Teachers need teachers to grow. *Teacher Education Quarterly, 31*(2), 113-125.

Judy Williams
Faculty of Education
Monash University

HELEN WATT, PAUL RICHARDSON AND NICOLE TYSVAER

10. PROFILES OF BEGINNING TEACHERS' PROFESSIONAL ENGAGEMENT AND CAREER DEVELOPMENT ASPIRATIONS

INTRODUCTION

Teacher educators, policy makers, and employing authorities have for too long overlooked the values, beliefs and motivations of those entering teacher education programs and insufficiently explored how these shape beginning teachers' aspirations for professional engagement and the trajectory of their career development.

> Unless teacher educators engage prospective students in a critical examination of their entering beliefs in light of compelling alternatives and help them develop powerful images of good teaching and strong professional commitments, these entering beliefs will continue to shape their ideas and practices. (Feiman-Nemser, 2001, p. 1017)

Continuing insistence on the need to reform teacher education derives from long-standing debates about the quality of the teaching workforce and scrutiny of the different programs through which teachers are professionally prepared. Concurrently, there is an equally persistent problem of teacher shortages – in Australia as in many other countries. Within our perspective, beginning teachers' perceptions impact their subsequent professional engagement, development, and quality of their work. Our 'FIT-Choice' [Factors Influencing Teaching Choice] theoretical model outlines these relationships over time (see Richardson & Watt, 2006). It is grounded in Expectancy-Value theory (Eccles (Parsons) et al., 1983; Wigfield & Eccles, 2000), which argues that individuals' choices and behaviours are shaped by their expectancies and their values, and we have elsewhere detailed the development and validation of our framework for the context of teaching as a career choice (Richardson & Watt, 2006; Watt & Richardson, in review).

In this chapter, we adopt a multidimensional approach to investigate participants' professional engagement and career development aspirations as they conclude their teaching degree. We focus on teacher graduands to tap aspects of professional identification at this critical final stage of initial teacher education. Specific facets we explore encompass planned effort, planned persistence, professional development aspirations, and leadership aspirations for when they enter the profession. Additional evaluation of satisfaction with the choice of a teaching career was included at both entry to and exit from teacher education,

A. Berry, A. Clemans and A. Kostogriz (Eds.), Dimensions of Professional Learning: Professionalism, Practice and Identity, 155–175. © 2007 Sense Publishers. All rights reserved.

permitting us to explore *changes* in satisfaction, and how these relate to professional engagement and career development aspirations encompassing cognitive, emotional, and behavioural aspects, being the different dimensions of engagement that prior research has emphasised (see Guthrie & Wigfield, 2000). All factors were averaged composites of survey scale items in Table 10.1[1], and demonstrated good reliability and construct validity.

Our investigation is based on longitudinal data from a large sample of 510 beginning teachers. Common sense suggests beginning teachers may differ from one another, and we explore whether there are different '*types*' having shared profiles of aspirations for professional engagement and career development. We adopt cluster analysis, a mixed-methods and person-centred approach with which to identify differing subgroups. Within identified profiles we frame our analysis of the qualitative data, and develop group-based explanations concerning the predictors and correlates for each beginning teacher 'type'.

Participants completed a graduate-entry primary or secondary teacher education degree at one of three Australian universities (119 University of Sydney, 214 Monash University, 177 University of Western Sydney), and all held a relevant prior undergraduate qualification. Participants provided data at two timepoints: on their entry to teacher education, and immediately prior to completion of their qualification. We draw on closed-ended quantitative and open-ended qualitative data from surveys administered during regular classes at both occasions. In our ongoing longitudinal study we will subsequently follow these and other beginning teachers through their early professional experiences, to better understand how, in the cauldron of professional practice in schools across a range of sociocultural contexts, initial motivations are confirmed or disconfirmed, and how these experiences begin to shape different professional identities – particularly those who are committed to and effective in the teaching profession.

Historically teachers have not received high returns in terms of salary or status and have been expected to look upon teaching more as a vocation than as strictly a job. Over recent decades there have been significant changes to the labour market which potentially impact on how those who undertake teacher education programs look upon teaching as a career choice. It is reasonable to expect these individuals will have different career trajectories in mind even at the outset, with some only intending to teach for a short period. The specific questions that our chapter addresses are:

- Can we identify different subgroups having distinct *profiles* of professional engagement and career development aspirations, and are we able to develop explanations to predict who is likely to fall into these different clusters?
- Do levels of satisfaction with the choice of teaching as a career *change* through teacher education, and are changes different for each cluster?
- What might this imply for teacher education programs, policy makers, and employing authorities?

Table 10.1. Factor items, reliabilities and pattern coefficients

Factor	Item	Stem *[1 (not at all) to 7 (extremely)]*	Pattern coefficient
Satisfaction with choice ($\alpha = .925$)	a12	How happy are you with your decision to become a teacher?	.70
	a9	How satisfied are you with your decision to become a teacher?	.68
Professional Engagement			
Planned effort ($\alpha = .915$)	a11	How much effort will you put into your teaching?	.85
	a8	How much will you work at being a good teacher?	.81
	a14	How much effort do you plan to exert as a teacher?	.80
	a5	How hard will you strive to be an effective teacher?	.72
Planned persistence ($\alpha = .962$)	a16	How sure are you that you will stay in the teaching profession?	.90
	a7	How certain are you that you will remain in teaching?	.86
	a10	How confident are you that you will stick with teaching?	.86
	a13	How sure are you that you will persist in a teaching career?	.80
Career Development Aspirations: "To what extent do you aim to…"			
Professional development aspirations ($\alpha = .914$)	b7	participate in professional development courses?	.85
	b3	undertake further professional development?	.84
	b9	learn about current educational developments?	.67
	b5	continue to acquire curriculum knowledge?	.59
	b1	continue learning how to improve your teaching skills?	.53
Leadership aspirations ($\alpha = .913$)	b4	reach a position of management in schools?	.85
	b8	take up a leadership role in schools?	.84
	b6	seek a staff supervision role in schools?	.80
	b2	have leadership responsibilities in schools?	.67

THREE 'TYPES' OF BEGINNING TEACHERS

Cluster Profiles

We identified three subgroups of beginning teachers in terms of their planned effort, planned persistence, professional development aspirations, and leadership aspirations. These clusters were supported in our hierarchical cluster analysis using Ward's method based on the cluster dendogram, the number of 'steps' in the scree-type plot of fusion coefficients relative to number of clusters and on the basis of substantive interpretability. The three different profiles are illustrated in Figure 10.1.[2] Cluster 1 contained 225 participants[3], and gave the highest ratings for all four factors. We named this group the 'highly engaged persisters'. Cluster 2 contained 132 participants, whose responses were similar to Cluster 1 except on *persistence*, where Cluster 2 responses were significantly lower. We named this group the 'highly engaged switchers'. Cluster 3 contained 136 participants, and exhibited significantly lower scores on our four measures of professional engagement. Although their mean scores on planned effort and professional development aspirations were still quite high relative to the 7-point scale, they were lower than for the other two clusters. In particular, their mean scores for planned persistence and leadership aspirations were relatively low *both* on the 7-point scale and compared with the other clusters. We consequently named this group the 'lower engaged desisters'.

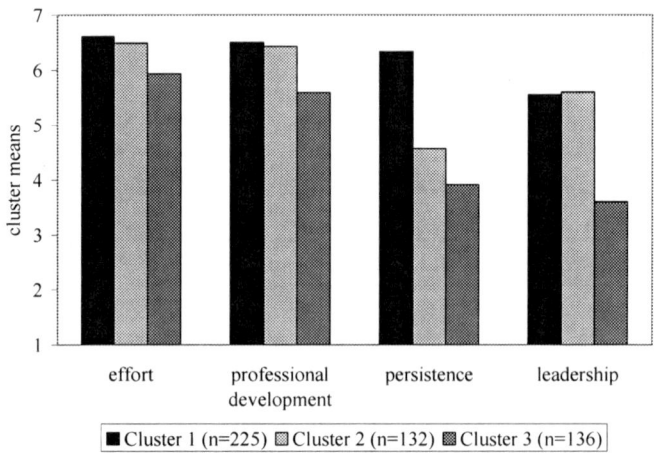

Figure 10.1. Mean professional engagement and career development aspiration scores for 'highly engaged persisters' (Cluster 1), 'highly engaged switchers' (Cluster 2), and 'lower engaged desisters' (Cluster 3)[4]

Different Professional Plans for Different Beginning Teacher 'Types'

How does our identification of these 'types' help our understanding about beginning teachers' development and needs? We next examined correlates and consequences of belonging to each cluster. First, participants' professional plans were explored through a question on the survey which asked them to select one of "I do not want a teaching career"; "I want to teach in the short-term but later want to pursue a different profession"; or "I want my whole career to be in the teaching profession". Those who did not want a teaching career wrote about why, and nominated their desired career. Those who wanted to teach in the short-term but then wanted to pursue a different profession wrote about why, what career they subsequently planned to pursue, and how many years until they planned pursuing it. Those who wanted their whole career to be in the teaching profession indicated why this was the case.

The overwhelming majority of Cluster 1 (87.3%) planned to teach for their whole career, in contrast to lower proportions for Cluster 2 (53.5%), with Cluster 3 the lowest (40.9%; Figure 10.2). The pattern was reversed for proportions of participants within each cluster who planned to teach in the short-term and then switch to another career: Cluster 3 had the highest proportion (52.3%), followed by Cluster 2 (45.7), and Cluster 1 (12.2%). Only small numbers of participants planned not to teach at all across the whole sample (2.8%): Cluster 3 had the highest proportion (6.8%), followed by negligible proportions within Clusters 2 (0.8%, one person) and 1 (0.5%, one person). All cluster differences in professional plans were statistically significant. To explore the reasons *why* individuals from each cluster held such different plans, we turned to participants' open-ended qualitative responses.

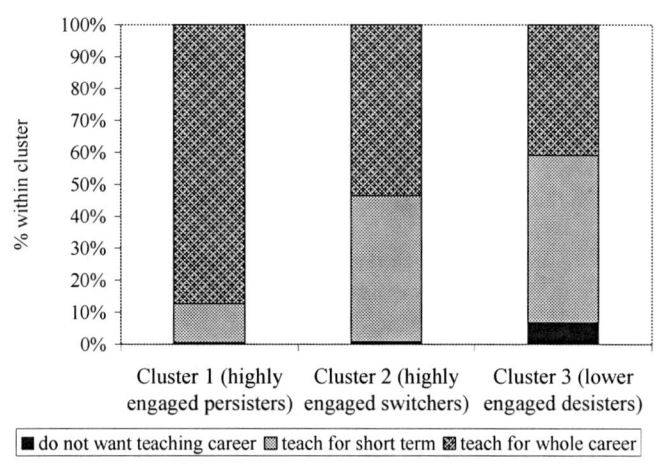

Figure 10.2. Professional plans for cluster groups

Reasons for Cluster Differences in Professional Plans

Cluster membership framed our analysis and reporting of participants' open-ended qualitative responses in relation to their professional plans – an approach we have found informative with previous samples of beginning teachers (see Richardson & Watt, 2005). Themes from participants' unrestricted open-ended reasons regarding their professional plans were developed within each cluster, to illustrate and elucidate within-cluster patterns and between-cluster differences.

Cluster 1 - Highly Engaged Persisters

As indicated earlier, the overwhelming majority of people in Cluster 1 intended to spend their whole career in teaching. This was true for participants who were in the younger age groups and for whom teaching was their first career through to those who were older and making a career change, some of whom had had more than one prior career. Open-ended comments foregrounded salient reasons for career choice. The most frequently nominated reason for wanting to teach was a passion for teaching which was for them satisfying, varied, and interesting. A related theme saw teaching as a 'dream ambition', a vocation or calling, and something they were 'supposed to do'. Their enthusiasm for the intrinsic rewards of teaching is captured in a sample of their comments:

Intrinsic satisfaction.

I love teaching students.

Because it is interesting and has varied tasks.

It's my calling.

I am passionate about teaching and know I can be beneficial to students.

This finding was also reflected in another study (Watt & Richardson, in review) where we have used additional quantitative data from this sample, and found that individuals high on intrinsic and altruistic motivations for initially choosing teaching were also those who, on completion of the program, planned to persist the longest.

A desire to work with children and adolescents to influence their learning and to make a difference in their lives was reassuringly central to the reasons people gave for wanting their whole career in teaching:

I enjoy teaching and I love working with kids to further their learning.

Because I enjoy working with children and find it rewarding

Love kids and like to learn 'how' they learn – general interest.

Because I want to make a difference in the lives of kids.

Because I like to share my knowledge with others and make a difference.

Clearly, people who do not want a career that involves working with children or adolescents would be ill-advised to choose teaching as their occupation. Working with young people to foster their learning of particular disciplines, and to exert a positive influence on their personal and social development, is something that these people believe a career in teaching provides. Cluster 1 also included people who had chosen teaching because it offered them a satisfying career and supported their family life including caring for their own children. Teaching allowed them the means by which to meet their career goals without sacrificing a quality family life:

It is a career that is satisfying, fulfilling and suits family situation.

Fits in with family as well as career goals.

Family reasons and my relationship with children.

In a previous study of an independent sample of people who switched careers into teaching (Richardson & Watt, 2005) we identified people who had given up highly paid, yet demanding, inflexible, and time-hungry careers in business and accounting for the opportunity to combine career with a lifestyle change focused on securing more time for family and the care of children. An emphasis on lifestyle change was again evident with some people in this sample who were seeking a combination of 'lifestyle and personal satisfaction', or a better balance of work with other aspects of their life. As one participant observed: "I've worked for *corporates* for a long time and now I want a lifestyle improvement". Others who were making a career change similarly expressed their hope that teaching would meet their expectations and they would not need to move on to yet another career path:

I have tried other careers and hope to settle.

I've made a major change late in life and intend to stick it out.

Moreover, there were those who were sure that on making a career switch in favour of teaching they had finally found an occupation that fitted more comfortably with their goals and ambitions than the previous careers they had pursued:

This is my fourth career choice and this is what I really want to do.

I have come to it as a second career and now know it's what I want to do.

I have worked a few years in industry and believe teaching is where I really belong.

I have already had a design career and wish to have a stable and rewarding career in teaching.

While the career switchers had tried other careers and arrived at teaching by a more circuitous route, others looked equally approvingly on the possibilities of a long career in the profession. Their comments focused on teaching as being enjoyable, allowing one to make a contribution to the lives of others, while also being personally rewarding and a morally good career:

It's a positive thing to do with my life.

I consider it a rewarding career.

Most real/rewarding profession available to me.

We contribute to something worthwhile.

Members of Cluster 1 may have been enthusiastic about their career choice but they were also very aware that the financial rewards are not very great; as one participant said: "It is a stable career and reward is OK". As we have seen above, others emphasised the personal and moral dimensions of the reward structure provided by the career; however it remains to be determined if less tangible rewards will be sufficient to compensate for the comparatively modest financial returns that a career in teaching provides.

Cluster 2 – Highly engaged switchers

We have characterised members of Cluster 2 as 'switchers'. That is, they were more likely to indicate they had career plans other than spending their whole career in teaching. Interestingly, people in Cluster 2 were already contemplating another career path as they completed their teacher education program, which they may have been contemplating prior to their entry. Many of them were able to nominate their reason for not wanting to stay in teaching, as well as when they planned to leave the career for something else. Timeframes ranged from 'now' through 15 years. This cluster drew together people who knew they needed new challenges over the course of their career and therefore sought to be involved in a diversity of occupations including business, other public services, health promotion, entertainment, the arts and crafts, design, and their own small businesses. They are perhaps best described as *restless spirits* – needing new challenges and a diversity of experiences including other career options such as working in policing, ASIO and foreign affairs, and overseas travel. Their restlessness and desire for variety and diversity is captured in these comments:

I like diversity and want to grow as a person always.

I will outgrow it and like new challenges.

I want to experience more than one career.

I feel that there are more things I want to try.

A further theme was the identification of a 'five year plan' for their career development – a plan that would see them teach for about five years, by which time they hoped to have positioned themselves to exit. These people looked upon teaching as a 'back-up plan' with which to build their personal and financial resources in preparation for another career. The comment "I'm on a five year plan" was indicative of the sentiments of many in this cluster. In the comments that follow, participants were more specific about what plans they had for the future and why teaching was for them a back-up career. It is not surprising that people who in the longer term were seeking careers in the entertainment industry and as visual artists (painters, photographers and designers) were also looking to secure a reliable income stream while attempting to establish themselves. Even though teaching offers a modest income, it nonetheless provided a degree of security that the performing and visual arts do not necessarily provide. While the longer-term careers of these people were elsewhere (nominated careers in parentheses), they nonetheless planned to pursue teaching in the short-term:

Teaching is my back up plan (Entertainment).

I enjoy teaching, and cannot as yet survive as an artist (Prefer art).

Never saw teaching as the only thing I wanted to do (Art related/self-employed).

Stability, build foundations (Photographer).

Money and broaden my life experience (Art/Design small business).

Want my own business (Interior Decorating).

For others, simply keeping their options open was more important than foreclosing on teaching as a career for life. For this group, teaching would afford them the skills and experiences that may be applied in other domains and contexts outside of school classrooms, and as such would function as a stepping stone into other professions. Thus individuals indicated their intentions of finding employment as a 'trainer in a software industry', being involved in nutrition and health promotion, working in corporate training, entering politics, being an academic, or just being open to 'a broad life perspective'. While some individuals in this cluster indicated a desire to continue working with children and adolescents, this would not be in classroom contexts. They were looking forward to becoming counselling psychologists, and in one case, entering into religious ministry with children. A desire to keep their options open was interpreted differently by some who, at the end of their teacher education program, were unsure about the viability of a career in teaching. They clearly did not identify with the prospects of teaching as a long-term career and remained undecided about how long they would persist. They would wait to see how things worked out. They were not enthusiastic about the profession and would weigh up confirming or disconfirming experiences. These people were less interested in teaching as a vocation and more focused on realising job satisfaction. The following comments revealed their hesitation and commitment only to the short-term:

Not sure and don't know if I really want to [teach].

It all depends on the experience I will have in first couple of years.

I am not going to stay in teaching if I do not like it?

Unsure as to how I'll enjoy teaching in a few years.

Not sure if it's for me.

It's worth doing this rather than doing nothing.

A substantial number of this group did not undertake a teacher education program intending to remain in teaching for their whole career. On the contrary, their intention had always been to operate on a 'five year plan' and not to persist in teaching. While they planned to be as effortful, engaged, and to do as good a job as those who wanted their whole career in teaching (Cluster 1), they also planned to then move on to another career.

Cluster 3 – Lower engaged desisters

Cluster 3 members contrasted with both Clusters 1 and 2. We have identified this cluster as the 'desisters' from teaching. They were the least likely to plan to persist, and if they took up teaching at all, offered many reasons why they were not planning on a long career in the profession. The sources of their disaffection were varied and stemmed in a minority of cases from unpleasant experiences at university and "bad practicum experiences". Others reported that teaching proved to be too demanding – it was "too much work", demanded "too much work preparation", and schools provided "too little administrative support". As a result, members of this cluster felt they would "not have enough energy when older", that they would become "jaded", and quickly suffer from career burnout. Comments such as "children don't value education" and "it does not suit my needs – the preparation and class management issues", and "don't want to work in a high school – will teach overseas to get money", point to experiences during the course of their teacher education program that took on a negative valence in relation to their tenure in teaching.

While the first themed set of comments from this cluster was concerned with the demands of the career, a second theme focused on the paucity of career prospects and rewards. A number of the people in this second set made the observation that they would receive more "pay and respect", and better "career progression" by working in other fields such as IT, business management, and consulting. The comments that it "takes too long to get a full time job!" and "teaching is not very stable" seem to point to the frustrations recent graduates often experience in shuffling between a wide range of schools eking out a sometimes very insecure living by undertaking substitute and relief teaching work before they can secure full-time employment. Given that members of this cluster generally had higher qualifications and a range of previous occupations, they may easily be attracted into other careers where their teaching qualification would be viewed as a marketable asset, especially in corporate environments where training is a feature of the workplace.

For some in this cluster teaching was not their 'first option'. Careers as research scientists and in the academy, together with further education and eventual careers in psychology and sports psychology, were more attractive options. Having other options as a journalist, in human resource management, or as an engineer perhaps made it possible for members of this cluster to evaluate their decision to undertake a one-to-two-year teacher education program differently. As with Cluster 2, this cluster contained a group of people who looked upon teaching as a 'stepping stone' into other careers such as working in art galleries, being a theatre director/actor, working in conservation, educational tourism, as well as those who wanted to combine part-time teaching with tourism, environmental consulting, the fine arts, and photography.

People in Cluster 3 did not necessarily want to teach at all and even though they may have enjoyed "children and teaching", they observed that they needed change and variety in their life and as a consequence did not "want to be stuck" in a career that from their perspective lacked "flexibility". As one participant wrote, "I can't see myself doing anything for 40 yrs!! I'll get bored!" while another contended that "Nothing is forever". These sentiments paralleled those of others who preferred "not to map out future", were "still uncertain whether to take up teaching – I don't have a plan", and those who were generally "not sure what to do – want to look after child".

The finding that a significant number of people in Clusters 2 and 3 only wanted to teach in the short term and that their longer term career plans were not going to be in teaching, begs the question as to where these people were intending to go with their career plans? While people in Cluster 2 identified non-education related careers in business, IT consulting, management, the arts, and health-related occupations; members of Cluster 3 were more intent on these careers than those from Cluster 2. Of the 77 people from Clusters 2 and 3 who were able to identify their longer term career plan, 34 saw themselves moving into careers that were broadly related to education or training. Taken together these people were seeking longer term careers in curriculum design and development, religious ministry to children and adolescents, youth counsellors and educational psychologists, research and academic careers, trainers in business organisational contexts, and as education officers at public art galleries, nutritional and health promotion officers, educational development officers in the police force, and music therapists. While they intended leaving teaching, they nonetheless hoped to move into education-related careers where the emphasis is on broader public educational activities than work in classrooms and schools.

CHANGING SATISFACTION LEVELS THROUGH TEACHER EDUCATION: A MECHANISM TO HELP EXPLAIN BEGINNING TEACHER PROFILES?

Cluster Differences in the Satisfaction with Teaching as a Career Choice

Is it because Cluster 1 is the most satisfied with their choice of teaching as a career that they more often plan to pursue their whole career in the teaching profession? Is it because Cluster 3 is the least satisfied that they are substantially less likely to plan this? Our data suggest this could be the case. Cluster 1 were significantly the most satisfied with their choice at the time of their degree completion, followed by Cluster 2, with Cluster 3 significantly the least satisfied ($F(2, 477) = 110.26$). Because we had collected satisfaction data both at the start and finish of participants' teaching qualifications, we were also able to investigate whether satisfaction levels remained *stable* through the course of their teacher education preparation, or whether the different clusters exhibited different *change* trajectories.

Interestingly, Cluster 1 did start out and remain highest, and Cluster 3 lowest, from their entry to teacher education ($F(2, 483) = 105.06$). Moreover, there was a significant interaction effect between cluster and time ($F(2, 483) = 4.83$), where Cluster 1 *increased* in satisfaction ($F(1, 220) = 10.78$), Cluster 2 maintained *stable* satisfaction ($F(1, 130) = 0.07$), and Cluster 3 showed a trend to *decrease* in satisfaction ($F(1, 133) = 2.76$; Figure 10.3). This implies Cluster 1 may well have become more 'turned on' to teaching while Cluster 3 were more 'turned off', through their teacher education experiences. Support for the idea that Cluster 2 had always planned switch to another profession is found in the stability of their satisfaction levels through teacher education. Because satisfaction changes were small where they occurred, we next examined the extent to which changes helped explain the three beginning teacher clusters.

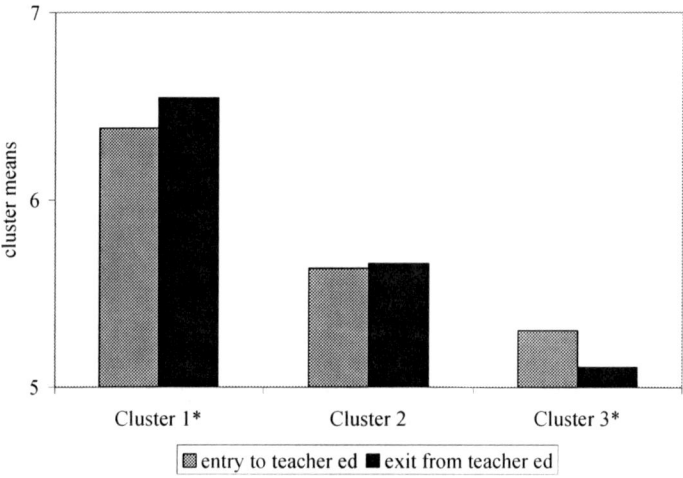

Figure 10.3. Change trajectories for satisfaction with the choice of teaching as a career for cluster groups (asterisks denote statistically significant changes within cluster)

Relationships between Entry and Exit Satisfaction Levels and Beginning Teacher Profiles

Could cluster-specific career choice satisfaction trajectories help explain the cluster profiles of professional engagement and career development aspirations for people completing their teaching degree? We expected individuals' levels of satisfaction would relate to their professional engagement and career development aspirations. Further, we anticipated that *changes* in satisfaction through teacher education would relate to these outcomes. Our two timepoint measurement of satisfaction with the choice of teaching enabled us to explore this question in several interesting ways.

Satisfaction with the choice of teaching as a career at the end of participants' teaching degree was moderately correlated with their concurrent planned effort, persistence, professional development, leadership aspirations, and professional plans. These relationships are presented in the first row of Table 10.2. Similar relationships were evident from participants' *initial* satisfaction levels at entry to teacher education, as presented in the second row of Table 10.2, although not surprisingly the strength of these relationships was weaker.

Table 10.2. Relationships between satisfaction with the choice of teaching as a career and change in satisfaction, with professional engagement and career development aspirations (Pearson Correlations with Listwise N = 473)

	effort	professional development	persistence	leadership	professional plans
satisfaction (on exit)	.528**	.493**	.686**	.348**	.460**
satisfaction (on entry)	.319**	.288**	.506**	.267**	.362**
satisfaction change (exit minus entry)	.226**	.222**	.196**	.088	.108†

** $p < .001$, * $p < .01$, † $p < .05$

These tests did not tap the more interesting question concerning whether the amount of *change* in satisfaction (from entry to teacher education through exit) related to the professional engagement and career development aspirations for these beginning teachers. We created an index of satisfaction change through subtracting entry satisfaction scores from exit scores, such that positive numbers indicated increased satisfaction, zero indicated no change, and negative numbers indicated decreased satisfaction. As can be seen from the third row of Table 10.2 – amount of satisfaction change did indeed relate statistically significantly to all the factors except leadership aspirations.

Because different changes in satisfaction relate to individuals' professional engagement and career development aspirations, we need to question *why* Cluster 3 became disaffected during their teacher education experiences, particularly since this group accounted for almost one-third (28%) of the cohort. From our large-scale ongoing longitudinal study, we actually know quite a lot about what factors shape teacher education entrants' satisfaction with their choice of teaching as a career (Richardson & Watt, 2006). Not too surprisingly, commencing teacher education candidates' satisfaction relates to their *motivations* for having chosen teaching as a career. The motivations which relate most strongly to high initial satisfaction levels include the altruistic-type motivations most frequently emphasised in the teacher education literature, as well as the intrinsic value individuals attach to teaching, and self-evaluations of their teaching-related skills (Watt & Richardson, in review).

We know less about what factors may alter teacher education candidates' career choice satisfaction during the course of their teacher preparation degree. Why would it be that some people's satisfaction levels increase, others remain the same, and others decrease? Is this something that we could predict from candidates' background characteristics, or is it intimately and idiosyncratically bound up with individuals' unique experiences during teacher education? At the individual level decisions about one's level of commitment may appear idiosyncratic but these patterns may be more readily discerned at the group level. The open-ended responses suggest that the experiences of those in Cluster 1 during the course of their teacher education program (including the practicum in schools) had dovetailed with their expectations, values and beliefs and that there was a matching of the person with the workplace environment. Such a fit resulted in increasing levels of satisfaction with their career choice, fostering expectations of planned effort, planned professional development, persistence, and a desire for leadership roles. Cluster 2 did not plan to stay in teaching for the long haul and although they would exert equally high levels of effort, professional development, and leadership to Cluster 1, they did not plan on their whole career being in teaching. Members of Cluster 3 were overwhelmingly less comfortable with the fit between themselves and teaching as a career path. They would not be around long enough to take an interest in leadership roles. Although this group had willingly signed up for further education in the hope of becoming a teacher, their experiences during teacher education, including the practicum experiences in schools, had in fact not confirmed their expectations, beliefs, and values.

CAN WE PREDICT WHO WILL BELONG TO WHICH CLUSTER?

Do Demographic Characteristics Make a Difference?

Are there any background indicators that would give us a clue as to which people are more likely to be 'highly engaged persisters', 'highly engaged switchers', or 'lower engaged desisters'? Gender was not a relevant factor in cluster composition, while language spoken at home was (English vs. other; $\chi^2(2) = 10.88$), with a greater proportion of Cluster 1 coming from non-English speaking backgrounds [NESB], compared with the other clusters (Table 10.3). Whether people had children also differed across clusters ($\chi^2(2) = 15.622$), with almost one-third of Clusters 1 and 3 having children, compared with 13% in Cluster 2 (Table 10.3). Undertaking primary versus secondary level teacher education had no relationship with cluster membership.

Table 10.3. Cluster composition by gender, home language, primary/secondary level, children, consideration and pursuit of other jobs, and prior qualifications

	Cluster 1 (n = 225) n (%)	Cluster 2 (n = 132) n (%)	Cluster 3 (n = 136) n (%)	Totals
male	65 (28.9%)	39 (29.5%)	33 (24.3%)	137
female	160 (71.1%)	93 (70.5%)	103 (75.7%)	356
English home language	177 (79.0%)	121 (91.7%)	118 (86.8%)	416
other home language	47 (21.0%)	11 (8.3%)	18 (13.2%)	76
primary	70 (31.1%)	41 (31.1%)	32 (23.5%)	143
secondary	155 (68.9%)	91 (68.9%)	104 (76.5%)	350

no children	156 (69.3%)	115 (87.1%)	95 (69.9%)	366
children	69 (30.7%)	17 (12.9%)	41 (30.1%)	127
other job not considered	77 (34.2%)	42 (31.8%)	31 (22.8%)	150
considered other job	61 (27.1%)	41 (31.1%)	47 (34.6%)	149
pursued other job	87 (38.7%)	49 (37.1%)	58 (42.6%)	194
undergraduate degree	160 (72.7%)	95 (73.1%)	85 (63.0%)	340
undergraduate Honours	37 (16.8%)	21 (16.2%)	27 (20.0%)	85
postgraduate degree	23 (10.5%)	14 (10.7%)	23 (17.0%)	60

Cluster 2 tended to be the youngest, while Clusters 1 and 3 were older ($F(2, 482) = 6.40$; Figure 10.4). Individuals' ages in Cluster 2 were also more tightly clustered together.

Cluster 2 came from higher parental income backgrounds than Cluster 1 ($F(2, 415) = 3.82$), while Cluster 3 fell in between. Figure 10.5 shows the distributions for combined parent income within each cluster. Participants were generally not from affluent family backgrounds and the modal combined parent income category was $60 001 to $90 000.

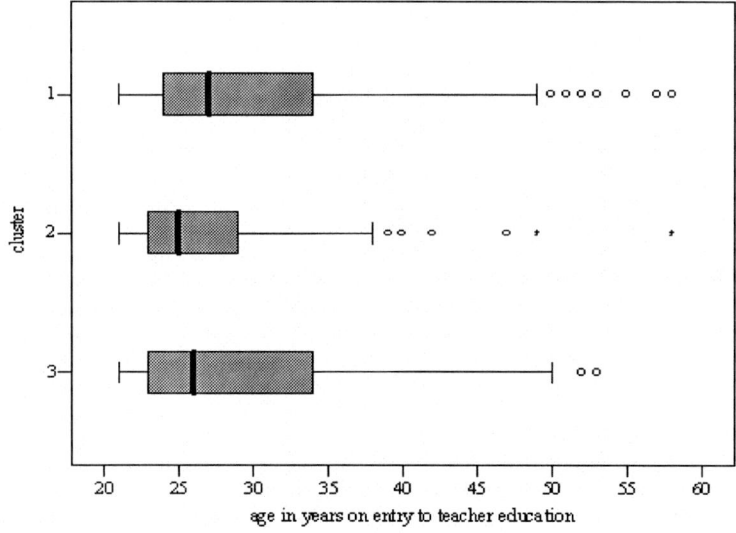

Figure 10.4. Cluster profiles for age of beginning teacher education[5]

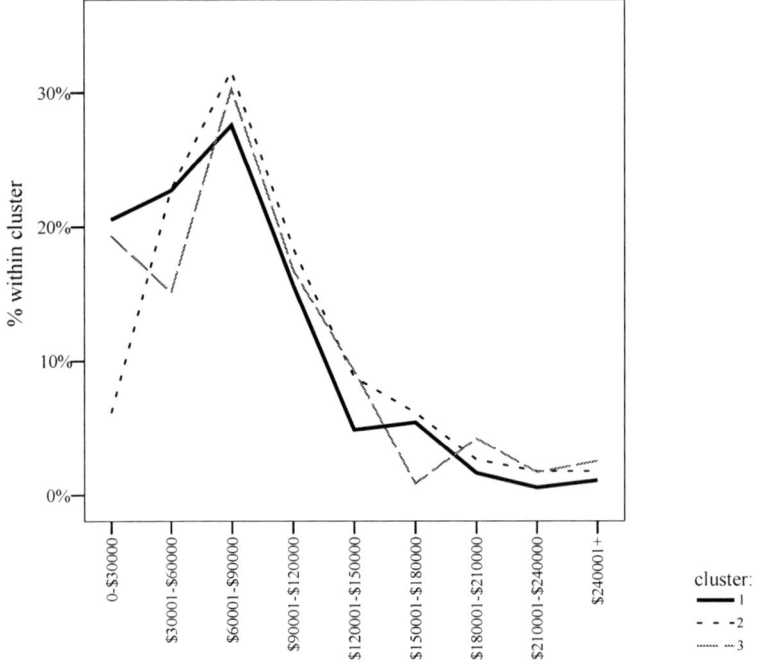

Figure 10.5. Cluster profiles for combined parent income (indicative SES background)
Career History, Prior Education, and Career Decision

Although the clusters did not significantly differ in terms of whether individuals had considered or pursued a different career prior to enrolling in teacher education (Table 10.3), or in their levels of satisfaction with previously *pursued* jobs; there were interesting differences in relation to the *types* of careers individuals from each cluster had pursued. We coded the occupational status of the jobs using O*NET – a comprehensive database of occupational information provided by the United States Department of Labor (US Department of Labor Employment and Training Administration, 1998), which ranks each occupation in the database from 1 through 5, based on factors including average salary and amount of educational preparation and training required (for details see Richardson & Watt, 2006). Of the 188 individuals who reported another career prior to enrolling in teacher education (Cluster 1: $n = 85$, Cluster 2: $n = 46$, Cluster 3: $n = 57$), Cluster 3 tended to have had careers higher in occupational status, Cluster 2 lower, and Cluster 1 in between ($F(2, 185) = 2.98$; Figure 10.6). There was also a trend for Cluster 3 to be more highly qualified than Cluster 1 ($F(2, 482) = 2.67$, see Table 10.3). For the 149 people who had previously seriously *considered* other jobs, there were no significant cluster differences in their occupational statuses (Figure 10.6).

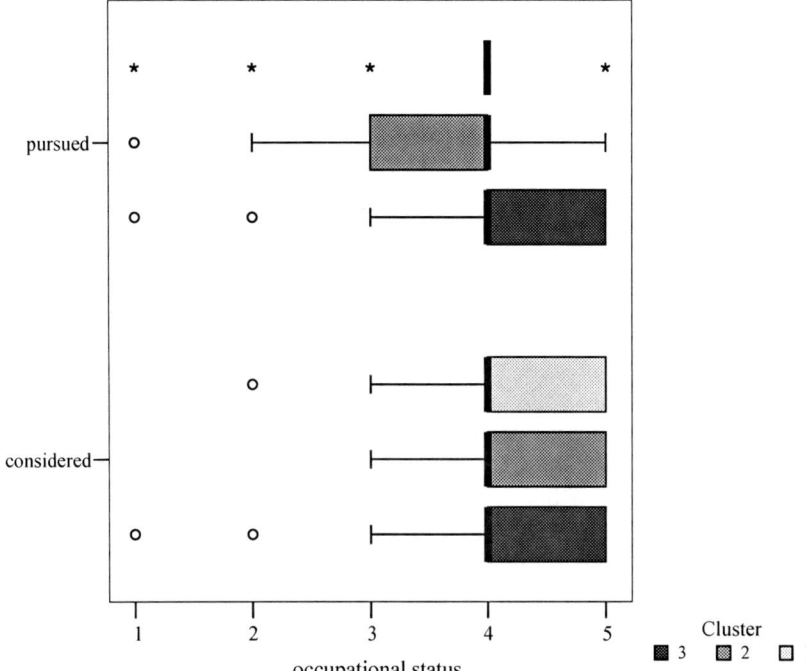

Figure 10.6. Cluster profiles of occupational statuses for previously pursued or considered careers[6]

The *timing* of when each cluster had chosen teaching as a career also differed significantly ($F(2, 472) = 6.84$), accounted for by Cluster 1 having decided to become teachers significantly earlier than Cluster 3, while Cluster 2 fell in between. On average, Cluster 1 had decided to teach 2.83 years ago ($SD = 1.76$), Cluster 2 had made this decision 2.50 years ago ($SD = 1.78$), and Cluster 3 had chosen to teach the most recently, 2.11 years ago ($SD = 1.73$). Taken together, distinguishing characteristics for each cluster paint the following summary pictures:

Highly Engaged Persisters (Cluster 1)

Highly engaged persisters were more likely to have children, tended to be older, to contain the greatest NESB concentration, to be from lower family income backgrounds, and to hold the lowest levels of prior qualifications. They had also chosen a teaching career the earliest, and for those who had previously seriously considered another career they expressed the lowest levels of satisfaction with career choices other than teaching. This cluster would likely be those preferred by teacher educators and school employers as holding the most desirable professional goals. These beginning teachers planned to exert high effort in their teaching, to undertake professional development to continue to improve their professional practice, to persist in the profession for a long time, and to aspire to positions of school leadership. Almost half the sample (45.6%) was described by this profile.

Highly Engaged Switchers (Cluster 2)

Highly engaged switchers were the least likely to have children, tended to have the lowest NESB concentration, to come from higher family income backgrounds, and to be younger. Their previously pursued careers were of lower occupational status, although this may relate to their relative youth. This cluster appeared very similar to Cluster 1 – except that they did not plan to persist for as long in the profession. We need to question whether this is necessarily a bad thing. Although there is a problem of teacher shortages at this point in time in Australia and elsewhere, for the time these commencing teachers plan to remain in the profession they aim to exert high effort, undertake professional development, and aspire to school leadership positions to the same extent as Cluster 1. In the modern world of career consumerism, where few professions expect to attract employees for the entirety of their working lives, it may be unrealistic to expect that teaching will be quarantined from the effects of labour market forces. Adequate succession planning and staff management will depend on teacher education providers and employing authorities acknowledging this beginning teacher 'type' – a profile representing more than a quarter (26.8%) of our sample.

Lower Engaged Desisters (Cluster 3)

Lower engaged desisters contained a low (although not so low as Cluster 2) NESB concentration. They tended to be more likely to have children, to be older, to hold the highest levels of prior qualifications, and to have chosen a teaching career the most recently. Their previously pursued careers were the highest in occupational status, and they expressed the highest levels of satisfaction with careers other than teaching that they had seriously considered. This cluster exhibited a less desirable profile, shared by more than a quarter (27.6%) of the sample. They planned to exert lower effort, to engage less in professional development, to persist less long in the profession, and hold lower leadership aspirations, than either of the other two clusters. Although their effort and professional development plans were lower, they were still relatively high in absolute terms. However, their persistence and leadership plans were low both in relative and absolute terms.

IMPLICATIONS AND CHALLENGES FOR TEACHER EDUCATION

We recognise that our study was conducted with a graduate sample where the teaching qualification may take just one or two years, and that as a consequence there is a lower level of commitment required to complete the program. Would we find the same profiles across an undergraduate sample? Perhaps not, since the people who are members of Cluster 3 may well have discontinued a longer program leaving a higher proportion of people committed to a career in teaching.

Our findings invite re-examination of recruitment efforts, aspects of teacher education programs, and current models of career induction and mentoring. We have demonstrated there are distinct 'types' of beginning teachers showing considerable variation in their predicted persistence in the profession. Whether participants had pursued a previous career and then come into teacher education had no impact on their cluster membership. Cluster 1 clearly exhibited the profile of people who are highly committed to a career in teaching, who will exert high levels of effort and commitment, and who see themselves having the potential for educational leadership. These people are highly positive about their choice of a teaching career, and exhibit the profile of aspirations for professional engagement and career development that the majority of teacher education programs would hope for in their graduates.

Cluster 3 by contrast, which is by no means a small or marginal group, have a profile that would not be anticipated as a desirable outcome of most teacher education programs. While most programs would acknowledge there will always be a small number of people who do not seek employment in teaching at the end of their program because they have realised that teaching is not a career for them, the robust size of this cluster is challenging. Cluster 3 included people who do not want to teach at all, others who are lower on engagement, effort, and leadership aspirations, and those who plan on leaving the profession as soon as possible. It is indeed surprising that Cluster 3 represents such a substantial proportion of the total sample. We have found that this group decreased in their satisfaction with their choice of teaching as a career through their teacher education, for reasons including confronting practicum experiences in schools, realising the demanding nature of teachers' work, and lack of school structural support. Attention to these factors and further exploration of other reasons for declining satisfaction levels may help educators devise ways to redress the pattern for this group. Fruitful emphases for teacher educators may include sustained supportive interactions through practicum periods, explicit investigation of teachers' multidimensional role in- and outside the classroom and in broader community contexts. At the same time, employing authorities and policy-makers need to attend to conditions in schools, including early mentoring of beginning teachers, school-university partnerships, and levels of structural and administrative support in schools which may overburden teachers with unnecessary work.

On the other hand, members of Cluster 2 plan to be effortful and highly engaged and to seek leadership roles during the period they are teaching, but have another plan and a desire for new challenges which will take them away from teaching. Although they are embarking on their teaching career explicitly intending not to persist, their high levels of engagement imply they will make a valuable contribution to the profession during the time they are in it. It is important that employing authorities and policy-makers be aware of this sizeable group in succession planning during the present teacher shortage. If, on the other hand, this group's career aspirations can be realised in the context of a teaching career, it may be possible to sustain them for a longer period. If within their five-year plan they can achieve leadership roles and have their desire for new challenges and opportunities, as well as their engagement and effort appropriately rewarded, then it is likely that their time in teaching might be extended.

Teacher education and teacher employing authorities need to take seriously the different planned career trajectories of people who come into those programs. Educators and employers must go beyond the assumption that a person coming into teacher education and into a career in teaching may well not hold with a traditional lifetime career model of job security founded on incremental age-related advancement and loyalty to the profession. Whether teacher education and employing authorities acknowledge it or not, teaching as a career has been influenced by the changing nature of work and shifts in assumptions about the nature of career structures, loyalty, and the psychological meaning of work. Employees have learnt a new work order characterised by performance, flexibility, and multiple changes of employers, with career advancement based on individual learning-related, portable skills (Miles & Snow, 1996). Professionals with a range of skills and work experiences across different domains now take responsibility for their own careers which they seek to develop across organisations where they have been employed. From the perspective of employees, and in such fluid work contexts, personal identification with meaningful work becomes a litmus test of persistence. For beginning teachers, their different profiles of goals, commitments, plans, and aspirations will inevitably lead to different pathways of professional identity and development.

ACKNOWLEDGEMENTS

This research has been funded by an Australian Research Council (ARC) Discovery Grant awarded to Paul W. Richardson and Helen M. G. Watt (equal co-Chief Investigators), and Jacquelynne S. Eccles (Partner Investigator); and by a Monash University Faculty of Education Small Grant awarded to Helen M. G. Watt and Paul W. Richardson. We would like to thank Dr Ray Debus from the University of Sydney and Professor Jacquelynne Eccles from the University of Michigan for valuable discussions about our ideas. Watt and Richardson contributed equally to the chapter

NOTES

[1] The exploratory factor analysis using image extraction and oblimin rotation (delta = 0) converged in 12 iterations, with 70.553% cumulative extraction sums of squared loadings. There were no cross-loading pattern coefficients.

[2] There was a significant main effect of cluster membership on each of the four factors ($F(2, 490) = 45.090$ for effort, $F(2, 490) = 71.803$ for professional development, $F(2, 490) = 399.963$ for persistence, $F(2, 490) = 217.139$ for leadership), and differences between cluster pairs were identified using Tukey post hoc tests.

[3] Note that totals add to 493 rather than to 510 because 17 people did not have full data across the four factors from which cluster groups were formed.

[4] 'effort': planned effort; 'professional development': professional development aspirations; 'persistence': planned persistence; 'leadership': leadership aspirations.

[5] The box length is the interquartile range and the solid bar represents the median value. "o" denotes outliers with values between 1.5 and 3 box lengths from the upper or lower edge of the box, "*" denotes extreme cases with values more than 3 box lengths from the upper or lower edge of the box.

[6] Ibid.

REFERENCES

Eccles (Parsons), J., Adler, T. F., Futterman, R., Goff, S. B., Kaczala, C. M., Meece, J. L., & Midgely, C. (1983). Expectancies, values, and academic behaviors. In J. T. Spence (Ed.), *Achievement and achievement motivation* (pp. 75-146). San Francisco, CA: W.H. Freeman.

Guthrie, J. T., & Wigfield, A. (2000). Engagement and motivation in reading. In M. Kamil & P. Mosenthal (Eds.), *Handbook of reading research* (Vol 3: pp. 403-422). Mahwah, NJ: Lawrence Erlbaum Associates.

Miles, R. E., & Snow, C. C. (1996). Twenty-first century careers. In M. B. Arthur & D. M. Rousseau (Eds.), *The boundaryless career* (pp.97-115). New York: Oxford University Press.

Richardson, P. W., & Watt, H. M. G. (2006). Who chooses teaching and why? Profiling characteristics and motivations across three Australian universities. *The Asia-Pacific Journal of Teacher Education, 34*(1), 27-56).

Richardson, P. W., & Watt, H. M. G. (2005). "I've decided to become a teacher": Influences on career change. *Teaching and Teacher Education, 21*(5), 475-489.

US Department of Labor Employment and Training Administration. (1998). *O*NET: The occupational information network*. Washington, DC: US Government Printing Office.

Watt, H. M. G., & Richardson, P. W. (In review). *Motivational factors influencing teaching as a career choice: Development and validation of the 'FIT-Choice' Scale.*

Wigfield, A., & Eccles, J. S. (2000). Expectancy-value theory of achievement motivation. *Contemporary Educational Psychology, 25*, 68-81.

Helen M.G. Watt
Paul W. Richardson

Faculty of Education
Monash University

Nicole M.Tysvaer
School of Education
University of Michigan

ROSEMARY VIETE AND ELEANOR PEELER

11. RESPECTFUL ENCOUNTERS

Valuing Each Other in Teacher Professional Learning Contexts

In class I always lived
Outside the minds of Others,
Invisible.
How things can change,
A word, a smile
Lend me a place to stay

INTRODUCTION

There is an edge in these voices, a desire. They are the words of students who wish to join a professional community. Their desire is to be respected for what they bring to that community and for the kinds of teachers they are becoming. This chapter is about the students whose words have been used in the poem. It is a chapter about belonging, becoming and being respected.

Respect may seem a fuzzy concept that is so overused that it is empty of meaning. Nevertheless, it is an ethical principle we feel is central to our efforts to shape positive learning spaces for learner teachers. Through stories of learner teachers' experiences of respectful encounters – and not so respectful ones – in their professional learning, and by interpreting these through theory on ethical interactions with others, we hope to indicate how we as teachers of new teachers can ourselves learn about ways of supporting their learning. In this sense the chapter discusses the "learning for all" invoked by Carroll and Ryan (2005). The learner teachers we discuss in particular come from cultural and linguistic backgrounds that form part of Australian society, yet are not dominant in our education system. They are also mainly international students with some local student representation, and are enrolled in postgraduate pre-service teacher preparation courses at a university in Victoria. Because these learner teachers study for only a single academic year after they have completed at least one full undergraduate degree, their efforts to achieve success must be resolute and intense. They need to be well supported in these efforts, certainly. They are also potential resources for the learning of their local peers and their teacher educators. The learning of all participants in this professional learning course can be deeply affected by the ways in which we are – or are not – attentive, responsive and respectful to each other.

A. Berry, A. Clemans and A. Kostogriz (Eds.), Dimensions of Professional Learning: Professionalism, Practice and Identity, 177–190. © *2007 Sense Publishers. All rights reserved.*

This chapter presents learner teachers' accounts of 'small' events in classes and schools, sometimes single interactions, which nevertheless impacted greatly on their learning. The stories have been written by us, the authors, from the descriptions offered in focus group interviews by 18 international students who attended our study groups, which complement the learning opportunities offered by formal classes and professional experience in school settings and which focus on language and cultural issues arising in the course. The focus groups were small but numerous, since they needed to be arranged at times that suited different students' commitments. This also allowed for greater opportunities for the learner teachers to each voice their opinions. Since students were very familiar with each other from the study groups, and were able to choose who they would attend with, they seemed to interact freely and disagreed and agreed openly with each other. Participation was active, and turntaking was enthusiastic but, they felt, respectful. In addition to engagement in the focus groups, students were invited to do some reflective writing on their experiences in and feelings about the course and the support activities.

We asked our learner teachers to tell us, with "affective colorations" (Prior, 2001, p. 59), about the kinds of interactions that helped them feel positive about themselves in their new professional spaces, and about those that affected them less positively. The stories we reconstructed from interview data and the learner teacher voices reflect the ways our own activities and those of other staff and students help these learner teachers experience a sense of becoming, belonging and being respected in the professional learning spaces of the course.

BELONGING, BECOMING AND BEING RESPECTED

The learner teachers' accounts of their experiences focus primarily on the opportunities they have to feel part of their targeted community. Kanno and Norton (2003, p. 241) point out the importance of the emotional investment learners have in their engagement in professional learning spaces, desirous as they are of belonging to their 'imagined community'. The issue of agency, closely linked as it is with the relations of power in the various spaces of the teacher education course is integral to students' sense of belonging to the community of learner teachers, of becoming members of the professional community of teachers and of being respected for their knowledge and skills. Learner teachers need to feel they can play a part in having their differences – and similarities – with others positively recognized and contribute to an expansion for all of the notion of who can be a teacher.

Belonging

Nao's two stories retold below are of exclusion and inclusion, of being rendered impotently inaudible and respectfully visible.

> ### Nao's story of exclusion – retold
>
> *Today's session was on multiculturalism and all the other 'isms' – pluralism, essentialism ... racism. She sat there, waiting, fearing, her breath held in anticipation. Surely the lecturer would ask her what it was like to be seen as visibly different, to be racialised, to be essentialised as belonging to a non-existent unity, an 'Asian', not an individual. Surely that was a topic she would be seen as having stories about. Hadn't she heard a friend being told by another student (also becoming a teacher) to 'get an Aussie accent', and hadn't someone hissed at her on the tram, to 'go home' as if they knew better where she belonged than she did herself?*
>
> *A classmate exclaimed in frustration: "Well, I'm not racist, but those students from Asia need to learn how to do critical thinking and stuff, 'cos they just learn passively, you know, so we have to help them".*
>
> *The discussion was energizing the class; they all had stories to tell and crowded all the spaces with their words – even the lecturer gave examples. But there was no silence she could fill, no patient moment for her to find voice, no-one who wanted to hear.*

The issue of belonging in classes in the course and in the school community was an important theme in the interviews. Much of the focus group discussions centred on **being included or excluded** in relation to teachers, peers, supervising teachers, school staff, and less frequently, school students.

Feelings of exclusion were expressed as being ignored, isolated, marginalized, or simply as feeling distanced. About some classes at university, Samy stated that when working with other students, *"sometimes I feel that I'm sort of being left out in the discussion and I have no idea what they're talking about, they didn't even ask me whether or not I understood what they're talking about, so I'm feeling like, can I be part of the conversation rather than **being isolated**?!"* Nao described this in one of her subjects: *"I feel that I'm really a **minority** in the classroom, and quite often I'm ignored"*. She was particularly upset about what she regarded as being actively omitted, by lecturer and peers alike, from discussion on topics about which she had expert, insider knowledge: *"We are about 5 or 6 international students. It's a lot! She ignores us for the whole two hours. It's a lot. Multiculturalism, social background, **it's all about us**! And we are **ignored**."* Satoko ascribed her feelings of *"being **a bit behind**, a bit marginalized ... just a little bit **isolated**, **marginalized**"* to her feeling that *"some teachers like to keep a **distance** between students and themselves, and in that way I feel very strongly that I am different from local students and I need to put more effort to participate in class, which is very different"*. Mei and Lin saw themselves as clearly unrepresented in lectures. This, they said, was because of the orientation of content to the Australian context.

Rei on the other hand indicated that she perceived her peers' kind intentions toward her, but still felt discomfort because *"They're trying to understand me, but some of them don't know how to, how to communicate with me ... probably ... they just feel strange. Some of them never talked to overseas students"*. Her experiences of belonging involved herself imagining the Other imagining her as Other. It was the distance of being seen and thinking about herself as Other that held belonging at bay.

For many (e.g., Rei, Asako, Samy, Satoko, Mei and Lin), feeling excluded also related to the fear that others would regard them as **less intelligent** than other students because they remained silent in class, or could not express their ideas as fully as they would have in their first language. Their ways of seeing themselves are socially relational, and language was seen as a negative marker of their belonging.

Exclusion, distance and othering are not the only themes in students' stories, however. They speak warmly of inclusive practices.

Nao's story of inclusion – retold

It was a nerve-wracking experience going into the staffroom. She knew it well from the first teaching round where she'd huddled in a corner without even a glance from anyone. Other student teachers had also been there, to her relief, but just the language teaching ones. It was as if they were second class citizens. Would this be the same? It could be much scarier! It was a bigger school and a 'richer' one too. Jimmy, her supervising teacher met her at the door to the staff room, shooed her in and took her to where some teachers were getting their morning tea. He introduced her by name (and by her status as a new student teacher) one by one to the five teachers – none of them were language teachers – and included her in the conversation they were having about the sports day coming up. One of them asked her whether she would like to help out. She was relieved that they didn't seem to expect her to know anything specific about the sports, but they clearly thought she could be good at organizing things. The five weeks ahead suddenly seemed full of promise!

Feeling included in the group was often the result of simple acts by teachers and peers, and also by these learner teachers themselves. For example, Satoko described the importance of positive teacher feedback in one of her classes when she was asked to take the role of Japanese teacher in a role play:

I had to say something from the teacher's point of view. Because I'm not a native speaker I couldn't say what I thought in my mind – a little bit less than that. I said [to the lecturer] my English isn't as good as other people's so I *couldn't say what I wanted to say. She said we understand that but it was still a good opinion, a good role play ... it's not about just the language issue, but it helped me very much. I **sort of found a spot, found a place in the classroom**, like **I could stay** in the classroom.*

Satoko made her concerns explicit. Her lecturer was attentive and appropriately responsive. This simple interaction built a new space for learning, and probably not only for her, but also for others in that classroom.

Asako showed how her peers explicitly included her in discussions: *"my classmates always asked me if I could understand what they were talking about and they asked me if I have got any opinions, so I could have a chance to join their conversation, which was really fortunate"*.

All of the learner teachers felt they were *"comfortable"* talking in the 'safe space' of the study group, though many of them experienced other places they could interact comfortably too. They characterized the study groups as *"relaxed"*, *"open"*, but confirming of *"direction"* (with assessed work), as spaces where *"peer support"* is readily available and the teacher *"cares"* about the students. Being comfortable meant belonging.

Becoming

Belonging to the community of learners is an important need for students. Feeling progression in their struggle to become members of the teaching community is equally important. The learner teachers trace the ways their interactions with others affected their sense of becoming competent teachers. It is heartening to see that these learner teachers see teachers as a community of diverse members. They do not homogenize 'teacher' and resist being positioned as members of a homogeneous group. This attitude is not always perceived as being shared by their peers.

A central theme for all in the transition to occupying the spaces of teaching is that of **confidence**. Clearly, as Jenny (a local student) observes, this is a common theme among all learner teachers, but it is particularly important to those operating in a second language and a new culture. The place where many local students feel safe, at university, is not necessarily a place where confidence grows for such students.

Rei speaks of the burden of not knowing what locals know.

I've just got so many things, so much information of teaching and what, and how, big responsibility and how difficult to manage a class. So many informations. My confidence is like this [holds fingers close together] and my expectations [holds hands wide apart]. But I don't think I'm the same as them, as local students. They know, they have experience of schools, but I haven't, and I don't have any idea of what will happen in schools. I've been in schools for just 10 weeks, so I don't know anything about school and my language as well and my culture, my background, everything is different from

181

them, so I have, not risk, but I have too many things, too many MORE things, that I have to think about than other students.

She talks of the loss of the confidence she always felt she had.

I never felt that. I think I lost so much confidence of mine. I'm thinking...I'm talented, I want to think like that, but whenever I go to tutorials, I feel like I can't do anything, so I'm not respected. Not always but...sometimes I feel that they're ignoring me. I want to, of course I want to contribute my idea to the groups, but I can't do that because it's too fast, and in my culture, I have to wait for them when they're talking and after that I can say what I want to say, but they talk and they overtalk and talk, so I can't find any chance to talk. [Responding to a question about the possibility of holding up a talking stick or a card] It's confidence to do that. I think if maybe my idea is not too good to stop everyone ... I don't know what they're thinking, but they might think that I don't want to contribute any opinions.

Rei has imagined the other imagining her, probably quite accurately. She recognizes that her peers may not want to pressure her, but this does not solve her problem, nor does it build her confidence.

Samy comments that in class, *"sometimes, if you have any questions regarding an assignment, sometimes you are not confident and don't want to ask the tutor, but in the study group you feel confident, you feel welcomed, respected, so you just ask questions. You know, so that makes us feel great"*. Asako points out that *"that kind of state of mind* [lack of confidence] ***affects my speaking of English"***. Others in the focus group agreed.

An aspect of agency in becoming a teacher in a new space is the resistance toward being defined by interaction that seems to position the student negatively as Other. Nao did not allow her students to see her proficiency in English as a deficit. If they seemed to comment on her English, she reported saying, *"What is wrong with my English? I speak Japanese as well. I'm a native speaker of Japanese and I speak English as well. I'm learning."* The flip side of this critical resistance is acceptance of new ways of working. Lin reported how she found Australians to be, on the whole, *"kind"*. As an example she explained that her supervising teacher had been kind to her in a very different way from that which would be used by a Chinese professional. The latter, she said, would do a lot for the student teacher, while the former *"tried to stand back"* to let her learn how to 'do her own thing'.

In his reflection, Samy professed the view that becoming and being a teacher was *"like a big wave"*. It was ever-changing, and *"it goes up and down (if you have a bad day, it does not necessarily mean that you will have a bad day tomorrow, and you will not always get a perfect class everyday"*. He said he used to think of teaching as a straight line, where one experience defined the next. After his supervising teacher told him that "tomorrow is always another day" he said he could see that particular interactions did not define him as a teacher, which allowed him to understand the space for his teaching as flexible and mutable.

These students' confidence and sense of agency in their own becoming was closely linked to their perceptions about the ways they were being respected.

Being Respected

Being respected meant many things to these learner teachers. They felt respected when they were treated as knowledgeable, when they were seen already as teachers rather than students, when the content included discussions of values and practices other than the local, when their right to speak about something meaningful was accorded and facilitated through teacher monitoring of appropriate grouping and turntaking, and when an international perspective was seen as requisite for good practice.

Being treated as knowledgeable. The learner teachers wanted to be seen as knowers, as intelligent, as bringing something special to the university and school settings. For them this was one aspect of being respected. However, they also felt that, if their teachers and peers did not understand or know about their cultures and values, they should at least seem interested and try to find out what was important, difficult or even taboo for them. Mei, Samy, Lin, Asako, Nao and Satoko all stated the need for their classmates and their teachers at university to understand and appreciate their cultural backgrounds. They felt respected in the study group, because the possibility of difference was acknowledged and diversity was explicitly discussed and valued. They most of all wanted teachers to draw on their knowledge and experience as resources in the class (e.g., on discussions of how racism affects learners), and to help local students without transcultural experiences to understand what it is like for people operating in a different language and culture. May spoke with delight about the class in which all the students with another language were asked to write something on the board in the language *"so that the class could see how hard it was to learn another language. It was great!"*

The knowledge they were seen to have should not of course be confined to the cultural, lest they be reduced to merely representing an essentialised cultural being. Satoko saw her supervising teacher in the school as being highly respectful of her as a teacher and knower of the English language (not just a student teacher). She felt her knowledge was respected and explicitly acknowledged in front of school students when her supervising teacher asked Satoko to correct her (the supervisor's) grammar. She was always asked explicitly for her view on teaching directions and was able to negotiate on these.

Being seen (introduced) as a teacher. Nao, Yuka, Asako, May and Samy all emphasized the importance of introductions as symbolic and constitutive of the way they were viewed (and respected) as professionals. Samy was upset at having been introduced thus: *"OK, here's a STUDENT TEACHER, and he'll be WORKING WITH US – (but not teaching you). So the kids didn't see me as the teacher.* He felt that *"things would have been different"* if the teacher had said: *"Here's your teacher and he'll be taking the class for the next few weeks".*

Grouping and turn-taking. All international learner teachers concurred that their treatment as knowledgeable, capable and intelligent in the learning spaces made available to them at university was heavily constrained by two factors, the turntaking conventions of Australian university classes and the ways groups were (or were not) arranged in these classes.

Referring to tutorials, Samy talked of needing *"time to think about what to say"*, *"structured time"*, while Rei spoke about how she could not *"find any chance to talk"* within the daunting pace of interactions and the dominance of the discussion by local students. Nao spoke of having ideas, but *"missing the time to interrupt"*. Yuka concurred: *"You know when you are having a discussion, actually some students asked me what do you think but I just couldn't answer immediately. They think oh she doesn't have any idea, but I was **thinking**"*. All agreed that wait time (and not simply what they felt was the teeth-grinding tolerance of exasperated silence) was an absolute requirement, but that more explicit assignation of roles in group work and some understanding and encouragement would help these learning teachers to feel their ideas were valued. Guidance in this respect, they felt, should come from teachers, and often did. Some mentioned the use of *"syndicate groups"*, which were groups whose membership was designated by the teacher, and which remained the same throughout the semester. These teachers usually assigned roles when assigning the task.

Jenny suggested that the problem of local lecturers and learner teachers not wanting to overburden international learner teachers with responding, or their inability to read the signs that one might be ready to take a turn, could be overcome by the use of a talking stick that would give in her words, *"a talking space"*.

Similar issues with group formation, group interaction and strategies to provide these have been discussed in the literature on teaching international students (see, for example Ryan, 2005; McLean & Ransom, 2005).

Being respected as language learners. A significant concern for international learner teachers is discrimination against their accented English. This causes extreme stress that can result in loss of confidence in their formal workplace contexts (Shergold, 1996). Such anxiety can make it impossible to continue to teach (Magazanik, 1991). Workshop situations can provide a forum for support and an opportunity for teachers to air their apprehension. It not easy to change an accent but some aspects of speech, such as word endings, can be addressed.

Our participants were concerned about their English use, but wished to concentrate mainly on fluency rather than on intelligibility and accent. They felt that much of others' attention to their talking and writing was focused on what they were not doing or had not yet learnt, and that this deficit view did not respect their achievements. They wanted the focus to be on their growth as language learners. Over one year, they felt they had come a long way, and indeed they had acquired competence in a broad range of demanding written genres previously entirely unfamiliar, and had learned to communicate effectively in oral English with a much wider range of people than ever before. Samy celebrated this learning as a great personal achievement.

Internationalising curriculum and pedagogy. Asako felt that the content of the course was too heavily oriented towards only local teaching settings and values, and rightly pointed out that the course should prepare its learner teachers for work around the globe, not merely in Victoria. She called for an internationalization of the content of the course, and suggested that lobbying for this would be an important task for us as support facilitators. Her focus group members concurred vigorously.

Much of what we have found is not new. Others writing about the experiences of international students have mentioned almost all of the experiences of isolation, positioning and intercultural disjunctions, as well as the many effective pedagogical strategies that ameliorate these adverse experiences (e.g., Carroll & Ryan, 2005). However, it is important to recognize that for all our good will and intentions, our international and migrant learners are still experiencing distress and sapping of confidence caused by both institutional and pedagogical practices that would benefit from only small changes in behaviour and thinking. Students indicate that the positive regard, the attentiveness and responsiveness to their own hesitations, the smiles in the corridors, the knowing of names, the invitation to be included on one's own terms, all make for happier interchange of ideas and growth of confidence. We need to learn how to show our value for each other more clearly. Concerted efforts among all staff, curriculum developers and school partners, as well as among all learners, are needed to ensure that the learning spaces are safe and productive for everyone. It is incumbent on us all to learn from our learners and make these changes.

RESPECTING THE OTHER: REPRESENTATION, RESPONSIVENESS AND RESPONSIBILITY

Many authors have discussed the vulnerability of learners from linguistic and cultural backgrounds that differ from those dominant in the new learning context. Ryan and Carroll (2005, p. 9) liken these students' experiences to those of "canaries in the coalmine"; their feelings about their learning atmosphere is also an indication of the healthiness of the learning spaces. This atmosphere, we contend, is constructed in the interactions that occur in these learning spaces.

How can interactions support and hinder learning? Why do we need to be respectful, attentive and responsive in our interactions and how can we achieve this? Our students' stories have shown us that these are important questions.

When we talk about our sense of ourselves in the world, we always 'are' in relation to some 'other' in our minds and perceptions. We are ourselves defined in our process of defining "alterity or otherness" (Hastings & Manning, 2004, p. 293). Levinas (1998) argues that to act ethically, and certainly to be ethical, we must inevitably and perpetually respond to the Other; our responses are 'commanded' by the Other (see also Atterton & Carlaco, 2005; Hutchens, 2004). Bakhtin (1986, p. 69) sees this process of active **responsiveness** as integral to all "real understanding". He argues that every speaker is oriented to responsive understanding, and thus "any utterance is a link in a very complexly organized chain of other utterances" (p. 69). And Prior (2001, p. 59), discussing Bakhtin, explains how this thinker sees discourse as being "never a neutral, anonymous system of referential meaning; instead it is infused with evaluative perspectives, affective colorations, and indexical traces of all kinds". Discourse or the utterance, Prior continues, is a site not only where "the personal and the social meet" but also "where the person and the society alike are produced", or rather "co-produced" (p. 61). In this way as we interact, we are perpetually in the process of becoming, and this always in relation to others.

This places a responsibility on us all – and certainly for teachers working closely with learner teachers as we do – for the ways in which we are responsive to others in every act of communication. Yet to be responsive in responsible ways we need to learn to be **attentive**. We need to learn more about how students construe and feel about what we do, and what others who teach and learn with them do, so that we can learn to be attentive, and help students be more attentive to the utterances surrounding them, and to understand how they impact on others and are themselves affected by them.

Linked to this notion of being **attentive** is Burbules' (1996, p. 6) call for a "respectful encounter" with people from other traditions and cultures *"on their own terms"*. **Respect** seems to require that there be an understanding that the rules of interaction are heterogeneous, that the terms of communication and knowledge are not one-sided. This requires an acknowledgement of difference, but also, as we see it, a **mutuality of attentiveness**. This mutuality is the central concern of Sennett (2003) who argues that being respectful of others on their own (cultural) terms does not mean remaining distanced for "fear of offending" (p. 21). Rather, it means forging a real "connection" (p. 37). This notion of **connectedness** as central to generative teaching/learning relationships is also proposed by Cadman and Hai (2001) in their discussion of "transcultural supervision".

We argue then, that the ways we are responsive and mutually attentive to each other as teachers and learners and to the texts and practices that we deal with in our complex contexts of learning, will shape the ways we learn and see ourselves as members of the professional community. We emphasise that seeking connections does not promote homogenising or essentialising discourses of cultural difference, but rather assumes heterogeneity, valuing it as generative rather than as marking out uncrossable boundaries. In our complex workplace, where institutional, societal and educational norms, values, needs and practices intersect and often collide, there are many challenges for teachers and learners moving among myriad social and cultural boundaries and experiencing the sometimes painful, sometimes generative abrasion of differences. For the process of teaching and learning to be a positive and generative experience for both individuals and the community, we need pedagogy that helps develop this mutual attentiveness, but does not ignore the context. To this end, we draw on the ideas put forward by Kostogriz (2005, pp. 202-203) who proposes a "critical pedagogy of space", one that actively promotes "productive-transformative activities" rather than ones working merely towards reproduction. His pedagogy in the "Thirdspace" denotes a dynamic process of growth and change. It is relevant to our understanding of what it is we do and should do as teachers of learners with different linguistic, cultural, disciplinary and experiential knowledge, and to our sense of ourselves in relation to others as writers, knowers and professionals.

As teachers and learners we work, learn and teach within institutional settings that are larger spaces where myriad competing, congruent and contradictory practices and values elide, collide, merge and vie for ascendancy, and where some seem to hold on to a static unitariness and others are marginalized and silenced. Kostogriz and Peeler (2004, p. 14) advocate an "ecological co-existence of differences" in negotiating such spaces and we believe that we must think and work more thoughtfully and systematically to promote an understanding of the value of diversity not only for the wellbeing of our students, but for our positive growth and the wellbeing of our social and institutional environment.

We learn best when we build on what we know, when we have confidence in our own ability and when we achieve some control over our own learning. Vygotsky (1962) has helped us understand that learning is a profoundly social activity. It is relational and essentially dialogic. Thus, being recognized and responded to as a knower is central to learning. If as teachers of learner teachers we do not explore, recognize and value the knowledge of our learner teachers and our own knowledge, and help them to do the same with their colleagues and students, then we may not be able to provide them with the conditions in which confidence can prosper and they (and their own students) can negotiate their own becomings and professional growth.

POSITIVE MANAGEMENT OF CHANGE: SUGGESTIONS FOR STAFF AND STUDENTS IN ONE-YEAR TEACHER EDUCATION PROGRAMS

We have explored how interactions in our courses can support or not the way learner teachers from other cultural backgrounds perceive themselves and others as acting positively in their learning spaces. We would like to reflect on how we as support providers might work with our colleagues at university and in schools to be attentive and responsive to our learners' needs and make a difference to these, our important assets in an environment of global movement and change. We propose strategies, many of which we all (teaching and support staff and learner teachers) already engage in, which may affect curriculum and pedagogy, support programs and the ways program and support staff work together to further foster the positive growth and respectful negotiation of identity and professional learning of all in the course (yes, teachers and other staff too!).

We emphasise the need to do these things collaboratively with all our students, so all can learn to build their professional identities in the new spaces they help to make available for themselves and others. In this way we can work effectively towards an ethical pedagogy of the thirdspace that promotes generative, transcultural learning for all.

Promoting an Explicitly Positive Focus on Diversity

Despite curriculum that emphasizes diversity as the source of opportunities for learning in schools, this value seems not always to apply to the professional learning context itself. We know from our students that it is important for staff to be explicit about their expectations that diversity be valued in their classes, and to model respect for diversity in their interactions. This means using teaching moments as opportunities for discussion about the positive aspects of using different ways of learning, speaking English in different ways (including different accents), speaking different languages, knowing different cultures, having different views about professional attributes. It also means helping professional learners explore their own prejudices (and doing this ourselves) about others, and help them/us find ways of re-educating ourselves about these. As support providers we feel it would be helpful to provide teaching staff with:

- Narratives about "how I learn" for understanding diversity and cultural influences in teaching and learning
- Englishes and International English – understanding the fallacies in the idealised 'native speaker' notion, and in the notion that accent equals language competence
- A collaboratively negotiated a list of 'Have you …?' ideas for all to use in classes (e.g., Have you learnt each others' names? Have you given positive feedback on others' ideas? Have you asked others what they think, and given them time to do so? Have you clearly negotiated the ways you should take turns in discussion? Have you made an effort to know your students' interests and expertise?). We could do the same for supervising teachers on teaching rounds (e.g., Have you negotiated with your student teacher how he/she would like to be introduced? Have you found ways of making your student teacher's strengths clear to him/her and others? Have you worked out with your student teacher ways he/she would like feedback to be given)?
- A reminder that when learner teachers map their own self-efficacy, they should be encouraged to consider their 'cultural capital' (Ryan, 2005), their knowledge and dual (or multiple) discursive competence (Kostogriz & Peeler, 2004).

Staff in professional learning programs are often drawn from the professional community on a part time basis. It is important that they are adequately mentored and oriented in the expectations of the program regarding respectful and productive interactions with and among students.

Promoting Equity in Classroom Interaction

Since sharing the talktime often seemed an insurmountable problem, we advocate more explicit exploration of group formation, group tasks and group interactions. To help learner teachers become more sensitive to other's values, feelings and needs in discussion role play tasks could be used. Moreover we recommend use of activities commonly known as 'jigsaw' tasks, where specialist groups and home groups are used to discuss different but related topics and report the diverse topics back, respectively. Such tasks give everyone a role to play. Matters such as wait time and thinking time could be explicitly negotiated.

Promoting the Development of Community

Students need to feel they belong to the professional community both at university and in schools. Organising places for community interaction outside of class is important, both for the larger community of all learner teachers and for smaller more specialized communities, such as study groups (staff or student-organised). Special lounges and designated rooms suit these purposes. Peer mentoring programs are also invaluable, but may need the official provision of physical and notional 'space'. Simple social events such as afternoon tea groups can develop the opportunities for learners to get to know each other as people rather than just professionals.

Internationalising Knowledge Orientation in Education

As a matter of urgency, we need to ensure that, while preparing learner teachers for local schools, we are also preparing them for work in the world, and are not encouraging knowledge that is narrowly focused. We need to use examples of good practice in teaching and educational policy from beyond our shores to encourage this broader vision. While our students may not all feel able to be sources of such knowledge, they are resources who may help us to think differently about matters such as intercultural issues in communication and interactions, approaches to knowledge, and understanding processes of learning. Without assuming any individual's difference from or similarity to others, we should encourage discussion of such topics.

CONCLUSION

In this chapter we have allowed our students' voices to demonstrate how important it is for all participants in the educational endeavour to be attentive and responsive to each other's conditions for learning. Learner teachers, teacher educators and support educators all need to learn from each other what constitutes interactions that are respectful of each other's professional (and personal) identities. This is best done in an atmosphere of openness, where assumptions are not made about others' views, but rather these views are explicitly elicited, discussed and valued. This has implications for changing the climate of classes from one of competitive argument and privileged knowledge to one focused on efforts to listen to silenced voices, to understand other perspectives and to foster the view that we continue to learn with each new interaction. It requires discussion among support educators and teacher educators too, so that we can come to a better understanding of our own professional work. Through explicit sharing of what makes us feel respected we can better enact our ethical responsibilities to build positive learning spaces for each other. The development of skill in respectfully encountering others in ways that value others on their own terms is not only a human responsibility as argued by Burbules (1996) and Levinas (1998), but a path to more effective professional learning. As teachers all, let us walk this path together.

REFERENCES

Atterton, P., & Calarco, M. (2005). *On Levinas.* Australia: Thomson Wadsworth.

Bakhtin, M. M. (1981). Discourse in the novel. In M. Holquist (Ed.), *The dialogic imagination: Four essays by M.M. Bakhtin* (pp. 259-434). Austin, Texas: University of Texas Press.

Bakhtin, M. M. (1986). The problem of speech genres. In C. Emerson & M. Holquist (Eds.), *Speech genres and other late essays* (pp. 60-102). Austin, Texas: University of Texas Press.

Burbules, N. (1996). Deconstructing 'difference' and the difference this makes to education. Retrieved June, 1999 from http://www. Ed.uiuc.edu?COE/EPS?PES-Yearbook/96-docs/burbules.html

Burbules, N. C. (1997). A grammar of difference: Some ways of rethinking difference and diversity as educational topics. *Australian Educational Researcher, 24*(1), 97-116.

Cadman, K., & Hai Than Ha. (2001). 'Only connect': Transcultural supervision as the 'Rainbow Bridge'. In A. Bartlett & G. Mercer (Eds.), *Postgraduate research supervision: Transforming (R)Elations* (pp. 215-232). New York: Peter Lang Publishing.

Carroll, J., & Ryan, J. (Eds). *Teaching international students: Improving learning for all.* London: Routledge.

Hastings, A., & Manning, P. (2004). Introduction: Acts of alterity. *Language & Communication, 24,* 291-311.

Hutchens, B. C. (2004). *Levinas: A guide for the perplexed.* New York: Continuum.

Kamler, B., Reid, J., & Santoro, N. (1999). Who's asking the questions? Researching race, ethnicity and teachers. *Australian Education Researcher, 26*(1), 55-74.

Kanno, Y., & Norton, B. (2003). Imagined communities and educational possibilities. *Journal of Language, Identity and Education, 2*(4), 241-249.

Kostogriz, A. (2005). Dialogical imagination of (inter)cultural spaces: Rethinking the semiotic ecology of second language and literacy learning. In J. K. Hall, G. Vitanova & L. Marchenkova (Eds.), *Dialogue with Bakhtin on second and foreign language learning: New perspectives* (pp. 189-210). Mahwah, NJ: Lawrence Erlbaum Associates.

Kostogriz, A., & Peeler, E. (2004, November). *Professional identity and pedagogical space: Negotiating difference in teacher workplaces.* Paper presented at the Australian Association for Research in Education Conference, University of Melbourne, Melbourne.

Levinas, E. (1998). *On thinking-of-the-other. Entre nous.* (M. B. Smith & B. Harshav, Trans.). New York: Columbia University Press.

Magazanik, M. (1991, November 30). Record award to teacher penalized for dedication. *The Age.*

McLean, P., & Ransom, L. (2005). Building intercultural competencies: Implications for academic skills development. In J. Carroll & J. Ryan (Eds.), *Teaching international students: Improving learning for all* (pp.45-62). London: Routledge.

Prior, P. A. (2001). Voices in text, mind, and society: Sociohistoric accounts of discourse acquisition and use. *Journal of Second Language Writing, 10*(1-2), 55-81.

Ryan, J. (2005). Improving teaching and learning practices for international students: implications for curriculum, pedagogy and asessment. In J. Carroll and J. Ryan (Eds.), *Teaching international students: Improving learning for all.* (pp. 92-100). London: Routledge.

Ryan, J., & Carroll, J. (2005). 'Canaries in the coalmine': International students in Western universities. In J. Carroll & J. Ryan (Eds.), *Teaching international students: Improving learning for all* (pp. 3-10). London: Routledge.

Santoro, N. (1999). Relationships of power: An analysis of school practicum discourse. *Journal of Intercultural Studies, 20*(1), 31-42.

Shergold, P. (1996, June). *Migrant women in the public service.* Paper presented at the Second Women in Migration Conference, Canberra.

Sennett, R. (2004). *Respect: The formation of character in an age of inequality.* London: Penguin.

Vygotsky, L. S.(1962). *Thought and language.* Cambridge, Massachussetts: MIT Press.

Rosemary Viete
Eleanor Peeler

Faculty of Education
Monash University

AMANDA BERRY AND SAMANTHA SCHEELE

12. PROFESSIONAL LEARNING TOGETHER

Building Teacher Educator Knowledge Through Collaborative Research

INTRODUCTION

The professional development of teacher educators is the focus of increasing attention worldwide. However, despite the growth of interest in their role, few formal opportunities exist for teacher educators to learn about their work as teachers of teaching (Lunenberg, 2002; Buchberger, Campos, Kallos & Stephenson, 2000). Research focusing on the nature of teaching about teaching that teacher educators might access is relatively limited (Korthagen & Russell, 1995), and examples of teacher educators as researchers of their own practice is a small, although growing, field (Berry, 2004). One consequence of this situation is that the professional knowledge development of teacher educators is generally informal, weakly conceptualized and concerned with *what* to teach prospective teachers more than *how*, or *why*.

The transition from school teacher to teacher educator can mean that while new teacher educators typically bring much expertise in terms of teaching skills and abilities, they bring little understanding of the different sorts of knowledge and skills required for their role as teachers of teaching, and the need to help prospective teachers prepare for "… an ill-structured domain where there are few clear right or wrong courses of action" (Mesa-Bains & Shulman, 1994, p. 9). Inexperience in their role combined with a culture of isolation in many faculties of education limit the development of knowledge of a pedagogy of teacher education (Korthagen, 2001). Teacher educators adopt a "telling and showing" approach (Myers, 2002, p.131) in which knowledge about teaching is delivered to prospective teachers in the form of stories, ideas and theories to be acquired and applied unproblematically in the practice context (Wideen, Mayer-Smith & Moon, 1998). Such a banking model of education (Freire, 1970), although widespread, is not helpful in influencing the practice of new teachers (Korthagen, 2001). One consequence of this situation is that transmissive approaches are perpetuated within teacher education. Teacher educators who choose to resist such a technical-rational view of teacher education face considerable challenges in constructing an identity and developing new kinds of knowledge for there are few role models and little in the way of published research.

This chapter explores our professional learning as teacher educators working collaboratively to understand better the relationship between teaching about teaching and prospective teachers' learning about teaching within the context of a

A. Berry, A. Clemans and A. Kostogriz (Eds.), Dimensions of Professional Learning: Professionalism, Practice and Identity, 191–205. © 2007 Sense Publishers. All rights reserved.

preservice Biology methods course. Sam accepted the invitation to be a participant observer in Amanda's classes to help Amanda to learn more about the ways her teaching intentions were interpreted and understood by her students. This collaborative venture also involved mentoring and shared development of the knowledge of practice through ongoing professional conversations about teaching. Our research arrangement was therefore intended to foster the professional knowledge development of each teacher educator that would "go way beyond a store of tips and tricks or the simple delivery of information about teaching" (Loughran, 2006, p. 18).

Driven largely by the concerns of teaching and the development of learning of all participants in the teaching/learning relationship (Hamilton, Pinnegar, Russell, Loughran & LaBoskey, 1998), self-study offers one approach to "unlocking the knowledge of practice" of teacher educators (Loughran, 2006, p. 7) in order to "yield knowledge of practice" (Dinkelman, 2003, p. 9). Hence, self-study is useful for both informing the practice of individual teacher educators and in contributing to and developing, a professional knowledge base of teacher education, and was clearly an attractive methodology for this study.

RESEARCH APPROACH

The research reported in this chapter was conducted over one academic year (2005), within a Biology methods subject of 25 students. The teacher education program at Monash University requires students to undertake studies in two methods areas as well as foundation subjects related to Teaching, Learning and Assessment; Professional Issues and Educational Contexts. Students also complete two five-week practica at two different schools. In terms of assessment, foundation subjects are graded, while methods subjects are ungraded, i.e., Pass/Fail grade only; a deliberate decision taken to encourage prospective teachers to explore different approaches to teaching and learning.

The main purpose for this study was to investigate how a tension experienced by teacher educators, between "telling and growth" (Berry, 2004), might be better understood and managed in teaching and learning about teaching. The tension of "telling and growth" is one of a series of tensions that dominate the everyday work of teacher educators who choose to challenge traditional technical-rational models of learning to teach. The notion of tensions captures the sense of ambiguity and struggle experienced by teacher educators as they learn to recognize and manage different competing pedagogical demands in their work. The tension between "telling and growth'" arises out of teacher educators' competing needs to 'tell' prospective teachers what they need to know about teaching while also acknowledging the important task of helping prospective teachers to 'grow', through providing experiences for learning about teaching for themselves.

The study described in this chapter aimed to explore the tension between "telling and growth" from the perspectives of the teacher educator (Amanda) teaching the class (through planning, teaching and reflecting post teaching), prospective teachers (in interpreting the teacher educator's aims for their learning, and possible impact on their approach to teaching) and a teacher educator colleague (Sam) who acted as a participant-observer in the research process.

Involving a colleague as a research partner is an important element of self-study as colleagues can "serve as critical mirrors reflecting back to us images of our actions that often take us by surprise" (Brookfield, 1995, p. 30). In this research, Sam's role was to talk with prospective teachers during Biology methods sessions about their experiences of their learning in order to gain a student perspective on how Amanda's intentions for their learning, as a process of activating and facilitating prospective teacher growth, were interpreted, understood and realised; and to act as a colleague for Amanda in interpreting, questioning and clarifying their various experiences of Biology methods sessions. In addition, as a beginning teacher educator, Sam's involvement in this collaborative research offered opportunities for her to consider her pedagogy as a teacher educator.

RESEARCH DESIGN

A variety of data sources were employed in this study to explore the teaching/learning relationship from a range of perspectives. These included:

1. *Participant-observation*: Sam attended Biology methods sessions (one 2 hour session per week) and talked with prospective teachers about how they interpreted the purpose/s for the different activities and their experiences of them. She made field notes that included a brief summary of Amanda's teaching approach, observations about student responses (verbal and non-verbal), and noted any other aspects of the class that struck her in some way as interesting or surprising. Importantly, Sam's role was to 'tune in to' the range of student experiences, to gain a perspective that can be otherwise difficult to access.

2. *Journaling*: Sam and Amanda regularly exchanged written journals to elaborate and explore issues that surfaced from our experiences of the research.

3. *Pre session briefing*: Prior to each Biology methods session Amanda discussed with Sam her intended aims in order to sensitize Sam to some of the issues that Sam might pay close attention to in her observations. (This pre-session briefing was suspended on several occasions after Sam had been surprised by considerable differences between prospective teachers' ideas of the aims of the session and Amanda's intended aims. Sam decided to test out whether she could discern Amanda's intended aims without having discussed them with her, in advance.)

In organizing the research, we were mindful of problems associated with teachers researching their students' views of their learning (Mayer-Smith and Mitchell, 1997). To some extent this issue was addressed through the structure of the teacher education program itself. Since methods subjects are ungraded the pressure on prospective teachers to tell us what they thought we wanted to hear was reduced. Additionally, Sam's ongoing presence in the class was organized purposefully so that she could "... get to know the students and to be accepted as an observer who had no … assessment status" within the class (Loughran & Northfield, 1998, p. 10). All student comments reported by Sam were anonymized. Conducting the research over a year also allowed time for trusting relationships to develop so that prospective teachers might come to appreciate that both Amanda and Sam had a genuine interest in learning about their experiences. And, just as the students needed to trust in us, so too we needed to trust each other, sharing and discussing feedback in ways that allowed open, honest, critique of Amanda's teaching. As we shared a mutual interest in the improvement of practice, Sam's feedback required honest and productive discussion and so any sense of personal criticism was considerably diminished.

RESULTS AND DISCUSSION

The findings are presented and discussed around three main foci: (1) Amanda's learning about how prospective teachers interpreted her aims for their learning and the insights she developed about managing the tension of "telling and growth"; (2) Sam's experiences of working in Biology methods classes as influencing her thinking about and approach to teaching prospective teachers; and, (3) Our learning about our collaborative approach to researching practice as a means of facilitating our professional learning.

(1) Amanda's Learning about Teaching: Intentions, Enactment and Interpretation

Two key themes emerged from the data with respect to Amanda's teaching approach and prospective teachers' learning. One theme relates to the complexities associated with enacting new approaches to teacher education, the other, to prospective teachers' expectations of their learning about teaching.

Intentions and enactment

The broad frame that underpinned Amanda's approach to her teaching was that prospective teachers needed opportunities to learn about teaching in personally meaningful ways, working from experiences and contexts that were relevant and motivating for them. Therefore, the emphasis was on creating an environment in which prospective teachers were encouraged to explore their own ideas, feelings and responses to different teaching/learning situations, to become more aware of their own development as learners and to take responsibility for their own professional growth; rather than relying on others (the teacher educator) to tell them what they needed to do and to supply them with a stockpile of 'fail-safe activities'. However, knowing what one intends to do and enacting these intentions is not a straightforward process and Amanda felt a continuing sense of uncertainty about balancing her responsibilities in supporting prospective teachers' needs and encouraging them to think of themselves as sources of knowledge about teaching. An extract from her journal illustrates this point:

I was keen to get them to construct their own knowledge about teaching from their experiences of teaching ... I see this as an empowering activity – they DO know stuff that matters. But do they think of it as empowering? Maybe they see it as unhelpful if I could be TELLING them what is right and wrong. I felt that strongly last week when Sam told me about how students felt that sitting around and talking about what they know could be done anywhere, anytime, what is it they come to uni for? ... I think about what are my responsibilities as a teacher educator and how do students view their part in the learning to teach process. I DO need to help them feel like I am 'giving' them things that they want but I am trying to create an environment where they can start to learn what they need ... and ways to fulfil [that] themselves. (Amanda, Journal, 21/03/05)

Learning to help learners to trust themselves and to look to themselves to develop their professional knowledge demands new forms of teacher educator expertise both in constructing and managing the learning environment. Feelings of self-doubt and vulnerability accompany the development of expertise as new situations are apprehended and responded to by the teacher educator. Sam was important in terms of personal support and in providing immediate access to prospective teachers' experiences of sessions that we could discuss and then consider ways of responding to consistent within the broader goals for prospective teachers' learning. For example, early in the year Sam learnt from her in-class conversations about some of the prospective teachers' 'need for notes'.

I [Sam] was shocked at the next comment, "We want more notes". They want to leave class with something concrete. I questioned them on the notes. "Do you think you will learn if you have notes?" They knew the implications associated with this question and responded by suggesting, "It is what we are used to from our degrees." (Sam, Field notes, March 14, 2005)

Sam's insights into these students' needs led Amanda to respond by modifying subsequent methods sessions, so as to incorporate more tangible products for students to take away, such as notes, but that were constructed using student input, rather than delivered 'pre-prepared' to students. In this way, Amanda attempted to balance the needs of her students with her goals for their learning. This example also illustrates the organic nature of the collaboration. New insights informed practice, as problems could be recognized, shared, and new alternatives trialed.

Intention and interpretation

As Northfield discovered (Loughran & Northfield, 1996), exploring individual learners' views of their experiences of learning raises a complex array of factors that impact the nature of the learning experience. Amanda and Sam also came to recognize the powerful influence of some of these factors and their unexpected effects as they sought to develop prospective teachers' understandings of teaching. Amanda felt that prospective teachers should know the reasoning behind her approach to teaching in Biology methods. Students needed to know why they were doing particular tasks and how these fitted into a broader picture of learning about teaching. So, in addition to explaining the aims for each activity, a whole group debrief was held at the end of each session to discuss participants' experiences of the session and to link the activities with different dimensions of knowledge about teaching in terms of: understandings of the specific biology content; structure of the pedagogical approach; feelings as a learner participating in an activity; and, implications for teaching arising from the different perspectives raised through the learning experience. Hence, there was a deliberate focus on making explicit the different elements that comprise a teaching/learning experience and their interconnections.

Despite Amanda's best intentions to make these goals explicit, prospective teachers' experiences of methods sessions revealed a different story. Sam's conversations with class members showed that a number of them regularly struggled to explain the aim of any particular activity beyond 'learning how to do [that] activity' or 'learning [specific biology] content', while others were not able to articulate any purpose at all for an activity ("… when I [Sam] asked one group the purpose of the activity … they came out and said they had no idea of Mandi's purpose for the task." – week 3). Rarely did students identify aims related to self-understanding as a learner or how a particular experience might influence practice as a beginning teacher. It was not for lack of frequent reminders either:

> Umpteen times during the session today, Mandi explicitly talked to the students about the model they had brought in. The focus was for them to have something to use to practice explaining something. When I asked several students why they did the activity their response was to help them in their teaching practice. None of them mentioned [learning about giving] explanations … (Sam, Field notes, April 4, 2005)

At the time, this finding surprised and frustrated us. What seemed self-evident as a way to support students' learning did not impact learning in the way we anticipated. In hindsight, reasons for this outcome are more obvious, but then, we did not recognize the influence of several important factors at work. These include prospective teachers' views of themselves as learners, the learning context, and understandings of 'telling', in the tension between telling and growth.

Prospective teachers' views of self as learner.   Prospective teachers carry strong views about themselves as learners and these views inevitably influence how they behave as learners (and later, as teachers). Learners accustomed to a transmission approach to teaching, where the learner occupies a passive dependent, uninformed role do not expect to know the purposes for their learning because the teacher is responsible for decisions about what to learn and how to learn it (Baird & Northfield, 1992). Learning is simply a matter of doing what the teacher says. It is only when the learner is active in the process of learning that she needs to know the purpose/s of the learning in order to make sense of those purpose/s and to control the learning process. For those prospective biology teachers whose self-perception was that of passive learner, Amanda's explanations were just another part of the classroom routine, but not something that required active attention.

Contextual influences. Many prospective teachers worry about the adequacy of their subject matter knowledge for teaching and/or the need to feel equipped with sufficient activities to be successful in the classroom. Concerns about personal adequacy as a teacher may, at least temporarily, override the capacity to consider more complex issues about teaching and learning, such as the relationship between what is learnt and how it is learnt. For these prospective biology teachers about to embark on their first experiences of teaching, and teaching a senior, externally assessed science subject, their primary concerns were (initially), focused around knowing the biology content well and having ways to teach it. Hence it was likely that these priorities were uppermost in their thinking when they talked with Sam about the purposes for different activities.

New understandings of "telling and growth". An additional factor influencing prospective teachers' learning about the aims for each session can be linked with the teaching approach employed. Although Amanda recognized that supplying knowledge about *teaching* to prospective teachers was not helpful, at the time she did not recognize that telling prospective teachers the aims for the various activities and expecting them to internalize them was another, more subtle variation of the same act since the "transfer problem" (Korthagen, 2001, p. 5) was again at work. Prospective teachers did not passively absorb Amanda's aims as their own; they constructed their own meanings for their various experiences based on their expectations as learners and their priorities in the learning context.

Sam's feedback helped Amanda to recognize that a problem existed, since it had appeared to Amanda that prospective teachers did mostly recognize her intended aims and their broader connections. In hindsight however, it was perhaps the voices of a dominant few who had influenced Amanda's thinking about the progress of the whole group. This learning through practice illustrates the subtle ways in which teachers can be blind to aspects of practice that contradict their beliefs.

These two examples from Amanda's practice (described above) highlight different ways of recognizing and responding to problems of practice as a teacher educator. In the first example, Amanda, with Sam's help, recognized a problem (that students wanted a tangible knowledge product) and was able to act on it. In the second example, recognizing the problem did not help in knowing how to act to address it at the time. We needed to develop a deeper understanding of the complex nature of the problem, an understanding that may well be only possible through researching practice.

Developing more sophisticated knowledge of practice through the research process impacts how we choose to respond to similar problems in future teaching. In this case, being explicit about one's purposes as a teacher educator is clearly important, but it is also not enough. Prospective teachers need time and encouragement to develop new understandings of learning and teacher educators need to watch for instances where prospective teachers' habits as learners can also be raised as experiences for discussion, thus impacting more personally on the learning process.

(2) Sam's Learning about Practice: Experience, Relationships and Reflection

A second area of focus relates to Sam's experiences of our collaborative research and its impact on her understandings of, and approach to, teacher education. For Sam, three key aspects were highlighted through the data: the role of experience in learning to teach; the influence of relationships in teaching; and, the value of reflection as a tool for learning.

The role of experience

From her conversations with students, Sam came to recognize the importance of particular skills required by the teacher educator, such as being explicit in instruction and identifying goals for prospective teachers' learning so as to reduce learner confusion and improve learning. However, she also came to acknowledge that no matter how clear and explicit the explanations of the teacher educator, there were some things that prospective teachers could not 'hear' until they had sufficient, relevant experiences. She reflected on this idea in her journal, linking her own experiences of teaching in teacher education with what she had learnt from Amanda's classes:

> I am discovering more and more that my aim to break down assessment tasks for my students to help them:
> understand how it fits into the big picture
> know what they need to do to fulfill criteria [assessment tasks]
> see the usefulness of task
> simplify the thinking of what needs to be done
> can only be successfully achieved once they have made a start on the task. I have banged my head against a wall with this. I have worked hard to be explicit, for what?? To be still asked the same simplistic questions. (Sam, Journal, May 24, 2005)

Sam recognized that it is only through stepping into an experience that prospective teachers can begin to understand the nature of that experience, including what they need to know in order to genuinely engage with it. Yet, because they do not feel sufficiently equipped to begin (in this case, an assessment piece) prospective teachers resist beginning (and continued to ask Sam the same questions about how to start). Sam's insight challenges a commonly held view of teacher education that prospective teachers "can only act by first being told" (Munby & Russell, 1996, p. 1) and illustrates the Meno paradox that is embedded in teacher educators' work. Inherent in this paradox is a view of learner as dependent on the teacher to show the learner what she needs to know, an act that is impossible since the learner cannot see what she needs to know until she has some experience of it. Sam also came to see this paradox play out in her interactions with prospective teachers during their practicum experiences as they complained about not having been adequately prepared for the situations that arose in classrooms. Although this was not the first time she had heard these kinds of comments from prospective teachers, Sam now recognized their comments as an important part of the experience of learning to teach so that instead of feeling frustrated that her messages weren't getting through to her students, she now "reframed" (Schön, 1983) her thinking in terms of learning progress, as prospective teachers developed "a need to know".

Learning the language of teaching. Sam recognized that through acquiring experiences of teaching prospective teachers also developed more complex understandings of the language of teaching and learning. This language development process is important in 'decoding' the teacher educator's intended messages. From her experiences as a teacher/educator Sam had come to attach particular meanings to words and ideas about teaching that then enabled her to construct meanings that were consistent with Amanda's intended messages. But, because prospective teachers had fewer experiences of teaching, they attached different meanings to these same messages because their interpretive frames were different. Sam's realization, that learning to teach involves learning to speak a shared language of teaching, developed as she reflected on her experiences of working with the prospective teachers over the year:

> It doesn't matter what the focus of the lesson was, when I asked students what the purpose of the lesson was, overwhelmingly it was not what Mandi's intended purpose was. I feel that Mandi is explicit in her teaching but I have learnt that it ultimately depends on who your audience is and where they are at on their learning journey. No amount of telling will improve their understanding. I hear the message because I am an experienced teacher that recognizes the key words, terms, etc. This language of learning ... is a language that I am fluent in but our students are only beginning to learn, so only now it is clear to me of course they can't make all the connections yet ... It will take time and experience for them to become fluent and be able to speak fluently with us. (Sam, Journal, October 15, 2005)

Prospective teachers take on the words and ways of speaking of the culture in which they are immersed. This they tend to do automatically, unreflectively. Becoming aware of this is a step forward. Trying out new terms (i.e., reframing the situation) is another step forward and may, if sustained, open up 'new worlds' and provide new possibilities to act. The role of the teacher educator then, is in creating conditions that enable awareness raising and support meaning making for prospective teachers.

Relationships matter

Another factor influencing the process of meaning making for prospective teachers that emerged for Sam was the role of relationships. Sam noted "the relaxed, easy going feeling in the [biology methods] room" that was established "in a few short weeks" and that this environment seemed to impact positively on prospective teachers' levels of engagement. Although she had always believed that developing positive relationships was important to learning, Sam's reasons for her belief were largely tacit. Being able to articulate her knowledge, that the feelings of individuals matter in influencing the teaching/learning process, affirmed her approach and led her to consider how she might act to establish and maintain positive and constructive relationships with the different individuals that she taught, as a purposeful and deliberate part of her future practice.

Reflection as a tool for learning

Although Sam already used reflective writing tasks with prospective teachers to facilitate their learning from their experiences, her experiences of researching practice helped her to articulate and refine her knowledge about the value of such tasks and her role as teacher educator in supporting and stimulating the reflective process. Sam identified specific indicators that she could look for in prospective teachers' reflective writing to help her recognize shifts in their journey from student to teacher. These indicators included: being able to write in a reflective manner about one's experiences, being able to read through one's reflections and extract some of the embedded 'big ideas' in terms of how learning occurs for that person, what impacts on the processes of learning and what shapes one's pedagogical decision making as a teacher. Sam noted too, that while these indicators are important outcomes of teacher preparation, they cannot be told to prospective teachers in advance, in a way that is meaningful for them. Hence her role was in finding ways to support students to engage in the process of reflecting on experience, to prompt them to think about their own developmental questions and to find ways to search for their own answers. That this process requires time was another aspect that was confirmed for her.

These examples of Sam's learning through researching practice, like Amanda's, are rich narratives of the development of our professional learning and as such, accord with research reported by Boshiuzen, Bromme and Gruber (2005, p.16.) who state, "apart from acquisition and accumulation of declarative knowledge, individuals acquire expertise as they participate in episodes of knowledge application that are personally meaningful to them".

(3) Our Collaborative Approach to Researching Practice

A third focus in this research relates to our approach to researching practice as a means of facilitating our professional learning as teacher educators. Implementing our research approach was challenging in terms of accessing the views of prospective teachers about their learning and in the ways that we conceptualized ourselves, and each other, in the research process.

'Playing the game of learning'

Sam discovered that the process of eliciting prospective teachers' views about their learning became more difficult over the year, as the way in which they engaged with her seemed increasingly to take the form of a ritual, rather than a genuine discussion of their thinking. This finding perhaps relates to their strongly entrenched routines as learners that re-emerged over time as the novelty of our research intervention faded.

> Disappointingly, as the year wore on, they [prospective teachers] became more attuned to telling me what they thought I wanted to hear ... On reflection I should have asked them individually and not in groups what the aim was ... They would look at each other and answer as a group and support each other's answers ... Perhaps this is why I was feeling I wasn't getting anywhere. (Sam, Journal, October 22, 2005)

Sam's insights raise important questions for teacher educators. How do teacher educators maintain an awareness of practice and prospective teachers' responses to it so that all are not simply reduced to 'playing the game of learning'? In this situation, Sam identified that changing the approach she used may have 'disturbed' prospective teachers' patterns of responding and helped her to better elicit the thinking she sought.

Developing a research agenda around "telling and growth"

Having invited Sam into her class as a researcher, and as the initiator of the research project, Amanda needed to explain to Sam the purpose of the research and help Sam to know about her role in it. At the same time, Amanda was conscious of the tension between "telling and growth" at work in explaining her intended purposes. Therefore rather than prescribing the questions and the research approach, Amanda encouraged Sam to find ways to explore prospective teachers' views of the teaching that made sense to her. Throughout the year we talked together about the purposes for the research, discussed possible questions that Sam might ask the prospective teachers about their learning and approaches for so doing. From Amanda's perspective it seemed as though Sam had a clear sense of her role, so it came as a surprise when later in the year Sam explained some of the difficulties she had encountered and her feelings of uncertainty about her task.

Developing a researcher identity

An important aspect of Sam's learning from this research experience related to how she came to conceptualize her role in it. Initially, Sam believed that if the research brief were sufficiently clear then it would be a relatively unproblematic task for her to uncover and report what was required. However, this was not such a straightforward process. First, she needed to negotiate a new role for herself as researcher within the methods classroom. She noted her feelings of "awkwardness" in deciding when to approach prospective teachers and what questions to ask them. It seemed that her experiences as a teacher educator were not so helpful in helping her know how to act as a researcher in this situation.

It was not until some time into the project that Sam began to make sense of the purpose in a way that was personally meaningful to her and that she could then act upon. Just as for the prospective teachers, Sam's learning was occurring "in the experience" (Russell, 1997, p. 39) of the research. Reflection on her experiences, through discussion and journaling, enabled her to identify some of the indicators of her own learning about herself as researcher.

> When I first began the project I realize now that I myself was very much like what Mandi has written in the [research proposal] abstract: '... *One consequence of such a view is that preservice teachers expect that they will be told how to teach in their teacher preparation, so that they, in turn, may teach their own students by 'telling' them.'* I guess I thought that it would be enough to be told what we were researching that I would understand and make the necessary links, ask the appropriate questions and provide Mandi with ... [what] she was hoping to uncover ... I think that even [half way through the year] ... the intentions for this research project were still not clear to me even though Mandi had spent a lot of time discussing them with me. I relate this back to the abstract again. Until I could find the connection personally with the questions/data I could not relate it back to the purpose. I found this out by having to continually ask Mandi throughout the first part of the year "tell me again what I am looking for?" I would also ask her to generate the questions [to ask prospective teachers]. I can now see that I was doing this not because I am lazy, but because I wasn't on top of what I should be looking for. I felt that if I could ask the right questions (Mandi's questions) then I would be on the right track. I now think that this should be avoided in future [research efforts]. I now see it would have been far more beneficial ... if I had understood the purpose more ... I feel just like the students that don't hear our messages in our teaching until they have a need for the knowledge themselves. (Sam, Journal, November 14, 2005)

Sam's journal entry reveals a powerful formative moment in her professional learning and offers insights into the tension between "telling and growth" as it played out in parallels between her experiences as a new researcher and the experiences of those new to their role as teacher. In the same way that prospective teachers needed to acquire experience before they could know what they needed to know, so too, Sam recognized her own feelings of wanting to be told what to do by Amanda, but then later realized that this was not really possible. She could not genuinely engage with the purposes of the research until they made sense to her, personally. Sam suggested that if she had conceptualized her researcher role as one that included the notion of herself as a learner then it might have been possible for her to reach these insights more quickly.

> I now see that this advice I have been preaching to my own students is completely related to my role as researcher as well. I had to generate a need to know so that I could understand the purposes [of the research]. Funny isn't it that we spend all year with our students talking about learning, etc., and that not once did I see myself as learner in this research role. Perhaps if I did

202

I would have been more open to the journey??? (Sam, Journal, November 14, 2005)

Our experiences of researching practice together have highlighted the tension between telling and growth as complex and multifaceted, and operating in ways that are both seen and unseen by those experiencing it. For both prospective teachers and teacher educators, there is no recipe for professional growth; growth is about being awake to opportunities for learning and being ready to act on them. Such a view of teacher education entails new roles for all participants.

"Telling and Growth" as a Means to Constitute and Express Professional Identity

Deeply embedded expectations about the role of 'teacher as teller' means that withdrawing from this role leads to feelings of discomfort and uncertainty for both the teacher educator and prospective teachers. Each needs to reconceptualise their identity as learner/knower (Coia & Taylor, 2006) and learn to be comfortable "building a working identity that is constructively ambiguous" (Lampert, 1985, p. 178). Reconceptualising and reframing practice are active processes of knowledge building that will occur best when situations and experiences are real and meaningful for participants, in order to create a need to know. One example of reframing is in understanding aspects of practice as indicators of professional competence rather than as weaknesses or deficiencies (e.g., vulnerability, doubt), another is in rethinking what telling means in the context of teacher education, as telling in this context becomes redefined. Ambiguities and complexities become more apparent through investigating practice and self-study acts as an important vehicle for such investigation.

Teacher Educators' Learning about Professional Identity through Self-study

Through attempts to question and understand the complexities of one's practice, the process of self-study can assist teacher educators to more deeply explore their own professional identities and facilitate the growth of knowledge of practice. Self-study supports the articulation of aspects of identity formation and transformation with a goal of enabling change in oneself and others. However, enhancing self-awareness as a teacher educator is itself insufficient as a purpose of self-study, unless the learning about self also serves as "a foundation for change in practice" (Loughran, 1994. p. 156).

This research demonstrates learning about practice that impacted both at the time of conducting the research and later, as we reviewed the data and developed clearer understandings of our pedagogy and how we might enact it more effectively. While in some ways the learning for each of us was intensely personal and the knowledge developed unique to our own selves and contexts, we also believe that through communicating our experiences and our learning that we might connect with, affirm and encourage the efforts of other teacher educators who are similarly concerned to enhance their knowledge of, and effectiveness in, the process of learning to teach. Understood in this way, self-study offers a bridge between what can be learnt by individual teacher educators and how an understanding of the work of individuals can contribute more broadly to the development of the knowledge of the profession of teacher education.

REFERENCES

Baird, J. R., & Northfield, J. R. (Eds.). (1992). *Learning from the PEEL Experience*. Melbourne: PEEL Publications, Monash University Printery Services.
Boshiuzen, H. P. A., Bromme, R., & Gruber, H. (2005). *Professional learning: Gaps and transitions on the way from novice to expert*. Dordrecht: Kluwer.
Brookfield, S. D. (1995). *Becoming a critically reflective teacher*. San Francisco: Jossey-Bass.
Buchberger, F., Campos, B. P., Kallos, D., & Stephenson, J. (2000, May). *Green paper on teacher education in Europe*. Paper presented at the conference of the Thematic Network on Teacher Education in Europe, Loule, Portugal.
Coia, L., & Taylor, M. (2006). Moving closer: Approaching educational research through a Co/Autoethnographic lens. In L. M. Fitzgerald, M. L. Heston & D. L. Tidwell (Eds.), *Collaboration and community: Pushing boundaries through self-study*. (Proceedings of the Sixth International Conference on Self-Study of Teacher Education Practices, July/August, 2006, Herstmonceux Castle, East Sussex). Cedar Falls, Iowa: University of Northern Iowa.
Dinkelman, T. (2003). Self-study in teacher education: A means and ends tool for promoting reflective teaching. *Journal of Teacher Education, 54*(1), 6-18.
Freire, P. (1970). *Pedagogy of the oppressed*. New York: The Seabury Press.
Hamilton, M. L., & Pinnegar, S. (1998). Conclusion: The value and promise of self-study. In M. L. Hamilton (Ed.), *Reconceptualising teaching practice: Self-study in teacher education* (pp. 235-246). London: Falmer Press.
Hamilton, M. L., Pinnegar, S., Russell, T., Loughran, J., & LaBoskey, V. (Eds.). (1998). *Reconceptualizing teaching practice: Self-study in teacher education*. London: Falmer Press.
Korthagen, F. A. J., Kessels, J., Koster, B., Lagerwerf, B., & Wubbels, T. (Eds.). (2001). *Linking practice and theory: The pedagogy of realistic teacher education*. Mahwah, N.J.: L. Erlbaum Associates.
Korthagen, F., & Russell, T. (1995). Teachers who teach teachers: Some final considerations. In T. Russell & F. Korthagen (Eds.), *Teachers who teach teachers: Reflections on teacher education* (pp. 187-192). London: Falmer Press.
Lampert, M. (1985). How do teachers manage to teach? Perspectives on problems in practice. *Harvard Educational Review, 55*, 178-194.
Loughran, J. J. (2004). A history and context of self-study of teaching and teacher education practices. In J. J. Loughran, M. L. Hamilton, V. K. LaBoskey & T. Russell (Eds.), *International handbook of self-study of teaching and teacher education practices* (Vol. 1, pp. 7-39). Dordrecht: Kluwer.
Loughran, J. J. (2006). *Developing a pedagogy of teacher education: Understanding teaching and learning about teaching*. London: Routledge.
Loughran, J., & Northfield, J. (1996). *Opening the classroom door: Teacher, researcher, learner*. London: Falmer Press.
Loughran, J., & Northfield, J. (1998). A framework for the development of self-study practice. In M. L. Hamilton (Ed.), *Reconceptualizing teaching practice: Self-study in teacher education* (pp. 7-18). London: Falmer Press.
Lunenberg, M. (2002). Designing a curriculum for teacher educators. *European Journal of Teacher Education, 25*(2 & 3), 263-277.
Mayer-Smith, J., & Mitchell, I. (1997). Teaching about constructivism: Using approaches informed by constructivism. In V. Richardson (Ed.), *Constructivist Teacher Education*. London: Falmer Press.
Mesa-Bains, A., & Shulman, J. H. (1994). *Facilitator's guide to diversity in the classroom: Casebook for teaching and teacher educators*. Hillsdale, NY: Lawrence Erlbaum.
Munby, H., & Russell, T. (1996, April). *Theory follows practice in learning to teach and in research on teaching*. Paper presented at the annual meeting of the American Educational Research Association, New York.

Myers, C. B. (2002). Can self-study challenge the belief that telling, showing and guided-practice constitute adequate teacher education? In J. Loughran & T. Russell (Eds.), *Improving teacher education practices through self-study* (pp. 130-142). London: RoutledgeFalmer.

Pinnegar, S. (2005). Identity development, moral authority and the teacher educator. In G. Hoban (Ed.), *The missing links in teacher education design: Developing a conceptual framework* (pp. 259-279). Dordrecht: Springer.

Russell, T. (1997). Teaching teachers: How I teach IS the message. In J. Loughran & T. Russell (Eds.), *Teaching about teaching: Purpose, passion and pedagogy in teacher education* (pp. 32-47). London: Falmer Press.

Schön, D. A. (1983). *The reflective practitioner: How professionals think in action.* New York: Basic Books.

Wideen, M., Mayer-Smith, J., & Moon, B. (1998). A critical analysis of the research on learning to teach: Making the case for an ecological perspective on inquiry. *Review of Educational Research, 68*(2), 130-178.

Amanda Berry
Samantha Scheele
Faculty of Education
Monash University

ALLIE CLEMANS

13. MOVING BETWEEN HIGHER EDUCATION AND VOCATIONAL EDUCATION

INTRODUCTION

This account of professional learning is set within Victoria, Australia in a context which, at the time of writing, is new and unique. Stephen and Catherine are two educators who work within a TAFE Institute[1] and whose teaching has been shaped by contrasting influences. Both teach music and performance to adult learners. They both move between higher education and vocational education and training (VET) because for the first time, the TAFE Institute in which they work has diversified from its traditional vocational offerings and has been accredited to deliver a suite of undergraduate programs. This means that teachers like Catherine and Stephen now teach across vocational certificates and higher education degrees. This chapter explores their developing professional identities as they move between vocational and academic learning spaces in the one institution. Are they the same in each space? What do they draw on in each setting to guide their own professional learning and that of the learners they teach? In what ways do their professional identities and the vocational and higher education spaces they move between shape their educational practice?

I approached Catherine and Stephen to talk with me about their experiences of teaching in VET and higher education in order to explore how they approached their work in each space. Stephen has taught in higher education settings for 16 years and in vocational education and training (VET) for five years. Catherine, on the other hand, has taught in VET for 25 years and in an undergraduate Bachelor degree program for just over one year. I had come to know them as students in an academic program that I taught and later, through work I undertook for the organisation in which they are employed. This work involved my facilitation of a 'community of practice' for newly practising managers and educators who were involved in the higher education courses delivered at the TAFE Institute. My comfortable connection with both of them over three years prompted my request to interview them, with the purpose of beginning to document and tease out the issues that arose for them as they moved between VET and higher education. Their stories of professional 'becoming' (higher education teachers in a VET setting) form the data described in this chapter, together with my 'reading' of their stories. Prior to that 'telling', I briefly present some key ideas from the literature that have framed my reading of their stories. In presenting this in the section that follows, I flag some of the ways in which these ideas connect to their stories that unfold later

A. Berry, A. Clemans and A. Kostogriz (Eds.), Dimensions of Professional Learning: Professionalism, Practice and Identity, 207–219. © 2007 Sense Publishers. All rights reserved.

in the chapter.

LEARNING SPACES AS CONTEXT FOR IDENTITY FORMATION

The stories of Stephen and Catherine are not told with the intention to generalize beyond them. They do, however, provide a glimpse into an educational institution that calls on the inheritances of two distinct types of educational provision – vocational education and training conventionally offered within TAFE Institutes and academic and liberal education conventionally associated with a university. These two forms of education provision have been part of what are known as the 'dual sector' institutions in Victoria, that is, those who have a separate TAFE and university making up a single institution. This is the first time, however, in which a distinctly vocational provider (a TAFE Institute) has extended its provision to include higher education (undergraduate degree) programs.

This initiative presents interesting possibilities. VET necessarily privileges the workplace in the development of vocational competency. The closer it reaches to workplace simulation (situated practice), the greater the chance for learners to place workplace knowledge in context. The synergy between workplace 'authenticity' that is strived for in VET and the place of the conceptual and the abstract that is prized within higher education is given potential for realization in such a blended setting. The connection of the local and the universal, the particular and the general and the integration of theory and practice stand to come together in exciting ways in such a learning space. Yet challenges confront those who work with such an initiative and particularly so, for teachers who move between this and other learning spaces. These call on the need to distinguish the educational purposes of each setting, to select appropriate practices to achieve the learning outcomes associated with each space, to fulfil the expectations of learners within higher education and VET and those of the institution as they work towards the development of professional musicians.

The learning spaces of VET and higher education are shaped by different inheritances and these respectively mediate the expectations that learners, teachers and society hold of them. A learning space is not without social constitution and the identities of those who educate and learn within it are formed and reformed.

> Spatiality captures the ways in which the social and spatial are inextricably realised one in the other; to conjure up the circumstances in which society and space are simultaneously realised by thinking, feeling, doing individuals and also to conjure up the many different conditions in which such realisations are experienced by thinking, feeling, doing subjects. (Keith & Pile, 1993, p. 6)

A learning space, as it is taken up in this chapter, is not seen as a neutral location but one which is situated within a social hierarchy, encompassing human subjects who portray "... distinctive roles, capacities for action, and [who experience] access to power within the social order" (Harvey, 1990, as cited in Rose, 1993, p. 18). The social construction of space then opens up a set of issues around the forms which particular spaces come to assume, the functions that are deemed appropriate in that space, the nature of those who inhabit those spaces and the power they enjoy within and beyond those places. Treating learning spaces in this same way brings their social construction to the surface, allowing the constitution of identity and place to emerge as a focus in this study. If space is then socially and culturally constructed to accommodate those who inhabit it, spatiality is also a significant aspect in the formation of human subjects. It becomes possible to talk of an intersection between identity, space and place.

This becomes particularly important in the context of the vocational and academic learning spaces in which Catherine and Stephen work. Woven into their stories is evidence of a socially constructed hierarchy of vocational and academic knowledges, and an associated set of practices and expectations that are perceived to apply to each. Stephen and Catherine live out the traditions they inherit at the same time as they disrupt them in interesting ways.

The learning spaces of VET and higher education in their stories reinforce and refuse a logic that presupposes fixed, coherent and bound identities. The professional identities of Catherine and Stephen are necessarily fractured and bound into the multiple spaces in which they work. The forms of these spaces and the practices they encourage construct their identities at the same time as Stephen and Catherine work on and shape the learning spaces they inhabit.

Rather than assert identity as fully formed, Hall (1996) sees it as always in process, conditioned by the symbolic and material resources required to sustain it. The marking of the symbolic boundaries of identity rely as much on what is left outside the boundaries to constitute what is within:

> ... actually identities are about questions of using the resources of history, language and culture in the process of becoming rather than being: not 'who we are' or 'where we came from', so much as what we might become, how we have been represented and how that bears on how we might represent ourselves. Identities are therefore constituted within, not outside representation. They relate to the invention of tradition as much to tradition itself ... They arise from the narrativization of the self, but the necessarily fictional nature of this process in no way undermines its discursive, material of political effectivity, even if the belongingness, the 'suturing into the story' through which identities arise is, partly, in the imaginary (as well as the symbolic) ... (Hall, 1996, p. 4)

Du Gay's work on identity (1996) similarly reinforces the constitution of contingent identity 'in relation to that which it is not' (Du Gay, 1996, p. 2). The making of identities is therefore contingent on, and subject to, difference. They necessarily "emerge within the play of specific modalities of power, and thus are more the produce of the marking of difference and exclusion, than they are the sign of an identically naturally constituted unity ..." (Hall, 1996, p. 4). Hall highlights that it is only through the relation to the Other, to what it lacks and what it is not, that identity can be constructed. Borrowing from Bhabha, Hall asserts that the sense of natural unity most traditionally associated with identity is, in fact, a constructed process of 'closure', through power and difference (Hall, 1996, p. 5). Identification requires the adoption of a subject-position at the same time that the subject invests in that position (Hall, 1996, p. 6). The accounts of Stephen and Catherine provide insight into the fluid constitution of their professional identities. They draw on multiple identities – as artist, educator, performer, learner and professional – to shape their professional identity and inform their practice. Their experiences as 'working performers' are particularly significant in bringing a distinctive orientation to their practice in both VET and higher education.

Hatfield et al. (2006) describe the complex negotiation of identities among people working concurrently as artists and art educators. The experience and creativity of artistic performance strongly pervades the educational work of Catherine and Stephen, as much as their teaching expertise. Yet occupations like teaching, founded on a strong ethic of care, have struggled with the basis of their professional identity and recognition of their professionalism. Vogt (2002) explored primary teachers' construction of their professional identity in a context where "[l]ike mothering, caring for young children in schools is regularly regarded as a natural sphere for women, making monetary incentives or public tributes unnecessary" (Acker, 1999, as cited in Vogt, 2002, p. 253). Drawing on the gendered conceptions of caring, it was expected that caring within teaching would evoke connotations of (female) service, of vocation and being a 'natural teacher' rather than (male) professionalism, expertise and authority (Vogt, 2002, p. 253). She found instead that teachers' construction of professional identity revealed discourses of both femininity and masculinity. An empathic stance adopted by both Stephen and Catherine, driven by reference to themselves as performers and manifested in their need to prepare future professionals for future employment, is a dominant strand in the constitution of their professional identity and practice.

The work of Stronach et al. (2002) on the nature of professional identity among teachers and nurses is particularly instructive for thinking through the construction of professional identity. Their work is intended to conceptualise the complex nature of professionalism. Their research distinguishes registers of performance into two – 'economies of performance' and 'ecologies of practice'. Economies of performance referred to the quantitative indicators of performance (measurement, effectiveness, improvement), often externally imposed, but which construct reality for professionals. Ecologies of practice refer to the individual and collective experiences, beliefs and practices accumulated in the course of professional performance. Their research strategy sought notions that "caught the in-between-ness of professional work" as professionals faced and negotiated the dilemmas they met in their work (Stronach et al., 2002, p. 126). They propose that the 'professional' comes to be constructed in the process of living and negotiating the tensions between registers of performance. They argue that:

> professionals walk the tightrope of an uncertain being. It is important, then, for theories of professionalism to hold on to these notes of ambivalence and contradiction, rather than try to reduce or resolve them … (Stronach et al., 2002, p. 121)

Importantly, they unsettle the 'becoming' of the professional. They critique conventional notions of 'becoming' which tend to speak of a prior unity 'undone' or of needing to be 'done up':

> What is the unaddressed weight of that 'becoming'? It implies a prior wholeness, and illustrates a pronounced tendency of accounts of the 'professional' to seek holistic succour in a mythicized past, or a utopian resolution in some future state of imagined grace. We intend our story of professionalism to resist such holistic temptations …, and to … keep tensions and movement in play, rather than acknowledged and backgrounded in the same dismissive gesture. (Stronach et al., 2002, p. 114)

In becoming higher education teachers, Stephen and Catherine do not 'undo' their professional practice and experience in VET. Nor do they seek ways to add skills and capacities that will conform to what they perceive to be acceptable professional academic practice. Rather they move between the formative influences which shape their professional identities, drawing on and from a range of professional and personal experiences in their teaching work. They acknowledge the dilemmas and tensions they experience as their discipline area (music) struggles to find a comfortable place in both VET and higher education. They juggle and negotiate constraining and enabling contexts in the professional commitment they make to music education. In this process, they find themselves shaped by the VET and higher education learning spaces in which they teach as much as they remake these spaces to accommodate values they espouse and practices they prize. Importantly, however, their professional practice is less defined by the traditions of VET and higher education and more so by their own artistic identities and experiences. It is these they yearn to integrate in the educational experiences they create for their learners.

PROFESSIONAL IDENTITIES IN VET AND HIGHER EDUCATION

Catherine and Stephen found it easier than I naively expected to downplay stark differences in the professional identities they assumed within VET and higher education. Each of them confidently asserted that they were 'the same' in both settings. But it was the basis of 'sameness' that differed for each. Stephen defined himself as a "higher education specialist" and generalised his approach to academic teaching across both VET and higher education:

> I have seen the products of this institution (TAFE) coming through to university for some time, and they were very well trained. Frequently not thinkers … frequently though their training was so excellent that they would articulate reasonably well and then you could awaken those other sides of them with the 'what if' sorts of questions. A good higher education teacher is someone who can provide the students with the questions that will help them inform their practice for the rest of their careers. It is also to place students in the broader landscape of the world and help them to know how much more is out there. (Stephen)

The educational practices of Catherine, on the other hand, were shaped by her strong motivation to support and guide learners to 'make it' as performers. Her practical craft knowledge drove her teaching work in both VET and higher education:

> I am a very practical person. Everything is directed by this need to tell them what they need to survive, and regardless of what level I teach at, that is my underlying need. So no, I don't think about any theoretical leanings. I have an urgency to teach them in the most effective manner I can so they can cope when they get out of here. (Catherine)

Irrespective of whether they taught in VET or higher education, each brought their particular approach to both forms of their educational work. They did not compartmentalize these learning spaces but rather remade them to 'fit' the values and consequent practices that aligned with their identities. Infused into Catherine's work was a pragmatic orientation that focused on professional preparation while influencing Stephen's work was a more traditional 'academic' stance aimed at critical thinking and questioning. But seen, too, in Stephen's sense of professional purpose was a connection between critique and career such that his learners' future performance aspirations were always the reference point for his teaching. The pragmatic, utilitarian and work orientation that has long been consistent with vocational education and training finds its way into higher education teaching. Both Stephen and Catherine point to this in their accounts of practice. Stephen, however, has learnt to let the values and practices that are associated with academic knowledge production and critique to lead his work, and he recasts his VET teaching to accommodate this.

Remaking both higher education and VET learning spaces is not without its dilemmas for both of them. It is in these dilemmas that the relationship between institutional and textual forms of governance and professional identity formation is visible – both for how they constitute identity and how identity constitutes professional and learning cultures.

CONSTRAINT AND RESISTANCE

Stephen and Catherine work in an institutional space that is governed by regulation and a distinct workplace culture. These forces act, in some cases, to impose limits on their professional identity and practice and in others, are transcended through the professional determination of Stephen and Catherine.

Both the VET and higher education course environment at the TAFE Institute is highly regulated. National and state accredited training programs offered in VET are competency-based and are known as Training Packages. Competencies direct the learning outcomes for learners and, as has been written about, impose a particular regime on teaching practice (Clemans, 1996; Jackson, 1994, 1995; Edwards & Usher, 1994). Higher education delivery within TAFE Institutes is regulated by state government authorities who require strict adherence to, and consistent requirements for, accrediting and monitoring procedures. This is unlike traditional university-based higher education programs which are nationally regulated. The accreditation of new courses and the quality of their delivery is monitored at the institutional level. As such, Catherine and Stephen feel the impact of state regulation and a dominant 'audit culture' at the level of their professional practice. In addition, developing musicianship in VET through a competency-based training process is experienced by them as inadequate to convey the dimensions of artistry necessary for learners' professional competence:

> VET at the moment is in a state of flux 'cos we are locked into the Training Packages, which the music department universally hates... It is real square peg in a round hole sort of stuff. We are trying to fit these competencies into what we know as working musicians ourselves ... that students need to cope with in the musical world. And because we have been able to design the degree courses ourselves, there is more satisfaction in that because there is a better sense of direction in the content you are delivering. ... The minutae of the Training Package is very frustrating. (Catherine)

> And this is where we tolerate the language of description the VET sector forces on us but we know the competency issues ... When I first came here, I would come in every morning resolved to quit each day – the alien-ness of the culture and the hopelessness of the VET mentality! Then I would teach the students and after an hour with them ... once I had got them to where I wanted them to be, I would think "how could I ever think of leaving this?" And then I would have to deal with some competency-based nonsense and I would think again "I am leaving tomorrow". I thought the darkness and mediocrity would swamp me but in the end, the culture has changed and I have been part of that (Stephen).

Stephen and Catherine speak more readily of the impact of the 'audit culture' on their VET practice as the infancy of higher degree delivery in their Institute has meant that the cycle of audit and regulation has not yet been fully implemented and directly felt by teachers. As such, their higher education involvement is painted as a liberatory experience, removed from the regulation traditionally experienced in VET. However, it is not just external forms of regulation that constrain their professional practice. The insertion of higher education programs into a learning and institutional culture that has grown around VET provision means that affordances that are traditionally part of the professional culture of university-based higher education are absent. Both Stephen and Catherine long for the kind of professional development that would feed their disciplinary knowledge yet acknowledge the 'foreignness' of their expectations for themselves and of students in the current organisational culture in which they work. Workplace cultures, practices and norms around VET provision are understandably entrenched and do not always easily accommodate the construction of 'professionalism' and the professional learning of higher education teachers:

> I need to know more about the voice and information coming in [about voice] is changing all the time. I would like to explore that and go to conferences. ...

[It's] still a bit foreign plus we are teaching in both areas [VET and higher education] so my classes will have to be covered in both. It is still 'nose to the grindstone' work. We also teach longer hours and have a lot expected of us. (Catherine)

It is very very difficult to work in that sector [higher education] unless things are resourced properly. Support – technical and staff support – so that things can function properly [is not always available]. The quality of students – we have terrific students … but it is a constant thing we have to look at. We are placed in a market place and there are questions about the prestige of different institutions. When I first came and people talked about 'PD' (professional development), I naively thought it might be connected with music or art or culture or even education. Frequently it meant learning how to operate computer programs so we didn't need secretaries … You would ask about [inviting] visiting musicians and you would be met with blank stares. The physical location of the TAFE is part of it. The vocational setting, too. Just to get the students here to pick up The Age [newspaper] and read the reviews is hard work. (Stephen)

Competency-based texts, organisational culture and the physical and social construction of the VET learning space constitute a context that constrains the professional practice of these educators. But that is not the end of the story. Both Stephen and Catherine point to examples whereby they resist the constraint and remake both higher education and VET practice. Teaching across VET and higher education permits a fluidity of practice across both. Their professional identities as academic educators permeate VET. Given the dominance of Stephen's higher education experience as a significant strand in his professional identity, he explains how he succeeds in incorporating higher education practices of exploration and critical questioning with his VET class by engaging them on their terms yet journeying with them on his:

[W]hen … I started teaching in one of the VET courses, my first frustration was when I walked into a classroom of a theory subject and showed a couple of ways of dealing with a particular music or artistic question. I [tried to] … engage the students in discussion about it and I was getting blank looks, and ultimately someone very frustratingly said "Don't ask us questions, show us how to do it". It took me some time to deal with that. I hadn't had that before. So … I gave them a simple exercise that could begin in the room and could develop into an actual product in the session – 16 bars of music based on the numeric intervals of their telephone numbers – and then started to demonstrate how those things could extend into developing a larger composition, but that there were still many questions that could inform the direction that composition went in … not simply a 'colour by numbers' … I was still determined not ever to teach in that system. (Stephen)

Catherine's professional identity was undoubtedly influenced by the dominance of 25 years teaching in VET. Her short-lived but obviously powerful experience of higher education gave her a new perspective, as she challenged and transcended the constraints of the competency-based VET curricula that had previously influenced her teaching:

> I now feel free to express myself in whatever … terms I wish to … I am … now carrying this through into VET. I was sneaking into the habit of slightly dummying things down as regards language … I teach at the lower levels. Now I thought, "blow that, I will use exactly the same language I would have used originally". The Training Package is the fly in the ointment here. I will teach to the level that I can drag my students too. So if I can't get them past crawling … but if I can get them flying, I will. (Catherine)

Tolerating difference and demonstrating resistance seems to come from the hybrid status of music as the teachers' discipline area and its uncomfortable home in both VET and higher education. Stephen suggests that a university looks at music "… sideways and says 'but you are teaching people to make music, where is the higher mind in that?'" Stephen sees music as "desperately trying to prove itself alongside maths and science and coming off second best." Music within VET struggles, too, and has to "tolerate the language of description the VET sector forces on us … [which] has nothing to do what we teach" (Stephen). Conceptual knowledge and practice come together in music to nurture the capacity to create and the integration of these knowledges struggle to find a home in both VET and higher education settings. Recognition of this seems to generate a perceived 'community' among music educators in the TAFE Institute, united for a moment by their shared commitment to the arts. Catherine expresses it well. "One of my colleagues always says 'it is all about the music!'". This shared professional and pedagogical commitment rests on acknowledgement of its uncomfortable location in the learning spaces which they inhabit. Their artistic experiences, however, rest on celebrating difference between them. Between these, a sense of 'community' amidst difference is formed:

> But they [the teachers] are musicians and what they know is not necessarily informed by VET practice. What they value is the music itself. It is a mistake to view them as VET practitioners. They are teaching music within a hostile environment so that binds us as well. [Yet] we are all different in the arts. (Stephen)

ARTISTRY, PERFORMANCE AND PROFESSIONAL IDENTITY

The particular characteristics and orientations of the learning spaces of VET and higher education within a VET context do have an impact on the professional identities of Catherine and Stephen. They move between them with relative ease but are able to mark the constraints and possibilities they present. It is not, however, the exclusive or multiple influences of one or the other that can be said to fully shape their professional identity and practice. It is their current experience as a working 'performer', 'musician' and 'artist' that become powerful dimensions of their identity and they are carried into the work they do in both settings. It is their success as working musicians that acts as a significant basis of their 'professionalism' and which is woven into their teaching work:

> ... we taught them from our experiences as working musicians. We just have this double life of educator and performer. ... I would have said a few years ago "I'm a musician first". We, as experienced educators and musicians say "this is what you need in the world". Everything is directed by this need to tell them what they need to survive and regardless of what level I teach at, that is my underlying need. (Catherine)

> As an artist, we are what we are all the time ... That is difficult in relationships with what we call 'civilians' ... It is every waking moment. So your home environment is a work environment. My home is a bower bird's nest of all the paraphernalia and equipment and resources that I will use in all of my teaching. It is every waking moment. I problem solve in my sleep. I write lectures in my sleep ... I think what I am going to say about Mozart tomorrow at 2 o' clock in the morning. It is part of who you are and I don't know if there could be any other way. ... I go for a walk in the forest and I will be writing a song while I do that because the rhythm of footsteps will do that for you. (Stephen)

The strength of Stephen's identity as performer means that he is ambivalent at times about the scope for his artistry in the context of a tenured academic position. He chooses to remain a sessional worker so that he can maintain his engagement with industry as a practitioner, a writer and a performer. Catherine tells me that she has recently undertaken her final 'job' as a performer but in the next breath, she assures me that she will continue performing in amateur theatre. The artist never dies!

Their experience as artistic performers shape their educational performance. Catherine considers teaching as performance. Stephen recounts his preparation for lecturing, needing time to get into his 'role' because he wants his "... telling of whatever story to be as seamless as any performance". Catherine adopts an empathic stance with her learners, based on her recollection of the way she 'became' a professional musician and her educational commitment to prepare her learners for that work:

> I have a lot of sympathy for kids who come in with virtually no background ... They have some skills and no theoretical background. That is exactly how I started. I could do it, I could sing, I had a really quick ear so I could cover up my lack of theoretical background. (Catherine)

Stephen holds a similar nurturing stance with his learners yet advocates the intersection of theory and practice as an effective means for their professional preparation. Here his artistic and educational identities merge. His practice hinges on the recognition of a range of flexibilities needed of students in order to gain employment but, as he says, "this needs to be informed by broader ranging

216

questions". His empathy with learners is clear as he resists what he perceives to be a traditional university teaching stance of detachment:

> The way I see it is that as an artist, we have a duty to notice what other people haven't noticed and hold it up to the light. That is what an artist does. And that means helping people cross bridges, it means holding their hands while they do that, I have always prided myself on being able to work from where the student is toward whatever that goal is... I am not going to stand here like a detached university lecturer ... I don't do that. I guess the breadth of my practice as an educator prevents me from thinking in that way. (Stephen)

LEARNING TO 'BECOME' A HIGHER EDUCATION PROFESSIONAL

There were three ways in which Stephen and Catherine described the professional learning most valuable to the development of their teaching work in higher education. First, professional learning emerges through their own evolution and experience as musicians and this has been addressed in the section above. Catherine seemed to incorporate her professional experience wholly into her higher education teaching whereas Stephen identified that this necessitated slight detachment from this identity. Success in achieving this separation was, he says, a process of 'trial and error':

> In the university setting I had to be a little detached from that persona – I had to demonstrate the reading and reflection I had done around the subject so that I could give the students some sort of critical perspective. (Stephen)

Second, both point to the importance of role models as having significant impact on their practice in higher education teaching. It is easy to see the alignment between Stephen and Catherine's respective role models and the current approaches they emulate. Catherine describes her role models as "inspirational":

> The inspirational ones were stunning. [They are] ... encapsulated in the ethos of this [her work] place ... They weren't confrontational, encompassing, very friendly – they embraced us and had no ivory tower mentality. (Catherine)

The nurturing and non-elitist qualities Catherine remembers are those that guide her higher education practice. She is not able to clearly distinguish between her practices in higher education and VET. It is the priority of 'the performance' that shapes her work in both spaces. Stephen, however, attempts to distinguish these two learning spaces and reproduce what he perceives as the fine qualities of his previous educators. The necessity of critical questioning and reflection appear as significant dimensions of his professional learning:

> I have always had some great models to look up to ... I can think of one or two ... I can go and visit their studios tomorrow and come away feeling I know nothing about teaching compared to that person ... because of the fine focus of their questions, ... their ways of directing the student have evolved

over such an amount of time and thinking. And there are those that come and observe my teaching. So there is that sense of questioning and reflection that is built into it. (Stephen)

Third, it is their current involvement in postgraduate study that has influenced their professional learning. Catherine has drawn from the templates and formats she has become familiar with in the course of her study and used these in her own higher education teaching. Stephen has found the process of watching other lecturers instructive.

But perhaps the most significant professional learning for both lies in Stephen's recognition of multiplicity and juggling identities:

... We do switch in and out of roles. I was in a play at the comedy festival where I had to play six different characters, and I was very aware of taking them on and off again. I have some shows I do when I am only at the edge of the spotlight and other shows I do when I am very much in the spotlight. Every lecture for is a performance in that sense. (Stephen)

Working with multiplicity seems to come easily to both as they necessarily draw on a range of professional identities in the course of their teaching work. They have an appreciation of 'role-playing' in their teaching work and a feel for the ways in which, and the times when, these identities must appear and recede.

CONCLUSION

The accounts of Stephen and Catherine moving between VET and higher education spaces have surfaced the "in-between-ness" of their professional work (Stronach et al., 2002, p.126) and the professional identities they assume. 'Performance' is a term that resonates for both. It is intimately connected to their artistic identities and significant in the impact and 'authenticity' of their teaching work. It is their experience of performance as working musicians that is the basis for their movement between these learning spaces. They recognise the constraints and possibilities inherent in these and overcome or realise them through their artistic identities. While it seems that only an inchoate distinction of the purposes and practices of VET and higher education is evident, Catherine and Stephen may even transcend the need for making such distinctions in the first instance.

They are working in spaces in which entrenched hierarchies of vocational and academic knowledges dominate. On the one hand, they subscribe to these and recognise how they shape their professional identity. Stephen describes the difference between VET and higher education as the difference between making a "wedding reception band player" (VET) or the "complete musician" (higher education). On the other, they resist these binaries by learning to blend academic and vocational knowledges within both learning spaces. In the course of their work, both Catherine and Stephen experience institutional constraints which create tensions in their identities. Becoming an academic in a VET dominant workplace cannot be learnt simply by looking to traditional university practices as a point of reference. They learn to make their professional identities as they negotiate the tensions in their movement between VET and higher education. 'In-between' their compliance and resistance, both Stephen and Catherine recast the learning spaces in which they work such that the traditions of VET and higher education are remade.

It is their identities as professional musicians that intersects both learning spaces and takes them beyond constraints imposed by the traditional inheritances of VET and higher education. Their teaching in VET is infused with critique and borrows from higher education thinking. Their teaching in higher education brings an appreciation for, and incorporation of, theory, critique and performance practice. The professional and educational identities of Stephen and Catherine are fluid and powerful. These educators appear to work easily with multiplicity as they move between higher education and VET in the same institution and, in the process, recast these spaces to reflect them.

NOTES

[1] TAFE Institutes in Victoria, Australia are vocational colleges which offer a range of fee for service and government funded programs. These programs are a mix of non-accredited and accredited certificates and diplomas.

REFERENCES

Clemans, A. (1997). Competencies and adult education: Working the gaps. *Education Links 55.* (Winter).

Du Gay, P. (1996). *Consumption and identity at work.* London: Sage Publications.

Edwards, R., & Usher, R. (1994). Disciplining the subject: The power of competence. *Studies in the Education of Adults, 26*(1), 1-14.

Hall, S. (1996). Introduction: Who needs identity? In P. Du Gay & S. Hall (Eds.), *Questions of cultural identity* (pp. 1-17). London: Sage.

Jackson, N. (1994). Rethinking vocational learning: The case of clerical skills. In L. E. D. MacLennan (Ed.), *Sociology of Education in Canada.* Toronto: Copp Clark Longman Ltd.

Jackson, N. (1995). 'These things just happen': Talk text and curriculum reform. In M. Campbell & A. Manicom (Eds.), *Knowledge, Experience and Ruling Relations,* (pp. 164-180). Toronto: University of Toronto Press.

Keith, M., & Pile, S. (1993). *Place and the politics of identity.* New York: Routledge.

Rose, G. (1993). *Feminism and geography: The limits of geographical knowledge.* London: Polity Press.

Stronach, I., Corbin, B., McNamara, O., Stark, S., & Warne, T. (2002). Towards an uncertain politics of professionalism: Teacher and nurse identities in flux. *Journal of Education Policy, 17*(1), 109-138.

Vogt, F. (2002). A caring teacher: Explorations into primary school teachers' professional identity and ethic of care. *Gender and Education, 14*(3), 251-264.

Allie Clemans
Faculty of Education
Monash University

ROSAMUND WINTER

14. TEACHER LIBRARIANS: THEIR METAMORPHOSIS IN THE GOOGLE AGE

An Australian Case Study

"Well, I suppose everyone will laugh at the idea," said Genghis, "but I want to be a librarian. I was a librarian at school and it was the only thing that kept me going. I catalogued the section on Historical Villainy and Dramatic Explosions. But I'll have to get glasses first."

"You don't have to have glasses," Prudence said. "It isn't a library rule these days."

"Maybe not," Genghis said, "but you need to be able to read fine print. You see, I don't want to be one of those progressive librarians trying to make the library the centre of community life. I want to be one of those scholarly librarians working with old newspapers, diaries, and so on, tracing obscure facts and running mysterious dates to a standstill before they vanish for ever."

"… Genghis can do our research for us – checking out recipes, new sorts of gardening ideas, or even old ones that are nearly forgotten, or television things – whatever we need to know." (Mahy, 1981, pp. 35 and 37)

The children in Mahy's *Raging robots and unruly uncles* are discussing something central to people's lives – learning about new discoveries, old ways of knowing, television programming, recipes, scholarly archives, good novels to read. They know they will find access to all these matters of curiosity, entertainment and scholarship in a library in which there is a librarian, with or without spectacles. When we use the word *librarian*, an image immediately comes to mind – usually, in Anglo-Celtic societies, a woman with a bun, twinset and pearls. The librarian stereotype is pervasive, and while usually female, is always stern about rules, order and quiet. There are positive images of librarians, and their praises as opponents of censorship and suppression are sung in unlikely quarters (Moore, 2002, pp. xvi-xviii); but whatever the image we have, it is always of a person, and in an environment populated by books and people seated at tables studiously reading and writing (with pen or keyboard). Librarians are people connected with collections, bastions of free access to recorded knowledge.

A. Berry, A. Clemans and A. Kostogriz (Eds.), Dimensions of Professional Learning: Professionalism, Practice and Identity, 221–234. © *2007 Sense Publishers. All rights reserved.*

IMAGES AND IDENTITY OF LIBRARIANS

What does Genghis's image of himself as a librarian have to say about the professional identity of librarians in 1981? The notion of a library and his image of a librarian came out of a long tradition of written collections and their custodians. Scholarly and organised, their professional roles were realised in helping people make use of the collections they managed. At the time, theirs were collections of physical resources, and access to the information they contained provided through careful indexing, and, more importantly, personal assistance. In 2006, these collections are no longer contained within the walls of the library, and management of all the information to which library users have access is vastly more complex. Gone is the image of the scholarly bespectacled librarian who needs to cope with fine print. And gone too, perhaps, the librarian's own conviction that it is her role to intervene when frowning library users look as if they need help.

With the rise of the Internet from the late 1980s, and the promise of immediate virtual access to information, the words 'library' and 'librarian' started to become tired. In 1988, the professional association in Australia changed its name from The *Australian Library Association* to the *Australian Library and Information Association*. 'Information management' began to encompass the work of librarians. Libraries and their staff were now about access to information online and on disc, and the people who staffed them needed to show themselves to be up with the times. This meant distancing themselves from book collections, providing access to 'information' through being experts in information systems and web authoring. The rhetoric of the Google Age would have digital access as paramount, ebooks replacing print, all information available at the touch of a screen. This view, however, ignores the complexity of what it means when someone has a question and needs help finding an answer. For Genghis and Prudence it is quite clear – you go to the person who knows not only the sources which may provide answers, but also knows how to help you find a way to make sense of them. Google helps provide instant access to information, but does little to scaffold learning.

What matters about librarians is that they act as a bridge between people who are seeking resources (which may not be information) and the resources themselves. It is their personal expertise interacting with others that matters, their work as educators. In schools this is particularly important.

From the 1980s to the present, the work of teacher librarians has changed significantly, and with it, a sure sense of what it is that teacher librarians should know and be able to do. Professional knowledge and concerns which can be seen in the contents of an association's publications, play themselves out through individuals and their sense of identity. This chapter will examine how that role has been articulated over the last three decades in Victoria, Australia.

THE 1970s: AN EMPHASIS ON READING AND LITERATURE

Although training in school librarianship commenced in 1956 at the Melbourne Teachers' College (Ward, 1976), and the 1960s saw the start of a major building program, it was the 1970s in Australia that saw the investment of millions of dollars in the establishment of libraries in all government schools, and federal and state funding was provided for the training of school librarians – people who were required to have training both in teaching and librarianship. In 1976, over one third of primary schools had trained teacher librarians (Ward, 1976, p. 5), and there was a growth in courses in librarianship; between 1973 and 1975, 13 new courses were registered across Australia (*Australian School Librarian*, 1975, *12*(2), p. 4). There was a recognition that children as young as possible needed to acquire the skills to follow not only their own interests in reading, but also to learn how to investigate and report on matters related to the school curriculum. This was a time when schools, some even with direct student input, designed their own curriculum with minimal government syllabus guidelines. Students were encouraged to construct their own knowledge, and to do this, needed solid grounding in the research skills that would facilitate this process.

Teacher librarians in primary schools had as their brief both grounding in good children's literature, the design of wide reading programmes, the encouragement of reading for pleasure and grounding in the basics of library research. Information literacy in the primary school consisted not in knowing Dewey numbers, but in understanding different kinds of texts, and the way in which these texts and the library itself were organised. In secondary schools, teacher librarians continued to promote children's literature, although sometimes to a much lesser extent (because students were now learning a specialist subject, English, which included in its curriculum the study of fiction texts). They were also responsible for developing much more sophisticated information literacy skills and an understanding of the research process. In secondary schools, teacher librarians have always had a less clear role. In primary schools, they were specialist teachers; in secondary schools, all teachers are specialist, and in the absence of a clear 'curriculum', the place of teacher librarians has not always been clear. It was taken as a given that secondary schools needed a library, and that librarians would be needed to staff them. The first edition of *Learning for the future*, published jointly by the Australian School Library Association and the Australian Library and Information Association in conjunction with the Curriculum Corporation in 1993, sets out such a curriculum. Exactly how the library related to the rest of the school curriculum depended on the way the school community worked as whole, in particular, in relation to the extent to which students were to be seen as independent learners.

An analysis of the professional journal, *Australian School Librarian*, from 1974-1980 reveals something of the professional concerns of teacher librarians. In a listing of noteworthy periodical articles, the following categories were identified: Libraries and librarianship; Children's Literature; Writers for children; Audio-visual; Reading and readers; and Science material (Gregory, 1974). Over that period, about half of the articles are concerned with library development and management, and the rest with teaching and learning, and children's literature and reading. Similar themes emerge from an analysis of the titles of the short dissertations from the Melbourne State College graduate diploma students in 1977; papers concerning some aspect of Children's Literature make up nearly half the number. Of particular interest, as this is not reflected in the professional journal articles, is the number of papers (just over 10%) concerned with library users from widely varying ethnic backgrounds (*Australian School Librarian*, 1978, *15*(1), pp. 16-19).

In this decade, it is clear that while teacher librarians see their responsibility for the management of resources as important, and are concerned to improve their skills with unfamiliar items such as non-book material and the new audio and video technologies, they are most centrally concerned with encouraging a love of reading. Books and their use for pleasure and research are important, and librarians speak of selecting good children's literature, both fiction and non-fiction. They also start to show their concern as teachers, writing about the way students carry out relatively meaningless and poorly constructed 'projects' in which no real questions are set up to be answered, and for which there is an apparent acceptance of copying verbatim from books (long before plagiarism became such a concern in academic writing). It is not until the 1980s and 1990s, however, that they reveal the emphasis of their work shifting from librarianship to teaching more strongly.

THE 1980s: TEACHER LIBRARIANS MEET THE DIGITAL REVOLUTION

The professional interests and expertise of teacher librarians changed markedly in the 1980s. This was the period when computers were introduced, in the beginning, to manage the library collection. As this decade neared its close, librarians saw that information needed to be managed in entirely new ways, the period when simple print indexes to the contents of periodicals became databases available at first on CD-ROM, and which in the 1990s would become massive aggregated databases, developing into full-blown fulltext access in the 2000s. It was a time which promised a new world of instant access to any information anywhere, and where notions of virtual collections first began to be imagined. More importantly, it was a time when the librarian began to be reconstructed as an 'information manager', when technical skills became those relevant to a digital environment, and the skills related to physical collections and the way people used them were less important. It was the time when the word 'librarian' started to become old fashioned, when the scholarly bookworm needed a technological makeover.

Teacher librarians wrote about networking of resources and central (card) cataloguing systems during this decade. The *Australian School Librarian* and its continuation, *Access* had many articles specifically on this subject, including articles on the use of computers in libraries. Interest in audiovisual equipment had almost disappeared. They still wrote about the history and development of libraries, and management issues such as collection development, but there was a marked shift to the expertise required for teaching and learning in the library. Articles on team teaching and the development of research skills, reading and Children's Literature, curriculum knowledge and support, copyright, sexism and multiculturalism, demonstrated the way in which teacher librarians saw themselves embedded in the teaching and learning activity in the schools. For the first time, too, they wrote about the need for innovation and change, and articles about staffing concerns included questions of performance and accountability. The late

1980s in particular showed the professional knowledge of teacher librarians as necessarily encompassing co-operative planning with classroom teachers, to improve the information literacy of students. The end of the decade foreshadowed the massive impact the information revolution would have on the work of teacher librarians (e.g. Dwyer, 1989).

'Resource-based learning' was a catchword of the late 1980s, and in schools which embraced the notion of a student centred curriculum, team teaching with teachers and librarians was central to such a program. It was in 1989 in Victoria that the curriculum of the final two years of secondary schooling was completely overhauled, with a huge emphasis on student-centred learning evidenced in the major assessment tasks which students themselves designed and researched. Articles describing teaching procedures and practices written by Victorian classroom teachers in 1989 highlighted the importance of library research skills (PEEL, 2005). Teacher librarians saw as one of their central roles that of ensuring access for senior students to resources which were beyond the immediate collection of the school. This meant not only working with fellow teachers but also other librarians as finite resources needed to be shared, and access to each other's collections made available across sites.

THE 1990s: WHAT IS A TEACHER LIBRARIAN ON THE INFORMATION SUPERHIGHWAY?

The 1990s saw the acceleration of publishing to the Internet, the rapid development of PCs, the takeup of home use and networked computers across public institutions that led to that astounding change we now no longer refer to as the Information Revolution. We take the Internet so much for granted now that it's hard to remember the first stumbling steps that professionals and families took then. For teacher librarians, this was a period both exciting and fraught. For some, their sense of identity was so tied up with the management of physical resources and the primacy of the written word that the shift to digital management was something they could not deal with easily. Prensky (2001) talks about those who grew up before the age of computers as "digital immigrants", and some librarians found assimilation very difficult. As online information became seen as a virtual replacement for many written materials, schools began investing in information technology infrastructure, and networked PCs in classrooms were seen in some cases as a replacement for visits to the library. Those librarians who were comfortable with new ways of managing information and could continue teaching with colleagues who recognized their value as specialist teachers, embraced new technologies which allowed an expansion of their substantive work – teaching students to find and make sense of information from a large variety of sources. That they saw the need to develop whole new skill sets, both in accessing and creating information sources, is evidenced in the articles they wrote in the professional journals.

In the 1990s, teacher librarians saw themselves more overtly as teachers. They spoke of cooperative curriculum planning, team teaching and the supporting of good information literacy and research practices. At the same time, however, many felt threatened by the extent to which they had to become experts in the use of new information technology tools, and saw themselves as being pulled in two directions: were they teachers or information specialists? The use of information sources they understood, but the need to create digital resources for their students required a steep learning curve, and the learning of a language that was just too difficult for some to grasp.

The articles in the journal *Access* (the continuation title of the *Australian School Librarian*) in the 1990s reveal teacher librarians examining their role in the school, particularly in relation to team teaching and the development of research skills, an understanding of student learning styles, and resource-based learning. (This was mirrored in the rise of numbers of articles by teachers concerning library research skills in *PEEL in practice* (PEEL, 2005).) There was still a significant number of articles dealing with management issues, including matters relating to performance and accountability. There was a growing interest in research into the effectiveness of the profession, and in particular, in 1999, on the impact of the school library on student learning. Children's Literature and student literacy remained important concerns. Overwhelmingly, however, the need for greatest professional development and expertise was seen to be in the use of information technology tools. The first issue of the decade featured seven such articles; as the decade progressed, the emphases changed, from learning and information skills in an information age, through plagiarism in the age of the Internet, to the use of LANs (Local Area Networks) and, by the end of the decade, web authoring, intranet development and online teaching.

Looking at the articles in a professional journal gives a glimpse into the concerns of a profession, but also the concerns of those who wanted to move the profession forward by sharing their experiences and expertise. Professional knowledge was gained and professional concerns played out by individuals and the way they saw themselves and their role. For teacher librarians struggling to manage libraries by themselves or with little paraprofessional assistance, there was a real conflict between developing those skills which they saw primarily as teaching skills – good management of the 'classroom' of the library, development of a good library curriculum, fostering a love of reading – and information management skills. There were mixed messages for teacher librarians about what their role should be, particularly from some administrators. For some teacher librarians, those digital immigrants unable to learn a new management language, this was too big a shift in identity. Others saw vacancies in libraries being filled by librarians who were not teachers; clearly, their teaching role was not valued.

It was a time when teacher librarians struggled with their identities as teachers, as those who bridge the gap between the research question and the location and understanding of appropriate resources. The language used by the librarianship profession more broadly concentrated on the management of information, not the meaning that students needed to make from it. School administrators were easily seduced into thinking that the Internet was a kind of virtual library (not realizing the careful organisation of resources that embody a *library*), and that clicking on

Google would supply students with all the infrastructure they needed to carry out research. Many teacher librarians wondered at their place in the school, as staff in libraries increasingly were employed for their technical skills and money diverted into information technology infrastructure and management.

WHAT DOES BEING AN *INFORMATION MANAGER* IN A SCHOOL LIBRARY MEAN?

The Information Age has had a profound effect on the profession. The mid 1990s saw the demise of both training courses and professional staffing levels in schools. The course in teacher librarianship that started in 1956 at the Melbourne Teachers' College was finally closed in 1994. Other courses across Victoria were closed down, and it is now no longer possible to study teacher librarianship on campus anywhere in the state. The Australian Library and Information Association lists all the courses available in Australia in Librarianship. There are twenty-six courses listed, of which only three are in teacher librarianship, all at the Masters level. Of the twenty-three generalist courses, only nine actually have the words *library* or *librarianship* anywhere in the course titles (ALIA, 2006). The language used in current courses in librarianship in Australia focuses on digital management. A search in Australian university websites reveals very few courses or units which mention the word *librarianship*, and the biggest school of library studies in Australia is situated in the Faculty of Science and Agriculture (Charles Sturt University, 2006). This change in language away from people and spaces to information and its management has impacted negatively on the centrality of the role of the librarian in the school, the interpersonal relationships so important to the work of the teacher librarian. Recruitment of teacher librarians is difficult, due to the drastic cuts in training opportunities. This presages a bleak future; if teacher librarians cannot be replaced, then the role of librarians in schools will of necessity be that of the provision and management of a collection, managed by librarians with no knowledge of education, or even technicians.

During the 1990s, both social and economic changes, and the exponential explosion of information, worked to reduce the importance of the librarian in student centred learning, and both financial constraints and the growth of the Internet forced a change in the way school principals began to see the place of libraries, particularly in primary schools. In Victoria, Australia, during the same period that the Internet was being seen as the future gateway to all information, even likely to replace print, a change in government in 1992, and a massive push to reduce state debt by reducing funding in the government sector, saw significant funding cuts to government schools. In primary schools in particular, this had the effect of drastically reducing the number of teacher librarians. Faced with the choice between increased class sizes and the loss of specialist teachers, principals opted for the continuation of smaller grades. In 1992, many experienced teachers left the State school system; many of these were librarians, either to move into mainstream teaching, or out of the system all together. These librarians have not been replaced. At the same time in secondary schools, principals increased the number of general staff in school libraries at the expense of teacher librarians; they were cheaper, and well able to organize collections and house computers.

"Where have all the teacher librarians gone?" Thus begins an article dealing with the decline in staffing of Victoria's primary school libraries in the 1990s (Reynolds and Carroll, 2001). Their study looked at the number of schools staffed by fully qualified teacher librarians, that is, "…a specialist teacher in a specialist classroom who, to perform the role must have specialist teacher librarianship training…not only trained in education and librarianship but also in the philosophy and pedagogy of teacher librarianship" (p. 32). Their study found that only 13% of primary school libraries were managed by qualified teacher librarians (cf. the 33% in the 1970s, and 55% in 1983). In addition, 12% of libraries were managed by people with no formal qualifications at all, in education or librarianship. In partial answer to their question about the disappearance of teacher librarians, they found that "sixty-two schools without a qualified teacher librarian in the library in fact had at least one qualified teacher librarian on their classroom teaching staff. In more than one instance, the school had as many as three qualified teacher librarians on staff but the library was being managed by someone with no teaching qualifications, library qualifications or no formal qualifications of any kind" (Reynolds & Carroll, 2001, p. 32).

In the same year a similar survey undertaken by academics at RMIT University showed the situation in secondary schools to be considerably better, but there were still 12% of schools that had no teacher librarians in their libraries (Cook, 2004). These findings were backed up by my own experience as a lecturer in Teacher Librarianship at Monash University; 50% of the part-time students were classified as librarians or technicians in schools, although some were carrying out the work of teacher librarians, and 27% of practicum placements were in schools which did not have established library programmes, and where students had special classes created for them to teach, or had no real opportunity to teach at all, except by using their initiative with students and teachers one to one.

For teacher librarians working during this period in state primary schools the message was clear. Their value as teachers lay in traditional classrooms only. The space called the library was not a specialist classroom; it was all about access, not about learning. For the librarians who left the system in 1992, it was the only way to retain a sense of themselves as teachers. For many of those who were retained in secondary schools, there was a loss of self confidence about what it was they should do, the expectations the school (through the principal) had of them. Were they merely fulfilling a legal requirement for supervision of students by qualified teachers? It was my experience visiting a few schools where the librarians supervising practicum placements told me they did not "have a library programme", that their job was largely a supervisory one. It was not uncommon in these situations for the school library to act as a private study space for students in the final years of school. Students coming in to these libraries presented a pass, to show they had permission to leave the classroom and come into the library. They did not come to the librarian with a question. In these situations, librarians demonstrated a professional timidity, and did not have a strong enough sense of their role to question the students about their purpose. They did not intervene as teachers in a learning situation.

21st CENTURY: BACK TO THE BASICS: HOW DOES THE WORK OF SCHOOL LIBRARIANS INFLUENCE LEARNING?

Teacher librarians were keen to articulate the role they play in supporting students' learning, central to their notions of professional identity. In 2002, the Australian School Library Association commissioned a report on research worldwide, but in Australia particularly, about the impact libraries have on student achievement. The ASLA commissioned report found a number of significant gaps in the research in Australia (Lonsdale, 2003). What had been of great interest worldwide during the 1990s and particularly in the early 2000s was a concern to show that school libraries make a difference to student learning (Lance, 1994; Kuhlthau, 1999; Todd, 2001; Koechlin & Zwaan, 2002; Oberg, 2002; Williams, Wavell, & Coles, 2001; IASL, 2004; OELMA, 2004). Since 2003 in Australia, in response to this research agenda, there have been a number of reports from practitioners outlining cases in their schools; the ASLA conference from 2004 had several such papers, as have the Australian, NSW and Victorian journals *Access, Scan* and *Synergy,* and there is a new study currently being completed at Charles Sturt University, replicating research undertaken in Ohio (Hay, 2005a, 2005b).

In response to a need for Australian research, in 2003, the School Library Association of Victoria added a peer reviewed journal, *Synergy,* to its suite of publications. In the six issues published so far, the ten research articles have dealt with teacher collaboration, electronic information and communication, and primarily with evidence of the effectiveness of Australian school libraries. Here we see a concentration on the work at the heart of teacher librarianship: the contribution they make to teaching and learning.

Not all teacher librarians have not been good at articulating what it is they do to improve students' learning. They have tended to report within their schools the work they do in terms of numbers of loans, visits to the library, classes conducted in the space, and so on. They have assumed that quantifying the usage of the collection and the space (since literacy and a love of reading is so self evidently what libraries are all about) makes a case for their role in student learning. Their job is not just about access. They haven't managed to communicate to the broader education community the role they play in helping students find a variety of sources, in different media, presenting different points of view, and then helping them find a way of organising their thinking and presenting their findings. It is specialist teaching, often conducted one-to-one, and therefore invisible, except to the students themselves.

"We all know that school libraries help students. Why must we have a survey about it? All schools need libraries, so let's not worry about the surveys. (Grade 11 female)" (OELMA, 2004, ppt). Such was the response of a student to a large scale study of school libraries in Ohio. Ross Todd, formerly an Australian teacher librarian and academic, now Director of the Research Centre for International

Scholarship in School Libraries at Rutgers, has been concerned for some time (Todd, 2001a, 2001b) that school librarians have failed to document the impact of their work. In 2003, a study funded by State Library of Ohio was undertaken by the Ohio Educational Library Media Association (OELMA) with Ross Todd and Carol Kuhlthau, into the impact of school libraries on student learning. Thirty-nine school libraries across Ohio participated; 13 123 student responses and 879 teacher/administrator responses to the survey were collected online. The results are available on the OELMA website (OELMA, 2004), and elsewhere (Todd, 2004).

Students were asked to rate questions around seven constructs of 'Help': how helpful the school library was with getting information you needed; with using the information to complete your school work (information literacy skills); with your school work in general (knowledge building, knowledge outcomes); with using computers in the library, at school and at home; with your general reading interests; when you were not at school (independent learning); general school aspects – academic achievement. There were also open-ended questions in which students were asked to describe critical incidents: "Now, remember one time when the school library really helped you. Write about the help that you got, and what you were able to do because of it" (OELMA, 2004, ppt.).

The Ohio study showed overwhelmingly that students value school libraries, and that they provide vital support. Most importantly, the study shows that it is the "instructional intervention" of the teacher librarians that matters. "What the data convey is the notion of an effective school library not just as an information place, but also as a knowledge space where students develop the appropriate information literacy scaffolds to enable them to engage with information, make decisions about the information they encounter in terms of its worth and appropriateness, and build their own understanding." Student comments included: "I needed help doing a project for government that had to do with presidents and they had so many books and then the librarian helped me find web sites. But then they gave me ways of sorting through all the ideas to extract the key points so I could get my head around it all." "It helped me find info on racism for a 10th grade project, and made me really think about that, especially I didn't realize how racist some of my ideas were." "I needed to write a paper and I went to the Library where I was ultimately able to write a paper successfully. My ideas were a mess and talking to the librarian gave me a way to organize my ideas and present the argument. I did really well!! I've never forgotten that – used it to do many other assignments" (OELMA, 2004, ppt.).

Librarians talked of the role they played with individuals and their recreational reading, and a love of Children's Literature and a commitment to it; fiction sections in many schools were large and well used, and in some libraries this remained central to what librarians did. The Ohio research showed, however, that students regarded this as comparatively unimportant, when talking about the libraries and what they meant for learning. Students spoke about the individual assistance of teacher librarians in their work preparation. The study clearly showed that librarians made a difference – and a difference as teachers, not as guardians of collections, or managers of good websites, important as this was.

WHAT MATTERS IS PEOPLE, NOT MANAGEMENT OF INFORMATION

What matters for schools is having *teacher* librarians – people who understand the nexus between research and resources; who talk of 'information literacy' and 'the research process'. When librarians present workshops for other teachers about, for example, setting up a good search strategy before looking for the available resources, teachers are often surprised at what they don't know, and once shown, approach their own work in newly empowered ways.

"I wish someone had taught me how to develop my information literacy skills through resource-based learning in these ways in school. I might not have had such a horrendous time of it when I came to university." So begins the reporting of a programme in Canada in which preservice teacher education students were teamed with teacher librarians both within the faculty and in district schools to plan units of work together, embedded in which was the teaching of information literacy skills (Asselin & Lee, 2002). I have had similar comments made to me by Masters students after conducting sessions showing them, for example, advanced searching techniques interrogating online databases to current literature. These skills are not simply acquired along the way; they need to be taught, in context, by specialists who understand the processes required for research, how people learn, and how information about sources is managed. This is not 'information management'. It is the expertise of teachers who understand both how information is managed and the requirements of individual researchers in understanding the process involved in developing their questions, finding sources, and organizing their ideas. It is about people and their skills, about the people as educators that matters, not their ability with computer architecture, database structure, and so on (important as this is) that really matters.

Administrators who see libraries simply as repositories of *things,* and the Internet as a major source of information, fail to understand what these repositories are *for.* If students cannot talk to people who understand what the things are for but only know how to organize and manage them, then they are being robbed of the opportunity to understand how to pursue their interests in not only efficient but also constructivist ways. 'The research process', central to the teaching of teacher librarians, is an immensely empowering one.

The information explosion is a cliché now, but it doesn't hurt to look again at what it means. It is, of course, what has led to the 'Information Managers'; without these particularly specialist librarians, who manage digital resources, the Internet and access to current literature would be impossible to deal with. The necessity for mastering information technology tools appropriate for student and staff support has been a difficult transition for some teacher librarians, although others have embraced this new form of information management. It was one of the concerns which dominated the local library literature and professional development activities during the late 1990s, and continues to be of concern for a greying profession (Todd, 2001a).

However, many people, including digital natives, those who have grown up with computers (Prensky, 2001), still seek information and recreational interests in more traditional forms like books, newspapers, journals, documentaries et cetera.

231

Collections of *things* are still important, and librarians are still needed to help ordinary people with straightforward tasks. Teacher librarians need to provide experiences for students at school that serve the ordinary recreational or information purposes they may have – how to work out what sort of heater to buy if they are concerned both with cost and global warming – and also to meet the more serious research purposes that they have now, and will have with greater complexity as students in the senior years of school and perhaps in tertiary education.

Todd's questions and the students' open ended answers show that teacher librarians help students refine their questions, think through concepts for searching for information, organise the notes they take from information sources, to put what they have discovered in a coherent way in a final product. And the comments clearly identify that it is the *librarians* that the students see as doing this. This is not to say that discipline based subject teachers do not do this; the good ones do help students understand this process. But they can't follow them all up, and don't have the brief to help out of the classroom situation. Librarians are in a different relationship with students and, moreover, are at the interface between the research process and the resources themselves. It *is* their job to make information accessible, and to work on a particular kind of literacy with students. Just as English teachers are seen as primarily responsible for helping students to express themselves and communicate clearly, they are not seen as solely responsible. In the same way, librarians are primarily skilled in the research process, but not solely so.

The Google Age has brought with it unprecedented access to information on many platforms that could not have been dreamed of in 1981. That access is now almost universal, even in countries for which there was no infrastructure a mere five years ago. People now have access to scholarly articles, archived photographs, digital artworks, music and films, as well as an overload of rubbish, in their own homes. New technologies will replace the information and communication platforms that the majority of us use today. It is a wondrous age, unimaginable such a short time ago, one that is taken utterly for granted by my digital native children. At the same time, however, it is an age when teachers still matter, thousands of years after they first became important in the lives of a lucky few. Teacher librarians of the Google Age need to spell out the contribution they make to the ways in which students in school make meaning out of the plethora of information available to them. As physical and virtual spaces move beyond the walls of the library buildings, teacher librarians need to reassert the importance of all that sits in our collective psyche about the notion of a librarian – the person who ensures free access to recorded human endeavour, and helps ordinary people of all ages find the strategies to answer questions and create new knowledge.

This is not Information Management: it is education. The strong adoption of the term *Information Management* by the librarianship profession has worked to diminish the importance of what it is that librarians do best. Interaction with people matters.

REFERENCES

ALIA (Australian Library and Information Association). (2006, August 15). *Education: ALIA-recognized librarianship courses*. Retrieved August 22, 2006, from http://www.alia.org.au/education/courses/librarianship.html

ASLA (Australian School Library Association) and ALIA (Australian Library and Information Association). (1993). *Learning for the future: Developing information services in Australian schools*. Carlton, Vic: Curriculum Corporation.

Asselin, M., & Lee, E. (2002). "I wish someone had taught me": Information in a teacher education program. *Teacher Librarian, 30*(2), 10-17.

Charles Sturt University. (2006). *Faculty of Science and Agriculture: Undergraduate*. Retrieved April 13, 2006, from http://www.csu.edu.au/courses/ug/sci/libinf/

Cook, M. (2004, April 26). Cracks in the halls of learning. Melbourne: *The Age* (Education supplement), pp. 6-7.

Dwyer, J. (1989). Information bomb: Dealing with the shrapnel. *Access, 3*(1), 10-11.

Gregory, A. (1974). Selected periodical articles. *Australian School Librarian, 11*(3).

Hay, L. (2005a). Hallmarks of school library programs to support student learning. *Connections, 55*. Retrieved April 20, 2006, from http://www.curriculum.edu.au/scis/connections/cnetw05/55hallmarks.htm

Hay, L. (2005b). Student learning through Australian school libraries. Part 1: A statistical analysis of student perceptions. *Synergy, 3*(2), 17-30.

IASL (International Association of School Librarianship). (2004). *School libraries make a difference to student achievement*. Retrieved April 15, 2006, from http://www.iasl-slo.org/make-a-difference.html

Koechlin, C., & Zwaan, S. (2002). Making library programs count: Where's the evidence? *School Libraries in Canada, 22*(2), 21-23.

Kuhlthau, C. (1999). Student learning in the library: What library power librarians say. *School Libraries Worldwide, 5*(2), 80-96.

Lance, K. (1994). *The impact of school library media centers on academic achievement*. (ERIC Document: ED372759). Retrieved April 18, 2006, from the ERIC database.

Lonsdale, M. (2003). *Impact of school libraries on student achievement: A review of the research*. Melbourne: Australian Council for Educational Research. Retrieved April 13, 2006, from http://www.asla.org.au/research/

Mahy, M. (1981). *Raging robots and unruly uncles*. London: J. M. Dent.

Moore, M. (2002). *Stupid white men ... and other sorry excuses for the state of the nation!* London: Penguin.

Oberg, D. (2002). Looking for the evidence: Do school libraries improve student achievement? *School Libraries in Canada, 22*(2), 10-13.

OELMA (Ohio Educational Library Media Association). (2004). Student learning through Ohio School Libraries: The Ohio research study. Retrieved April 18, 2006, from http://www.oelma.org/StudentLearning/SLFindings.asp

PEEL (Project for Enhancing Effective Learning). (2005). *PEEL in practice*. Accessed August 22, 2006, from http://www.peelweb.org/index.cfm?resource=pip

Prensky, M. (2001). Digital natives, digital immigrants. Part 1. *On the Horizon, 9*(5), 1-6.

Reynolds, S., & Carroll, M. (2001). Where have all the teacher librarians gone? *Access, 15*(2), 30-34.

Todd, R. (2004). How effective are school libraries? Students' perspectives from Ohio. *Orana, 40*(1), 9-21.

Todd, R. (2001a). Pathways to the future: Knowledge construction and evidence-based practice. *Connections, 39*. Retrieved April 13, 2006, from http://www.curriculum.edu.au/scis/connections/cnetw01/39pathways.htm

Todd, R. (2001b). A sustainable future for teacher-librarians: Inquiry learning, actions and evidence. *Orana*, November, 10-20.

Ward, J. (1976). Current trends in school libraries. *Australian School Librarian, 13*(1), 5-7.
Williams, D., Wavell, C., & Coles, L. (2001). *Impact of school library services on achievement and learning: Critical literature review.* London: Department for Education, Skills and Resources: The Council for Museums, Archives & Libraries. Retrieved August 23, 2006 from http://www.rgu.ac.uk/files/Impact%20of%20School%20Library%20Services1.pdf

Rosamund Winter
Faculty of Education
Monash University

CONTRIBUTORS

Amanda Berry is a Senior Lecturer in the Faculty of Education, Monash University where she works mainly in the areas of preservice and inservice science teacher education. Amanda's research focus is the self-study of teaching practice, an interest that began during her career as a high school teacher before joining Monash University. She has a keen interest in the collaborative learning about teaching that can take place between teacher education colleagues and in the power of modeling in teaching about teaching. Amanda has published widely in the areas of teacher education and science education.

Allie Clemans is a Senior Lecturer in the Faculty of Education, Monash University, where she works in the areas of adult learning and development. Allie teaches in both undergraduate and postgraduate programs and undertakes a range of development work with community-based and vocational education organisations locally and internationally. Allie's research interests lie in approaches to adult education and training in diverse learning contexts, the nature of work in adult learning spaces and the community learning space as a site for transformative learning.

Deborah Corrigan is a Senior Lecturer in Science Education and a former Associate Dean (Teaching) at Monash University. After working as a Chemistry and Biology teacher for 10 years, she has worked at Monash University for 15 years in Teacher Education, particularly in Chemistry and Science Education and Professional Practice. Her research interests include documenting professional practice particularly through professional portfolios, mentoring and learning logs, industry and technology links with chemistry curricula, and an active involvement in many vocational educational programs for students and teachers. However, her main research interests remain improving the quality of chemistry and science education so that it is relevant to students and improving the professional practice of teachers and other industry professionals.

Russell Cross has recently completed his doctoral thesis in foreign language teacher education at Monash University. His research interests lie in the knowledge base of language teaching, foreign language pedagogy, immersion and bilingual education, and Vygotskian sociocultural theory. He is currently a lecturer at the University of Melbourne.

Joanne Deppeler is a Senior Lecturer in Psychology & Inclusive & Special Education in the Faculty of Education at Monash University. She has written extensively on issues in inclusive education and has been involved in a number of projects in Australia and internationally that have focused on improving outcomes for students through teacher professional learning.

Brenton Doecke is an Associate Professor in the Faculty of Education at Monash University. He has published a range of articles on teacher professional identity and change, as well as English curriculum and pedagogy.

Trevor Gale is an Associate Professor of Education at Monash University and Immediate Past President of the Australian Association for Research in Education, an association with a membership of 1400 researchers in education. His research interests are in the sociology of education, particularly policy sociology, social justice and teaching for diversity and difference. He is author and co-author of three seminal books in the field, *Just Schooling* (OUP, 2000), *Engaging Teachers* (OUP, 2003) and *Rough Justice* (Peter Lang, 2005), and frequently publishes in international journals. He is editor of the journal *Critical Studies in Education* (formerly *Melbourne Studies in Education*).

Margaret Gearon is a Senior Lecturer in the Faculty of Education at Monash University. Her research interests include the use of the target language in foreign and second language classrooms; the development of biliteracy and bicultural identity by teachers in community languages' schools; and the ways in which languages' teachers respond to professional development programs. Her current research projects are the evaluation of the oral and written language development of students in late partial immersion French programmes in a school in Victoria and the development of biliteracy skills and bicultural knowledge in early years in two community language programs.

Bella Illesca teaches in the English Education program at Monash University. She has taught English in government and independent schools in Australia and in the U.K. She has completed a Masters degree titled, 'Literacy and Accountability: The changing shape of English teachers' work'. Her teaching and research interests include language and literacy, professional learning and teacher professional identity.

Alex Kostogriz's career in education spans 15 years, and he has taught English for students from diverse language and cultural backgrounds both in Australia and overseas. He is a Senior Lecturer in languages (TESOL) and literacy in the Faculty of Education, Monash University. He is involved in undergraduate and graduate pre-service programs and in Masters level courses in TESOL and TESOL-International. His research interests are sociocultural perspectives on language and literacy learning, teacher education and professional learning, and spatial analysis of learning environments.

Ian Mitchell spent 23 years teaching science, chemistry and maths in secondary schools. For the last 14 of these, he was seconded half-time to the Faculty of Education at Monash University. In 1985 he co-founded the Project for Enhancing Effective Learning (PEEL) at Laverton Secondary College, Victoria. This unfunded initiative involved a group of 10 teachers who were dissatisfied with passive learning in their classrooms and volunteered to meet regularly in what we would now call a Professional Learning Team to research and develop ways of meeting their concerns. PEEL has since spread to many other schools and Ian has a long history of leading such groups, working with teachers running them and acting as critical friend for schools setting up initiatives in this area. For the last 8 years he has been full time at Monash where he is now a Senior Lecturer.

Jane Mitchell is a Senior Lecturer in the Faculty of Education at Monash University. Her research interests focus on teacher education curriculum, policy and practice.

Joce Nuttall is a Senior Lecturer in Early Childhood Education in the Faculty of Education at Monash University. Joce's research interests are in teachers' practice and professional learning, early childhood curriculum and policy, and cultural-historical approaches to understanding educational settings. Joce is the editor of *Weaving Te Whaariki: Aotearoa*, New Zealand's early childhood curriculum document in theory and practice (NZCER, 2003).

Eleanor Peeler offers academic and language support to undergraduate and post graduate students in the Faculty of Education at Monash University. She has a keen interest in the transitions of overseas-born learner teachers in their practical placements in the Australian educational system. This was the focus of her doctoral thesis which explored how they developed a professional identity.

Paul Richardson is a member of the Faculty of Education, Monash University, where he has held significant administrative and leadership positions in teaching and learning. His current research focuses on motivations for teaching as a career choice, teacher self-efficacy and career development; as well as adolescent identity development, adolescent literacy, and teaching and learning in higher education. He was a visiting scholar at the University of Michigan 2004-2006, where he worked as a Research Scientist on the large NICHD-funded study: Social and Cultural Influences on Adolescent Literacy Motivation and Development.

Samantha Scheele is Science Co-ordinator and senior teacher at Emerald Secondary College, Victoria. She is also a part time Lecturer in Education in the Faculty of Education at Monash University. Sam has been actively involved for many years in teacher professional learning and classroom research, both within her own practice and as a member of PEEL (Project for Enhancing Effective Learning), a collaborative action research group based at Monash University.

Libby Tudball has been actively involved in Studies of Society and Environment (SOSE) education as a teacher in state secondary schools from 1976 to 1984, and since then as a teacher educator, researcher and writer. Libby is the lecturer in charge of SOSE method and teaches other education subjects at Monash University. Her publications include school curriculum materials, teacher professional learning programs and academic articles. Libby is actively involved in teacher professional development and is currently engaged in research in teacher professional learning, Civics and Citizenship education, studies of Asia, values education and the internationalisation of education. She is vice-president of the Social Education Association of Australia, and a life member and active participant in the Victorian Association of Social Studies Teachers. Libby is a regular contributor to the Australian Teachers of Media journal, Australian Screen

237

Education.

Nicole Tysvaer is a PhD precandidate in the School of Education, University of Michigan. With a Masters in Public Policy specialising in outcomes-based evaluation methods, Nicole has over a dozen years' experience working with educational programs that serve children and youth. Her current research interests are teacher motivations, adolescent literacy development and children's out-of-school time use.

Rosemary Viete, after teaching English in Venezuela for 12 years, has spent the last 15 years providing support in academic literacy and study skills for international and local students in Education courses at Monash University. Her research has consistently focused on cross-cultural issues in the negotiation of diverse academic requirements, including English proficiency entrance requirements for pre-service teacher education courses, requirements for the approval of research along ethical guidelines, and voice in research writing. Her teaching and research have also reflected on pedagogical issues in the teaching and learning of international students and those with language backgrounds other than English.

Helen Watt works in the Education Faculty at Monash University, and has previously held positions at the University of Michigan, University of Western Sydney, University of Sydney and Macquarie University. Her interests include motivation, mathematics education, gendered educational and occupational choices, motivations for teaching, teacher self-efficacy and quantitative methods. She has received national and international early career research awards, attracted substantial external funding, and published in leading journals.

Judith Williams has been a primary teacher for approximately 25 years, recently resigned from the Victorian Department of Education and Training. She is a PhD student in the Education Faculty at Monash University, and also does sessional teaching (primary undergraduates) and research assistant work. Her main research interests are mature aged/career change students in teacher education and teacher professional learning in general.

Rosamund Winter has worked as a teacher librarian for many years in primary, secondary and tertiary libraries. She currently lectures in Teacher Librarianship Education in the Faculty of Education at Monash University, and works closely with students and staff across the faculty as a librarian in the Faculty's Library & Media Resources Centre.

INDEX

FURTHER READING

Understanding and Developing Science Teachers Pedagogical Content Knowledge
John Loughran , Amanda Berry, and Pamela Mulhall, *Monash University, Clayton, Australia*
There has been a growing interest in the notion of a scholarship of teaching. Such scholarship is displayed through a teacher's grasp of, and response to, the relationships between knowledge of content, teaching and learning in ways that attest to practice as being complex and interwoven. Yet attempting to capture teachers' professional knowledge is difficult because the critical links between practice and knowledge, for many teachers, is tacit. Pedagogical Content Knowledge (PCK) offers one way of capturing, articulating and portraying an aspect of the scholarship of teaching and, in this case, the scholarship of science teaching. The research underpinning the approach offers access to the development of the professional knowledge of science teaching in a form that offers new ways of sharing and disseminating this knowledge. Through this Resource Folio approach (comprising CoRe and PaP-eRs) a recognition of the value of the specialist knowledge and skills of science teaching is not only highlighted, but also enhanced. This book is a concrete example of the nature of scholarship in science teaching that is meaningful, useful and immediately applicable in the work of all science teachers. It is an excellent resource for science teachers as well as a guiding text for teacher education.

paperback: ISBN:90-77874-23-2 hardback: ISBN:90-77874-24-0
April 2006, 240 pp
SERIES: PROFESSIONAL LEARNING 1

Competence Oriented Teacher Training: *Old Research Demands and New Pathways*
Fritz K. Oser, *University of Fribourg, Switzerland,* **Frank Achtenhagen,** *Georg-August-University Göttingen, Germany* and
Ursula Renold, *Bundesamt für Berufsbildung und Technologie, Bern, Switzerland* **(eds.)**

Internationally leading experts from four continents provide new views and pathways to teacher education and training. How can teachers be effectively and efficiently trained to master the complexity and the process conditions of teaching-learning situations? The chapters as a whole demonstrate that subtle knowledge of the conditions and variables of instructional processes is necessary. They provide new insight into the classroom. But the chapters also stress the necessity of reflection: Teachers have to learn how to judge and justify that knowledge and its use. Reflective behaviour, thus, is seem as the overall goal of teacher education and training. The authors are aware that this goal might be classified as "idealistic" and present, therefore, complex examples for successful conducting instructional processes. They open the view on hidden or neglected dimensions of teaching and learning, discuss standards for teacher behaviour, present critical situations together with possible solutions and give hints for the use of technology. Together, these chapters present new perspectives for successful teacher actions and the corresponding preparation for successful instruction.

paperback: ISBN:90-77874-68-2 hardback: ISBN:90-77874-69-0
April 2006, 306 pp

Teaching, Learning, and Other Miracles

Grace Feuerverger, *Ontario Institute for Studies in Education, University of Toronto, Canada*

Feuerverger wrote this book to tell how School can be a magical place where miracles happen. She shares narratives about her school teaching years, about her university teaching and about her research work. Unifying these is a story of how language, culture and school serendipitously all came together in her childhood to offer her a way to survive - a path towards repair and restoration. In an era of narrow agendas of 'efficiency' and 'control' in schools, this book dares to suggest that education is and always will be about uplifting of the human spirit. It advocates for the priceless opportunity that good public education can give to students of all backgrounds. Every chapter of this book offers both inspiration and direction, discussing in a multiplicity of ways the act of creating and of being in classrooms as sites of cultural encounters and spaces for possibility and community and knowledge. Each classroom calls out for a witness. Each student is an angel in disguise. Each lesson is a work-in-progress. Each teacher is both an artist and a muse.

paperback: ISBN:90-8790-000-7 hardback: ISBN:90-8790-003-1
2007, 180 pp
SERIES: TRANSGRESSIONS 5

Printed in the United Kingdom
by Lightning Source UK Ltd.
127797UK00001B/104/A